LETTERS
FROM
THE EDGE

ALSO BY THE AUTHORS

As Told at The Explorers Club

The Explorers Club

THE EXPLORERS CLUB PRESENTS

LETTERS FROM THE EDGE

Stories of Curiosity, Bravery, and Discovery

JEFF WILSER

CROWN
NEW YORK

CROWN
An imprint of the Crown Publishing Group
A division of Penguin Random House LLC
1745 Broadway
New York, NY 10019
crownpublishing.com
penguinrandomhouse.com

Library of Congress Cataloging-in-Publication Data is on file with the publisher.

Hardcover ISBN 978-0-593-24003-8
Ebook ISBN 978-0-593-24004-5

Editor: Matt Inman
Assistant editor: Fariza Hawke
Production editor: Sohayla Farman
Text designer: Aubrey Khan
Production: Jessica Heim
Copy editor: Mimi Lipson
Proofreaders: Lisa Brousseau, Alissa Fitzgerald, and Miriam Taveras
Publicist: Josie McRoberts
Marketer: Mason Eng

Manufactured in the United States of America

1st Printing

First Edition

The authorized representative in the EU for product safety and compliance is Penguin
Random House Ireland, Morrison Chambers, 32 Nassau Street, Dublin D02 YH68,
Ireland, https://eu-contact.penguin.ie.

CONTENTS

LETTERS
FROM
THE EDGE

INTRODUCTION

FOR NEIL ARMSTRONG, going to the edge meant walking on the moon. For Jane Goodall, the edge meant studying chimps in Tanzania For Edmund Hillary and Tenzing Norgay, it meant summiting Everest. For Amelia Earhart, it meant circumnavigating the globe.

So, what is "the edge"?

Andrés Ruzo thought he knew the answer. A geothermal scientist, Ruzo trekked through the Amazon to chase down the legend of a "boiling river" that once haunted conquistadors. The river was not on any maps, and many believed it to be a myth. When Ruzo discovered this river that boiled—emitting vapors that glowed in the moonlight—he stood at what he thought was the edge. But now those words meant something else entirely. "The world is bigger, more incredible, and more mind-blowing than I could ever have imagined," says Ruzo. "Awe lies at the edge—the edge is where you find God."

If you ask one hundred explorers to define the edge, you'll get one hundred different answers. This is not an exaggeration, and this is not theoretical. While preparing this book, we asked members of The Explorers Club—the home to the world's greatest explorers since 1904—to share their own meaning of the edge.

Over 140 explorers responded. For one mountaineer, the edge means "not knowing if you will live to see tomorrow." Others view it as an internal challenge. "Pushing my limits taught me resilience," says Meg Haywood Sullivan. "Growth occurs when challenging the boundaries of emotional security, physical comfort, and the status quo."

The edge can refer to the edge of a cliff, the edge of consciousness, the edge of the known world. But almost every edge has one thing in common. "The edge means risk," says Will Roseman, the Club's longtime executive director. And it's the explorer's job to calculate and manage and minimize risk, weighing the pros and cons of climbing that next ridge. Sometimes the plan goes sideways. And when it does, says Roseman, "It takes all their wits and all their efforts to save themselves from falling off that edge."

We're fascinated by the edge, in part, because it strips away the quotidian aspects of "normal" life, highlighting the most dramatic aspects of exploration. "The edge is the place, one step past what you think you can endure, where humanity is distilled into its strongest stuff," says Donna Oliver, who, in 1975, became the first woman to solo-winter in the Antarctic Circle.

This book shares excerpts from letters showcasing this "strongest stuff," as well as their accompanying stories. Many of these are gripping tales of adventure, yes, but they're also something more, something deeper, something universal. By seeing how world-class explorers operate at the edge, we can gain insights, instruction, and inspiration for how we can navigate the edges in our own lives.

For all of us have our own version of the edge. "The edge, to me, is that invisible, theoretical, metaphorical boundary that defines your comfort zone," says lifelong hiker J. R. Harris. "Some people like to stay at its center, where life is more stable and comfortably consistent. Others, like me, like to explore the periphery, where life is less predictable but more exciting."

This book also explores what it's really like to navigate the edge—with the spotlight on actual flesh-and-blood human beings, not exalted heroes. (Even if these humans are in many ways heroic.) So we'll get into the grime and the weeds and the muck. "The edge is not always full of glory, like some people may think," says Jessica Glass, whose letters from the edge include salty details like "New PhD low: fishing in the Seychelles Islands on a researcher's budget, casting under a bridge at 5:30 a.m. with no luck, as you stand under a sewage pipe that periodically reeks of shit and—best part—sprays sewer water on you."

And that brings us to the letters themselves. For millennia, explorers have wandered from their homes and then sent dispatches from afar. These letters have helped us move the needle of human knowledge. Charles Darwin could not write *On the Origin of Species*, for example, without first traveling to Patagonia, exploring its ecosystem, and then scribbling his thoughts in a series of letters. An explorer's work isn't finished when she reaches a new destination or makes a discovery; she needs to somehow share what she's learned.

From the Silk Road to rovers on Mars, letters have always told the tale. But they do more than that. Letters give us comfort in the knowledge that the explorer is alive and safe—or warn us when they are not. Letters can be intimate. They provide the benefit of immediacy, giving unfiltered insight into what the explorer was feeling in the moment, whether excitement or fear or despair or wonder. They allow us to clearly hear the voice of the explorer, sometimes in triumph and sometimes from the grave.

For millennia, letters from the edge were exactly what they sound like: handwritten notes on sheets of paper. Technology changed, but the concept endured. So we'll widen the scope of "letters" to include all the ways that explorers have captured their thoughts and shared them with the world: email, text messages, field journals, blog posts, ham radio, tweets, scientific studies, fax, telegrams, drawings, data packets from space, and holograms intended to reach the far side of the galaxy.

Yet, in one final sense, the letters are not really about the far side of the galaxy or even the edge. They have a secret dual purpose. When explorers go to the edge, they're on a quest to learn something. That could be discovering the South Pole, researching climate change, studying other cultures, or rocketing through space. They share what they've discovered, and the world is enriched by that knowledge. Even probes to distant corners of the universe, ultimately, help us better understand Earth's place in the cosmos. For astrophysicist Gregory Matloff, the edge means that "The universe is huge, and we are tiny. We can't conquer it, but we can explore it."

Going to the edge, paradoxically, is a way to gain perspective at the center. Understanding the edge is a way to understand ourselves.

1

The Edge of the Known World

For much of human history, exploration focused on the edge of the known world. So this is where we begin. In 1921, The Explorers Club's president, Vilhjalmur Stefansson, sent a team to the Arctic on a three-year mission. It did not go as he had planned; thankfully, we have the letters to tell the tale.

Flash forward a century. The edge of the known world evolved to mean outer space, so we'll hear from astronauts on the far side of the moon. And sometimes what's meant by "the known world" is less obvious. Meg Lowman, for example, discovered an "eighth continent" above our heads, looming over us in the canopy of trees. And finally, the psychologist Donna Oliver, by attempting to solo-winter in the Antarctic, reminds us that even if a place has been "discovered," we still have much to learn.

The edge of the known world can mean loneliness, resilience, despair, sacrifice, hope, illumination, and not knowing if you will make it back alive.

THE ACCIDENTAL EXPLORER

Vilhjalmur Stefansson
and Ada Blackjack

VILHJALMUR STEFANSSON JOINED The Explorers Club in 1903, four years after its founding. He served as the Club's president in 1919, and then once again in 1937. He was a legendary Arctic explorer who was known for deeply appreciating Inuit culture and customs, discovering new Arctic islands, and focusing on scientific pursuits.

In many ways, Stefansson held a thoroughly modern view of exploration. He would heartily agree with the Club's current distinction between exploration and adventuring, the latter of which he deplored. "There is absolutely nothing heroic in Arctic exploration," he wrote, "for exploration, like any other work, is easily resolved into certain simple rules, which, if properly followed, render it as safe and about as exciting as taxicab-driving or a hundred other things which are done in civilization and done without a suggestion of heroism."

Stefansson's record, however, is not without blemish.

In the 1920s, he wanted to dispel the idea that the Arctic was a scary, dangerous place. He wanted to see people move there. He longed to set up camps and communities and even cities. "I think that anyone with good eyesight and a rifle can live anywhere in the polar regions indefinitely," he liked to say. He even boasted that "Given a healthy body and a cheerful disposition, a family can now live at the North Pole as comfortably as it can in Hawaii."

So in 1921, while serving as president of The Explorers Club, Stefansson had a new idea for an Arctic expedition. He wanted five men to set up camp and live on the desolate Wrangel Island, which is located between modern-day Alaska and Siberia.

Stefansson had three reasons for this expedition: (1) He wanted to claim the island for Canada or the U.K. (it had been explored before, but now it was abandoned); (2) he thought the island could be a future hub for an aviation base; and (3) it would help prove his theory that the Arctic is as pleasant as Maui.

To recruit the men whom he would send to the edge, Stefansson wrote a letter outlining the qualities he was looking for:

> I am planning a three-year polar expedition. This year I want to send north to a point within the Arctic Circle an advance party, consisting of a Topographer, a Botanist, a Zoologist, a Geologist, and one or two other men.
>
> My experience has been that generally the younger the man the more readily he adapts himself to northern conditions. For that reason I should prefer to get men just out of college. The chief qualification is temperamental. There should be no tendency to imagine that you are a hero or that it constitutes remarkable hardships to be away from movies and operas for a year or two.
>
> Moderately good health is desirable. The man should be especially a good walker; his circulation should be at least so good that there is no marked tendency to numbness of hands or feet, and the eyesight should be above the average. No man is useful in midwinter work in the far north who is not able to get along without glasses. . . . The wages would be nominal—$1,800 a year. The man should at the very least have specialized as an undergraduate in Botany, Zoology or Geology; preferably he should have had at least a year's post-graduate work.
>
> This letter is confidential.

Stefansson did indeed find four men who fit his description. They were ecstatic to be selected. A nineteen-year-old picked to join the mission—the youngest of the bunch—wrote to his parents:

I am simply overjoyed, yes tickled to death. Out of this whole
bunch Stef had to choose me. . . . Is this not enough as yet to show
you that there is something besides just lollypopping around, if it
isn't, GOOD NIGHT!

Then Stefansson was thrown a curveball. There was also a fifth
explorer, and this was not someone he expected. This explorer didn't
fit any of Stefansson's criteria, except perhaps that of being a "good
walker" with reasonable eyesight.

The fifth explorer wasn't a young man or a college student or a
botanist or a geologist.

The fifth explorer was an Inupiat woman named Ada Blackjack.

* * *

ADA BLACKJACK WAS twenty-two years old. She'd grown up in
the city of Nome, Alaska. Thanks to the legacy of explorers like
Matthew Henson and Robert Peary—who relied on Inuit help to
reach the North Pole—perhaps most Arctic explorers, at the time,
simply assumed that every Inuit knew how to do things like shoot
seals, build igloos, and survive years of frozen winter darkness.

Ada knew none of those things. She had no outdoors or survival
training. She had a paralyzing fear of polar bears. And she had lived
a hard life. At age sixteen, she married a man named Jack Blackjack
who later abused her, starved her, and then divorced her. She lost two
babies. Her sole remaining son, Bennett, was plagued by tuberculo-
sis. Ada was impoverished. She worked as a seamstress and house
cleaner. Because Bennett's health was precarious and she had no ability to get him the care he needed at a hospital, she was forced to leave
him in an orphanage.

Nome, coincidentally, was on Stefansson's path to the goal of
Wrangel Island. Ada learned of Stefansson's mission. Stefansson
planned to hire Inuit families to join the four men and help with the

sewing and hunting and overall surviving—everyone, by then, knew that Inuit were key to an Arctic mission's success.

Ada thought about the offer. It would pay fifty dollars a month, a sum that dwarfed the pennies she made as a housecleaner. The money might make it possible for her to regain custody of Bennett and get him to a hospital. She knew she would be away from Bennett and her mother and her home for three years—an unfathomable stretch of time—but this felt like her one ticket to solvency.

Ada was leery of joining four white men in the Arctic, but was assured that she would be part of a larger Inuit contingent. She would be with her people. She had no survival skills, but perhaps other Inuit could teach her. Besides, her job was just to sew and cook, and she could do this well.

Then, on the date of departure for Wrangel Island, no other Inuit showed up. They all decided the expedition was too dangerous and not worth the money. This concerned Ada for obvious reasons. She thought about quitting. She almost did. But Ada had given her word to join the expedition, and she was a woman of her word.

She would go to Wrangel Island, risks be damned.

· · ·

WRANGEL ISLAND WAS nominally a Vilhjalmur Stefansson expedition, but he did not personally join the crew. He was its figurehead, funder, and chief strategist, but he merely set the team in motion and then hoped for the best. The men didn't mind; Stefansson was a legend, and they were happy to be in his orbit.

So the four men and Ada settled into their makeshift camp at Wrangel Island, cut off from the rest of the world. Ada sewed and cooked. The men hunted and hiked and conducted scientific research. "She was shy and desperately afraid of bears, but a good, hard worker, and they all got along fine," writes Jennifer Niven, author of *Ada Blackjack*.

Then, somehow, the group dynamic shattered. The prevailing theory of historians is that Ada developed feelings for the leader of the expedition, Allan Crawford, but that this was unrequited. "She decided that she loved him and she wasn't afraid to let the others know it," writes Niven. "She had made up her mind. She planned to marry him and become Mrs. Ada Blackjack Crawford."

Crawford was firm with his lack of interest, and Ada slid into a deep funk, lonely and homesick and full of regret for joining this thankless frozen mission. Some historians suggest she had "Arctic hysteria," a psychological condition that can lead to suicide—especially since Ada had grown up in a city and had no preparation for this grueling terrain.

At one point Ada tried to run away. She stopped cooking and sewing. She threatened to poison herself. She was convinced that one of the men, Lorne Knight, hated her and planned to kill her.

The men retaliated, and their retribution was harsh. They mocked her and called her "Oofty" and "Nymph." (Aside from Ada's fleeting crush on the leader, there is no evidence of any amorous impropriety.) Their journals refer to her as "the foolish female." They laughed at her. When Ada refused to work, Knight tied her to a flagpole in the cold, letting her freeze for hours. They starved her, telling her that she must work to eat—for two weeks she subsisted only on stolen bread.

Lorne Knight grumbled in his journal:

> She will not work and sits about and disobeys orders and eats up
> our food and is being paid fifty dollars a month for doing the op-
> posite always.

Ada's funk did not last long. She shook it off, she resumed her cooking and sewing, and the group continued as before. But now a bigger problem loomed: Wrangel Island was not the cakewalk Stefansson had promised. Game was scarce. It was cold. In theory, the group could have brought enough food to survive for years, but Stefansson had insisted they travel light to prove they could live off the land. Now this looked dicey.

The group's morale plunged.

· · ·

PEOPLE CAN FORGET HISTORY, both in life and in exploration. Stefansson, as president of The Explorers Club, was well aware of the tale of Adolphus Greely. The two had met. They mingled at Club headquarters. Stefansson even wrote the introduction to one of the early Greely books, *Abandoned: The Story of the Greely Arctic Expedition.*

Anyone who read Stefansson's introduction knows that after the first year of the Greely expedition, a resupply ship attempted to bring the crew food. But the ship departed too late in the season, the shipping lanes froze, and the crew was in peril. Nineteen of the twenty-five explorers died. The nearly miraculous fact that six (including Greely) survived was thanks largely to the resourcefulness of Greely's wife, Henrietta, who marshalled the nation to come to their rescue. Now history repeated itself.

After the first year at Wrangel Island, a ship was supposed to bring fresh supplies, food, and even new crewmates, in case the original four men were injured. They botched the job. Stefansson's ship left too late in the season, just like Greely's, and it couldn't penetrate the ice. There would be no relief.

Unbeknownst to Ada Blackjack or the four stranded men, news of this failure became public. Now the families of the four men began to worry, and they wrote letters pleading that action be taken by Stefansson or the Canadian government. (No one wrote letters on behalf of Ada Blackjack.)

One of the men's fathers sent a telegraph that pleaded:

> Is there nothing we can do? Is it too late and dangerous now to send another boat?

Stefansson was unconcerned. He wrote letters to the families, reassuring them that all was fine. After all, their children were just in the Arctic! The friendly Arctic. It was as comfortable as Hawaii.

There is no more need to worry about them than if they were in some European city or an ordinary place and were merely not in the habit of communicating with you. In other words, the only worries you need have for Allan are the same which he may reasonably have about you, and his chance of being safe and well next fall is the same as your own.

He also wrote:

As I see it, there is no cause for special anxiety about the men on Wrangel Island. They are as likely as you or I to be safe and well a year from now.

And to another parent, Stefansson cheekily wrote:

They are just as safe on their island as Robinson Crusoe was on his—a little more so because there are no cannibals in that vicinity.

• • •

MEANWHILE, back on Wrangel Island, the winter was dark, the days were cold, and the food was dwindling. The team feared starvation. But even with these bleak conditions, the men kept their faith in in Stefansson. One wrote a letter to Stefansson reaffirming his loyalty:

Of course I am not afraid of starving to death or freezing (thanks to the things I have been taught by you) but I am well aware that accidents are liable to happen to one in this country as well as on the 'outside.' So if I pass my 'checks' kindly send whatever remuneration I am entitled to, to my mother or father at McMinnville, and rest assured that I am ever grateful for the favors you have shown me, and the opportunities that you have made for me.

And now the men began writing letters to their families in case of their death, careful to say that this would only be caused by an "accident," and accidents can happen anywhere.

> As accidents are as likely to happen to one in this country as any-
> where else, I am leaving this letter for you. I am also leaving a let-
> ter for the manager of the Stef. Ex. & Dev. Co. asking him to send
> whatever money is due me, to you. However, if something does
> happen to me I will be thinking of you until the very end with all
> the love any one ever had for their Mother. This also applies to
> Dad & Joseph.

The journal of Lorne Knight, in particular, shows a deterioration of both conditions and spirits.

> The going ahead looks very bad, and as we only have five dogs in
> poor condition and the weather is very cold, it is needless to say
> that going is very difficult.

A bedrock principle of Stefansson's was that the Arctic would provide unlimited game—an endless buffet of hunting. The team found something quite different. One wrote a letter to his wife saying:

> There is not adequate food for all, there being only ten twenty-
> pound cases of hard bread and three pokes of seal oil to last until
> next summer. The prospects of getting game between now and
> next summer or sealing season are very poor.

The men wrote more letters to next of kin:

> My dear Mother, I am leaving this letter behind in care of
> Knight . . . in case an accident should befall me. Should the worst
> come to pass, I want you to know Mother that I have only myself
> to blame for my ending and that I'll remember to the last mo-

ment, the kind loving tenderness you have shown me as my mother all through my life. I have not once forgotten it, nor shall I ever forget. Farewell! A long farewell to you and all.

Three of the men decided there simply wasn't enough food on the island to support all five, so they decided to trek back to civilization, on foot, in a desperate mission to get help: Allan Crawford and his crewmates Fred Maurer and Milton Galle (who was just nineteen). They were scientists and explorers who perfectly fit the description that Stefansson had outlined in his letter. They were brave. They were adventurous.

They were never heard from again.

In one of exploration's open mysteries, we still don't know the fate of these three men. Some assume they starved to death. Some think they drowned in a makeshift boat. Still others think they were captured by the Russians, who claimed Wrangel Island as their own. One hundred years later and we still don't know. What we do know is that Wrangel Island, in the winter of 1922, now had only two inhabitants: Lorne Knight and Ada Blackjack.

. . .

KNIGHT WAS INTENDED to be the rock of the expedition. The anchor. He had joined one of Stefansson's prior journeys to the Arctic, nearly dying of scurvy but still eager to return. Knight was smart, hardy with a rifle, and had top-notch survival instincts. He had beaten the Arctic before—when most of the crew perished—and he knew he could do it again.

But early on, Knight felt something peculiar on his skin, in his lungs, in his bones. It was something he had felt before. Knight contracted scurvy. At first he kept the scurvy from the other men, from Ada, from himself. Then he could no longer deny the truth. He felt pain in his legs and arms. In his diary he confessed he felt "weak as a kitten."

After the other men left, Knight declined further. He soon found it difficult to hunt. This was alarming, because it was his job to provide food for both himself and Ada, who had never fired a gun. He lost his appetite. He lost weight. He lost his ability to chop wood, which was essential to keep the two of them warm. Eventually, he couldn't even leave his bed.

Suddenly, with the rest of the crew gone and Knight bedridden, every aspect of surviving the Arctic fell on Ada Blackjack.

Ada grabbed Knight's rifle. "I must learn to shoot," she wrote in a journal that she'd just begun to keep. She practiced on targets as Knight lay moaning in bed. The rifle had a brutal recoil that punished her shoulder, so she built a gun rest that cushioned the blow.

At first she was a lousy shot. Knight even made jokes about it, but with practice she got better. Then she became an ace. Ada, who grew up in a city and had no training or experience surviving in the Arctic, taught herself to crawl on her belly and sneak up on game, killing and then skinning her prey. She cooked the game for Knight. When he grew weaker, she fed him with a spoon. She chopped wood to keep them warm. She cleaned Knight's bedpan. And through all of this she kept thinking of her son, Bennett, who far away was battling tuberculous. She often wrote of him in her journal.

> If anything happen to me and my death is known, there is black stirp for Bennett school book bag, for my only son. I wish if you please take everything to Bennett that is belong to me. I don't know how much I would be glad to get home to folks.

Ada taught herself to set traps for foxes. She snapped their necks to kill them and skinned them. When she was too exhausted to hunt, she read Knight's Bible—with his encouragement: first the complete Old Testament and then the New. She continued to spoon-feed Knight and keep him clinging to life.

Knight's repayment for her generosity?

Cruelty. As he became woozier, perhaps enraged by his own impotence, he barbed her with insults. He laughed at her. He even expressed sympathy for Ada's ex-husband, who had abused and starved and divorced her. Knight said, basically, that he could see where the ex-husband was coming from.

As Ada vented in her journal:

> He never stop and think how much it's hard for women to take
> four mans place, to wood work and to hund for something to eat
> for him and do waiting to his bed and take the shiad out for him.

Ada tried to keep her spirits up, but Knight's meanness was tough to swallow. She wrote:

> This is the wosest life I ever live in this world. Though it is hard
> enough for me to wood work and trying my best in everything and
> when I come home to rest here a man talk against me saying all
> kinds of words against me then what could I do.

She kept her sanity, in part, by focusing on Bennett. Her journal is full of instructions on how he should be raised if she died. Above all else, she dreaded the possibility that the custody of Bennett would revert to her ex-husband.

> If I be known dead. I want my sister Rita to take Bennett my son,
> for her own son and look after every things for Bennett she is the
> only one that I wish she take my son don't let his father Black Jack
> take him, if Rita my sister live. Then I be clear.

Ada continued to care for Knight. And finally, after weeks of inexplicable resentment and hostility, Knight began to soften. Then he expressed gratitude. He could no longer ignore the extraordinary courage, grit, and resourcefulness shown by Ada. He gave her tips on hunting duck. He'd tell her, "Pretty good shooting."

The two became friends. Knight told her that when he died, he wanted her to have his most beloved possession, his Bible. He even wrote an inscription for her.

Ada, for her part, now saw Knight as a beloved companion. Though he was on his deathbed, she was grateful for the company. She even thought of him as a baby that needed help.

> Mr. Knight is sick now just like a little baby and I will take care of
> him just like my own little babies that are sick and die.

. . .

MEANWHILE, thousands of miles away, the four families—unaware three men were missing—demanded some kind of rescue mission Stefansson insisted that all was well. He wrote to Knight's father:

> The men on Wrangel Island are not "stranded" there. From my
> point of view they are a colony, no more stranded than were the
> early settlers of Nova Scotia or Plymouth Rock.

He continued:

> Illness is, of course, possible but the danger of that is no greater
> than it always has been on our expeditions. It is a very healthful
> climate, the danger of illness is less than it would be in a city, and
> about the only drawback on Wrangel Island from that point of
> view is the absence of surgical care.

. . .

SURGICAL CARE WOULD have been useful to Lorne Knight, who continued to wither. For days he could hardly speak, unable to eat anything. Ada would gently feed him part of an egg. He would lie barely conscious.

As Knight drifted closer to death, Ada realized she would need to shoulder even more responsibility. One of the expedition members, the nineteen-year-old Galle, had lugged a typewriter to the camp. He forbid Ada from using it, but the three had been gone for months, and Ada decided it was okay.

She taught herself to type. Her grammar was poor but the ideas were lucid, forceful. Every morning she dashed off an update on her whereabouts when she went out to hunt, both for posterity and in the case Galle and the others returned that very afternoon, wondering where she was. (The letters from this typewriter, incidentally, are how we know much of what happened on Wrangel Island.)

Ada's first dispatch from the typewriter:

> Dear Galle, I didn't know I will have very important writing to do. You well forgive me wouldn't you. Just before you left I've told you I wouldn't write with your typewriter. So I made up my mine I'll write a few words, in case some happen to me, because Mr. Knight he hardly know what he's talking about I guess he is going die he looks pretty bad.
>
> I hope I'll see you when you read letter. Well, if nothing happen to me I'll see you.
>
> The reason why I write this important notice I have to go out seal hunding with the rifle. Of course Knight wouldn't eat any meat he always say he's got sore throad.
>
> That's about all I well say in this notice I write. I may write some more some times if nothing happen to me in few days. With lots of best regards to your self from me
>
> Yours truly

Then, finally, it happened. For weeks it had been hard to tell if Knight was alive or dead. One morning Ada realized that he was no longer breathing. She was devastated to lose Knight—by now they clung to each other—and now she felt even more alone.

This was on June 23, 1923. We know this because Ada thought it important to record the date in her journal, sensing it would be of future interest to Knight's family and Stefansson. She wrote:

> The daid of Mr Knights death He died on June 23d I don't know what time he die though Anyway I write the daid, Just to let Mr Stefansson know what month he died and what daid of the month

But that was not the last word from Lorne Knight. Before he passed away, he'd written this poem in the journal that he gave to Ada:

> Here lies a Polar Explorer so valiant and bold
> Who devoted his life to snowstorms and cold
> All for prominence, so I've been told
> And a few pieces of yellow filth called gold.
> For nourishment he had snow and scenery
> Which reminded him of the grim beanery
> The grim beanery so greasy and
> grim Would look like Paradise now to him.
> Oh! Bring on your roast pork, apple sauce and pie
> And some whipped cream before I die
> Some of that wonderful potato salad, too
> And sliced tomatoes with lots of goo-goo
> And beans. Oh! Beans, that wonderful fruit
> And then to end it all, just to make things suit
> About a gallon of mother's canned fruit
> And then a wonderful bewitching smoke
> For as tobacco is concerned I'm dead broke.
> But I'm going now where it's always hot
> Where blizzards ain't and cold is not
> Where everyone's happy and anthems ringing
> But having no voice I'll be out of the singing
> Don't weep for me now, don't weep for me ever
> I'm going to do nothing for ever and ever.

. . .

AS KNIGHT WROTE his final lines of poetry, across the globe, Stefansson's expedition was becoming something of an international scandal. When they had first landed on Wrangel Island, the men hoisted the Union Jack and claimed the island for the United Kingdom. There was only one problem: Russia had claimed the island many decades before, even though they later abandoned it. Now the Russian government conveyed in the press that, if necessary, they would reclaim the island by force. "The Siberian Government is outfitting a vessel at Vladivostok for a voyage to Wrangel Island with the avowed intention of capturing the little band of British explorers," the Associated Press wrote, "and taking possession of the island in the name of Russia."

The British government's response? That if Russia followed through on capturing the Arctic explorers, this would be "equivalent to an act of war."

. . .

ADA BLACKJACK, of course, was not concerned about geopolitics. She just wanted to survive. Her journal reveals her determination to make it off this island, even if the four men were gone.

> June 24th.—I'm going to the other side of the harbar mouth do some duck hunding.

As always, she was afraid of polar bears, but she began to keep her anxiety in check.

> I saw two polar bears going in shore from the ice way over west of the camp. It's four o'clock now. I write down when I saw them. I don't know what I'm going to do if they come to the camp. Well, God knows.

Nearly two years earlier, when Ada arrived at Wrangel Island, the mere *thought* of a polar bear would seize her with terror. Now she knew precisely how to scare them away.

> I clean the seal skin today and lat this afternoon polar bear and one cub was very close to the camp and I didn't take any chances. I was afraid if I didn't hit it right I'd be in danger. I just shot over them and they wend away. I was glad thank the living God.

Ada even kept her sense of humor. One entry reads:

> I am glad it is not me polar bear eats.

She knitted herself gloves. She made Bennett a pair of slippers, decorating them with little beads. And then Ada, who was never taught any survival skills, figured out how to build herself a boat. She lashed canvas to driftwood and made a seaworthy vessel.

> After Knight die and birds and seal come I work hard to make a little boat so can get anything I shoot in the water.

Later, Ada turned introspective and philosophical, and even exculpated Stefansson for bringing her to this frozen rock. She accepted the responsibility.

> It was no one's fault but my own that I went up there, for no one would have forced me to go, but I wanted to go and thought I would never have another chance to go so I took it.

• • •

BY NOW TWO years had passed since Ada had left her home. She had no idea if Bennett was alive. And Stefansson, until the final hours, insisted that the four men (Ada was never mentioned) were perfectly safe. "One good hunter," he confidently wrote, "can provide food for ten dependents so long as his ammunition holds out."

If Stefansson had had his way, perhaps no relief ships would have ever been sent. However, thanks to a fundraising effort inspired largely by the explorers' families—and that included well-wishers in the larger exploration family, like Orville Wright—a relief ship did indeed depart from Nome in August of 1923.

It took ten days for the ship to navigate through the ice floes, and on August 20, 1923, the relief ship reached Wrangel Island. The captain of the ship, Harold Noice, expected to find Knight, Crawford, Maurer and Galle. Instead, when he paddled to the shore, he saw a young Inupiat woman. "She had the look of a hunter, he thought," writes Niven. "She was dressed in furs, from head to foot, with a snow shirt worn over a reindeer parka trimmed with wolf skin. Her face was lined and dirty, toughened by brutal winds and cold and hardship."

Noice looked at Ada.

Ada looked at Noice.

Both were surprised by what they saw.

"Where is Crawford and Galle and Maurer?" Ada asked. The three had left ages ago to find help, and Ada assumed that now her missing companions had finally returned.

Noice, for his part, couldn't comprehend what he was seeing.

"There is nobody here but me," she said. "I am all alone."

Ada told him what happened to Knight. Then she could keep it inside no longer. "I want to go back to my mother," she said. "Will you take me back to Nome?"

*   *   *

THE RELIEF VESSEL, at last, safely returned Ada to Nome. She was reunited with her mother and her sister. And she was reunited with her beloved Bennett, who she could now afford to remove from the orphanage. They later moved to Seattle, where she hoped to find a hospital with better medical care.

Vilhjalmur Stefansson, meanwhile, had some explaining to do. The tone of his letters changed on a dime, and he was stuck with the sober task of writing condolence letters to the families of the other four explorers. The communication was terse. To the families of the fallen men, Stefansson simply sent the following telegram:

Deepest sympathy over terrible news.

As for the legacy of Ada Blackjack? Some seemed to understand the inspiring role she played on the island. Knight's parents were grateful for her kindness. "How I wish I could make some suitable reward for Ada Blackjack," Knight's father wrote, after learning of all she had done. "She is the heroine of the whole expedition. If it is ever in my power to suitably reward her, I hope I may not overlook the opportunity."

The question of whether Ada was ever "suitably rewarded" is complicated. On the one hand, when she returned, she briefly became a sensation in the press. Newspaper articles called her "the Heroine of the Arctic."

Others tried to profit from this fame, including Stefansson. He sought access to both Ada's and Knight's journals, obtained them, and later wrote a book, *The Adventure of Wrangel Island*. He gave Ada some cash, but she received no royalties. Her side of the story was never fully told.

Ada did the best she could to give Bennett a healthy and happy life, but medical issues would long shadow her son. He contracted spinal meningitis. He became deaf and blind in one eye, but he managed to live to the age of fifty-eight.

With little interest in speaking to the press—especially after a series of nasty articles charged that *she* was the reason Knight died and the expedition failed—Ada found work as a housekeeper, struggled to pay bills, married and divorced again, and quietly faded from the news. Her story was forgotten by most. She lived to be eighty-five years old, passing away in 1983.

One of the rare public celebrations of Ada Blackjack came from the Alaska legislature, which, upon her death, honored her with an official citation for heroism. The citation read, in part:

> Not many Alaskans remember this soft-spoken and vital woman. In the years following her heroic feat she was forgotten by most people who knew of her ordeal. . . . We urge Alaskans to become familiar with the story of Ada Blackjack Johnson who recently passed away in Palmer. From her story we can each gain an insight into the life and personal courage of a resident in our state who survived under unbearable circumstances, only to be forgotten by her friends and neighbors. It is our duty and obligation to honor Ada Blackjack Johnson for her astounding courage, her spiritual strength, and her commitment to her fellow man.

THE FLAG FROM THE MOON

Jim Lovell

IN 1970, ASTRONAUT JIM LOVELL planned to bring a flag from The Explorers Club to the moon. Lovell's mission, unfortunately, happened to be Apollo 13.

As everyone who saw the eponymous movie knows, Lovell's crew, against all odds, miraculously returned home alive. What the movie did not show was that Lovell had The Explorers Club flag with him the entire time. So he later returned the flag to the Club, along with a polite letter of apology, explaining that "since we were unable to land, the plans were disrupted."

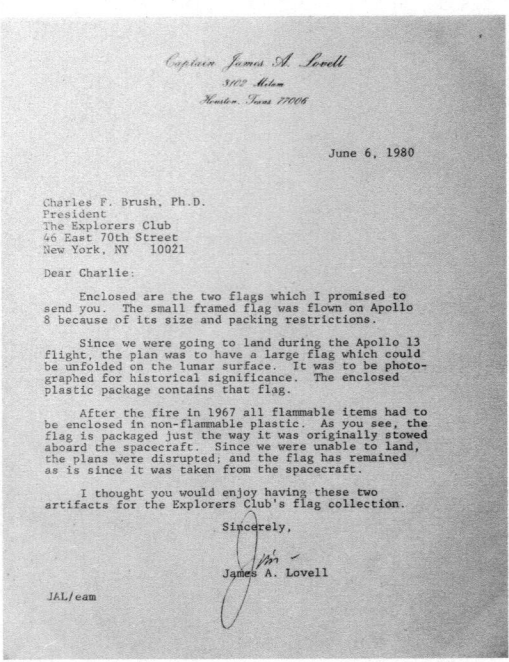

TWEETS FROM SPACE

Mike Massimino

LETTERS FROM THE EDGE play a crucial role that's often over-looked: They preserve sanity. Ada Blackjack did not have the ability to communicate back and forth with her loved ones, so all of her letters were one-way dispatches. Modern explorers can do more.

Lovell's Apollo 13 crew, of course, was able to communicate with NASA to crack all the daunting engineering challenges. For decades astronauts could speak with their colleagues and their families. And in 2009, NASA astronaut Mike Massimino—his friends call him "Mass"—ushered in a new era of space communication.

Mass, who flew in the space shuttle to perform critical repairs on the Hubble Space Telescope, knew that communication was critical—on both a personal and professional level. "You miss a lot," says Mass. "You're off the planet. You're going to miss birthdays and holidays. The birth of a child. You'll miss the day-to-day Little League games. And that does affect morale."

The astronauts sent emails to their families when they could, and they communicated more broadly with the world at large, sparking the public's fascination with space exploration. He also knew that communication helped NASA. "Part of our jobs," he says, "was to communicate what we're doing for taxpayer dollars."

So Mass took advantage of a relatively new communication platform: Twitter. He was the first astronaut to do so. As Mass trained on Earth for the mission, he gave quick updates of his journey. He shared details that were intimate, humorous, self-deprecating—exploration didn't need to be stuffy.

Cooking dinner . . . we are having tostadas, too bad I can't make them in space (would be too messy)

Quick visit to the doctor for a nose culture to make sure I am bacteria free before flying in space

Just got out of the motion simulator after a morning of shuttle re-entry simulations, we are 19 days from launch

On May 11, 2009, the space shuttle *Atlantis* blasted off from iconic Launch Complex 39A at the Kennedy Space Center, the same site that serviced the Apollo missions. Mass knew he'd become the first astronaut to tweet in space. So he asked some advice from a friend of his, an Apollo astronaut who knew about sending a dispatch from the edge—Neil Armstrong.

"I didn't really think much about it," Armstrong told Mass, referring to "one small step." Instead he focused on the mission. And that was his advice.

"So I wasn't thinking about it," says Mass. "I was worried about the mission and getting that done. And then whatever came to mind, I put out there in the first tweet."

On May 12, 2009, Mass wrote the first tweet from outer space:

From orbit: Launch was awesome!! I am feeling great, working hard, & enjoying the magnificent views, the adventure of a lifetime has begun!

Over the rest of the mission, he used Twitter to give real-time updates of what it was like to live and work in the space shuttle:

From orbit: Eating chocolates in space, floating then [sic] in front of me then floating and eating them like I am a fish

From orbit: Listening to Sting on my ipod watching the world go by—literally

> From orbit: We see 16 sunrises and sunsets in 24 hrs, each one spectacular as the sun lights up the atmosphere in a spectrum of colors

> From orbit: The Earth is so beautiful, it is like looking into paradise

Mass then gave a clearer sense of what it's like to soak in that beauty:

> From orbit: Viewing the Earth is a study of contrasts, beautiful colors of the planet, thin blue line of atmosphere, pure blackness of space

> From orbit: The stars at night in space do not twinkle, they look like perfect points of light and I can clearly see the milky way galaxy

And finally:

> From orbit: My only regret when viewing the Earth is that my wife & children are not with me to see it (along with all of you following me)

After Mass landed, he kept tweeting and shared what it was like to reacclimatize to the planet.

> Getting re-adjusted to gravity, let go of a small bag of groceries and must have expected it to float, luckily no damage

Over fifteen years later, Mass looks back at these tweets with a chuckle. He knows they're not in the same league as Armstrong's "One small step," or John Glenn's "Zero G and I feel fine," or the Apollo 8 crew's reading of Genesis on Christmas Eve, and he's okay with that.

← **Post**

Mike Massimino ✔
@Astro_Mike

From orbit: Launch was awesome!! I am feeling great, working hard, &
enjoying the magnificent views, the adventure of a lifetime has begun!

4:33 PM · May 12, 2009

💬 97   🔁 687   ♡ 3.6K   🔖 115   ⬆

Instead, he takes pride that his tweet was immediately roasted on
Saturday Night Live. Then–Weekend Update host Seth Meyers read a
portion of the tweet—"Launch was awesome!"—and dryly noted
that "In forty years we've gone from 'One giant leap for mankind to
'Launch was awesome.' "

Meyers then went on to say, "I assume if we ever encounter intelligent life in the cosmos, this is how we'll be notified: *Alienz, you
guys! :-O*"

Mass takes this all in stride, amused. "I got a little street cred out
of it."

THE EIGHTH CONTINENT

Meg Lowman

YEARS BEFORE SHE CHALLENGED our definition of "the known world," Meg Lowman faced a far more basic problem: She didn't want to climb trees.

Since childhood she had been obsessed with nature in general and trees in particular. She remembers thinking as a kid, "Nature didn't bully you, nature didn't yell at you." Trees, in addition to "not yelling at you," could even help guide your way. One of Lowman's childhood heroes was Harriet Tubman, and Tubman had navigated the darkness of the Underground Railroad, in part, by using the illuminated moss of trees.

Did she really have to climb them?

In 1979, for her dissertation, Lowman studied the leaves of Australia's rainforest canopy. No one knew much about these leaves. How long did they live? What made them flourish or die? How did they fit into the larger ecosystem? Most people, at that point, only knew about the rainforest from what they could see standing at the bottom of the tree's trunk, but this was only 5 percent of the picture. That would be like staring at the ocean from the beach and concluding you know its secrets.

Lowman had to get raw, firsthand knowledge of whatever grew above the forest canopy—one hundred to three hundred feet in the air—but she wasn't exactly a sporting daredevil. In fact, she'd never played any sports. (Before Title IX's passage in 1972, many American girls weren't allowed.) She didn't love heights, so she thought about ways she could study the tops of trees from the ground. Maybe she could train a monkey to climb up the trees and fetch samples? Maybe she could use binoculars? Or maybe she could just lie on a hammock and hope the leaves would fall into her lap?

Lowman knew all that was ridiculous. She knew what she had to do. She would climb the damn trees.

Near Cairns, Australia, the rainforest canopy was more than 125 feet from the ground—high enough to get her killed. (Lowman loved trees, but she also loved living.) She knew she couldn't climb without any ropes or equipment. She considered using the tree-climbing equipment available at the time, but none of it suited her research purposes. Some arborists had harnesses, for example, but those weighed fifty pounds and were designed to accommodate chainsaws.

So she invented her own tree-climbing gear. She called it "the slingshot."

First, Lowman found a piece of metal and a chunk of rubber tire. Then she rustled up some fishing line, fishing weights, and a spool of sturdy nylon. She got some funny looks when she brought all this into the university's welding shop—although she was used to funny looks, as she was the only female in the entire graduate program.

She welded this gizmo together. And once she'd built a crude prototype of the slingshot, she brought it with her to the trees of the rainforest that stretched up as far as the eye could see. (She also brought along Oreos for sustenance, a habit she would keep for decades.)

Here's how the slingshot worked: She tossed a fishing wire over a nearby branch, using a fishing weight (imagine a small stone) to guide the line. She caught the fishing weight after it dropped down—this took some practice—which gave her a loop of wire that slung over the branch.

Now she was in business. The fishing wire, of course, was too light to use for climbing. So she took one end of the wire and hooked it to the sturdy nylon rope, then snaked it back over the tree branch. Now she had a loop of sturdy nylon. She attached the nylon to a harness she'd made from the rubber tire, she tied another rope to the ground for safety, and now she had a slingshot.

She still had that fear of climbing, and at first the work was tricky and slow. The trees had spikey leaves with bugs eating them, and she worried that the higher she went the more bugs and ants there would be to eat *her*. One of the branches could have termites, and maybe it would snap off and fall to the ground.

But soon she got the hang of it. She even got fast. Lowman kept tossing that fishing wire over branches above her, snaking the nylon through, reattaching the harness, and then climbing a bit higher.

Lowman traveled up ten feet. Twenty. Fifty. The ground looked small, and the canopy above her loomed larger. Her fingers got blisters, but she didn't care. She hugged the tree with her knees, and her legs burned with exhaustion, but she kept going. What would she find?

She thought it might take her all day to scale the tree, so she was surprised when the slingshot helped her do it in thirty minutes. And finally, when she reached the top of the trunk, she peeked her head above the dense ceiling of leaves.

And she saw bugs.

So many bugs.

Every leaf was swarming with them. Caterpillars, bees, ants, you name it. But these bugs didn't look gross or icky or scary. They were glorious. They were signs of pulsing life. And she saw a kaleidoscope of colors that pierced her heart—greens and yellows and reds and even silvery blues.

It was the most amazing place she'd ever seen. She didn't want to leave. Lowman took a quick break to munch on some Oreos, then snapped a few photos. She had discovered a goldmine.

After that first discovery, Lowman returned again and again. The climbs weren't just for kicks; she had questions about leaves, and she wanted answers. So Lowman concocted a systematic process of identifying and marking leaves throughout the canopy, returning frequently to see how they changed. Each leaf told a story. She began to build a map of the leaves and the canopy.

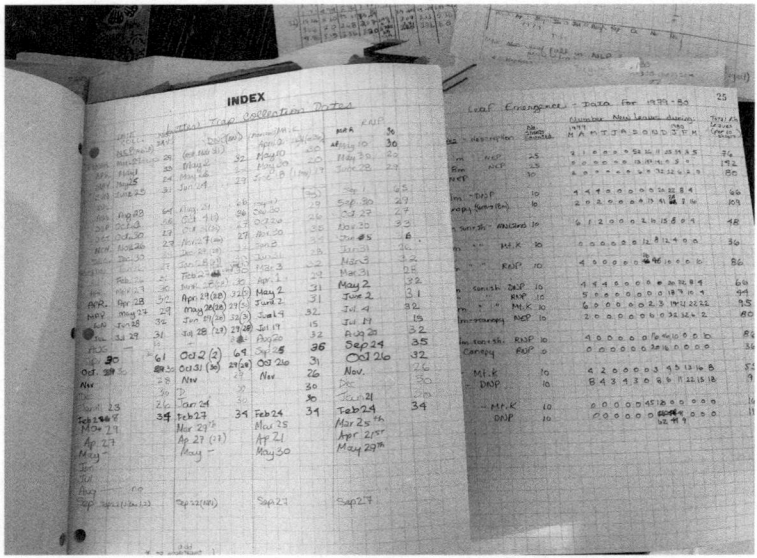

*Lowman's field notebook meticulously documents "leafing events";
she monitored thousands of leaves each month to record
bud burst, insect damage, storm tearing, and death.*

Lowman helped the world discover what she calls the "eighth continent," the planet's forest canopy.

And the world now knows her as Canopy Meg. She helped us understand that a jaw-dropping 80 percent of the world's biodiversity lives on this eighth continent.

Before Lowman, when we thought about trees, we only really cared about the trunks. (Mainly because we liked to chop them down.) Thanks to Canopy Meg, more of us are considering the whole tree. Decades after that first climb, she still speaks with wonder when she talks about trees and leaves. "The leaf is the unit that keeps us alive and keeps the trees alive," says Lowman. The insects eat the leaf, and animals eat the insects.

Once you spend some time with Lowman, it's tough to look at trees the same way again. "They produce oxygen for us. They take in the carbon dioxide that we pollute and store it in their trunks," she

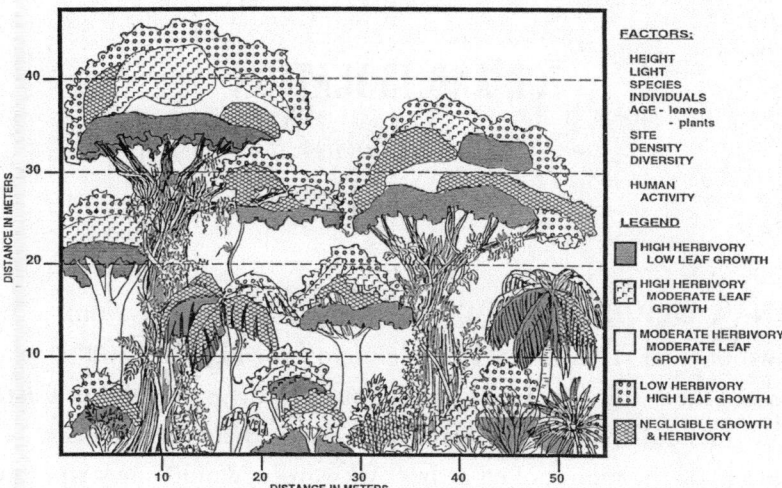

Fig 3. Schematic representation of 'hotspots' in the canopy, where herbivores are attracted to foliage that is more susceptible, and where insect abundance will be highest. 'Hotspots' will vary over time, due to the differences in phenology and foliage qualities among species.

says. "They provide us with chocolate and cherries." They provide us with protection from climate change.

Decades ago, she was afraid to climb trees. Then she perfected the "slingshot" and developed increasingly sophisticated climbing tools. She later wrote a manual on how to climb trees. And then she realized that she could make the eighth continent even more accessible to people who are not able to climb. Now there are canopy walkways around the world that can be enjoyed by all. Young children, the elderly, the disabled, and those with a fear of heights—now all can see what Lowman has seen. "We need to make sure trees are inclusive," she says. "That's what will save them."

ICE AND ISOLATION

Donna Oliver

DONNA OLIVER STOOD in a warehouse, the only woman in a crowd of men. The men began peeling off their clothes and stripped down to their white skivvies. Soon they were nearly naked. They started trying on cold-weather survival gear, seeking their correct sizes.

Some of the men looked at her awkwardly. Would she strip down as well?

The problem was solved when someone found a broom closet and suggested Oliver step inside. They had her try on gear in the stuffy little closet, but the gear itself was designed for men. No one had considered the possibility of a woman wearing it.

This was in 1976. Oliver, a psychologist, had just signed up to be stationed in Antarctica for 194 days during the darkness of winter. Along with her husband at the time, she would be part of a seventy-eight-person team to winter at the frozen McMurdo Station, and she had two goals: (1) to conduct pioneering research on isolation psychology; and (2) to prove that a woman could survive just as well as a man.

The men didn't want her there, and they told her so. Of the seventy-eight-person team, sixty-nine were military support personnel, and they voted unanimously that she not be allowed to join. But they had no choice. The Supreme Court had just ruled, under Title IX, that it was illegal to ban women from the workforce. So, for 194 days Oliver would be the only woman, from any nation, on the continent of Antarctica. She was only the fifth woman in history to winter beneath the Antarctic Circle, and the first to winter without another woman.

Oliver soon settled into Antarctica life. It was dark in the morning, dark all day, dark all night. It was minus forty degrees Fahrenheit outside. They'd neglected to install bathrooms for women, so throughout the day, Oliver needed to put on all her gear, step outside into the icy darkness, and hoof it across the base to use her one bathroom.

She kept a detailed journal of Operation Deep Freeze, eventually writing 640 handwritten pages. The journal gives a sense of what isolation is actually like at the edge of the known world, both physically and psychologically. Consider her entry from August 13, 1977, which she titled "Perceptual Changes":

Why have none of the gloomy prophesies of rape and the like occurred this winter? What have I done on my side to encourage things to go smoothly?

First of all, I behave as if I expect the men to treat me decently. I believe that people usually act the way they are expected to act. However, at the same time, I have also been cautious to keep an eye out for any exceptions to the above general rule. I avoid a few people I do not trust and places where the men tend to get particularly rowdy or drunk.

My whole set of perceptions has changed. My sense of time is geared only by the clock (the light/dark outdoor conditions are not a clue to the time, nor is my perception of being rested/tired, alert/sleepy). Making mealtimes is the most restricting regulatory time-keeper. . . . I have become so acclimated to the cold that a calm -15 degrees F seems like a lovely warm day.

My level of alertness is way under par. No matter how much I sleep I frequently feel tired. My motivation and level of production are also way down. . . . My attention span must be equivalent to that of a kindergartener.

Both my recent and remote memory are lacking. I sometimes forget simple vocabulary words that I have known for perhaps twenty years. Or, I walk to get something and forget what it was 2 seconds later. (For example: I walked into the biolab, decided to do some photographic work, and headed for the darkroom. When I arrived at the door I felt a draft [and] I wanted my slippers. I headed toward my office to fetch my slippers. When I arrived at my desk I thought to myself, "What are you doing here, Donna? You are supposed to be in the darkroom." So I returned to the dark-room and remembered I needed the slippers. I went through the above cycle several times before I finally "got it all together." . . .

My senses are much more sensitive:

1. Sounds: I react to unexpected or loud noises with a nervous jump. . . . The sound of the wind seems more at home to me than the occasional motor vehicle driving by. I wonder what my reac-tion will be to the variety of noises of a bustling modern-day city?

2. Sight: My eyes are more bothered by unexpected bright lights (a drafting light table or xerox machine). I also spend more time blankly staring at something without really seeing it.

3. Touch: . . . I am better able to withstand the cold and enjoy heat less. The air is extremely dry and my skin has become tough and dry. I feel, hear and see (if it is dark) numerous little static electricity shocks throughout the day (when straightening the bed sheets, touching a door handle, etc.).

4. Smell: My sense of smell has become heightened to the few odors which are available here. For example, deodorant and hand creme, which were undetectable to me in the "real world," are strong here.

5. Taste: This is difficult to detect and confusing with my crav-ings for unavailable "freshies," etc.

I believe that movies, dreams, daydreams, etc., become more important here because they are one of the few sources of variety. Also, more of my otherwise non-consciously remembered memo-ries come to the forefront of my awareness. I enjoy the warm, comfortable ones, and have an opportunity to "work through" those which are hassling. At home this happens less frequently because many more new, demanding stimuli come and go and come and go and occupy my attention.

I can remember periods of time (about 10 to 12 years ago) when I yearned to get away to a hideout (monastery) for a while.

At the time I thought I was trying to escape problems by running away. Perhaps instead my inner need for balance was telling me to get somewhere where I could become caught-up and have time to work through hassles in the method explained above. I believe that meditation provided another means to "get caught up."

Throughout the six months of darkness, Oliver tried to focus on the positive, and sometimes she reread Alfred Lansing's classic book on Ernest Shackleton, *Endurance,* for motivation. "I would read that from beginning to end and say, 'What are you complaining about, Donna?'" Oliver says now. She also found inspiration in Viktor Frankl's *Man's Search for Meaning,* embracing a can-do spirit that Ada Blackjack would appreciate.

And the foundation of Oliver's psychology itself had a streak of positivity. As you might expect, she kept a watchful eye on the negative consequences of prolonged isolation—such as impaired cognition, memory lapses, sleep loss—but she also took what she calls a more "humanistic" approach that considered the surprising upsides.

Oliver's research had some counterintuitive results. For starters, a stunning 87 percent of people who went through the winter considered it a positive experience. "You get back to normal when you get back," Oliver says, and in some ways you're even better than normal. "The things that stick with you are good," she says. "People are more capable of intimate contact in their life, and they learned to be more inner-directed. They become more cooperative. They become more capable of intimate contact."

As her PhD dissertation, Oliver wrote "The Psychological Effects of Isolation and Confinement in an Antarctic Winter-Over Group." She then moved on with her life and focused on other career objectives, not giving much thought to polar research. Decades passed.

Oliver was recently stunned to see a resurgence in the study of field isolation—with her 1970s work as a foundational layer. Suddenly, her work has urgency; just ask anyone who plans to stay on the moon or on Mars.

But isolation research was only half of Oliver's original goal. From the beginning, she wanted to prove that a woman could be just as effective as a man in the punishing winter of Antarctica. Originally the men balked. Gradually, after seeing her in action, they warmed and welcomed her into the fold. They even invited her to their weekly poker nights.

And on the final poker night of the winter, they told her, "Donna, you really did survive the winter well." Then they added a devastating caveat: "But we don't know any other woman who could." The men took a vote on whether women should be allowed to winter at Antarctica. Once again, they voted no.

Oliver was livid. *What more did she need to prove?* The men had tried to reconcile their old position (women don't belong) with their uncomfortable new data (Oliver exceeded expectations) by suggesting that she was an extraordinary woman, and most couldn't hack it.

She then wrote a detailed, respectful letter to the person in charge, the commander of Operation Deep Freeze, to protest the decision and make her case. It began:

> Wintering over at McMurdo Station this past season was one of the most rewarding experiences of my life. I accomplished a great deal professionally and grew personally from the unique experience. I see no reason why qualified female military personnel should not winter in the future. I realize that careful planning and selection of the women will increase the likelihood of a smooth transition from a traditionally all-male to a male-female community. Therefore I would like to offer a brief summary of my W/O '77 experiences and a few suggestions.

She also clearly articulated the structural problems that so many women face, not just in Antarctica but in so many realms where they've been traditionally excluded:

Antarctica has historically been a "man's world" and women were not officially allowed to work or live on the continent until 1969. This fact gives us a realistic understanding of why so few women work here now. I am in favor of a much more equal sex ratio as long as qualified and willing participants are available. The low female-to-male ratio is probably the most severe psychological strain that most women experience at McMurdo. It can be stressful to be a "rare bird" and frequently in the limelight.

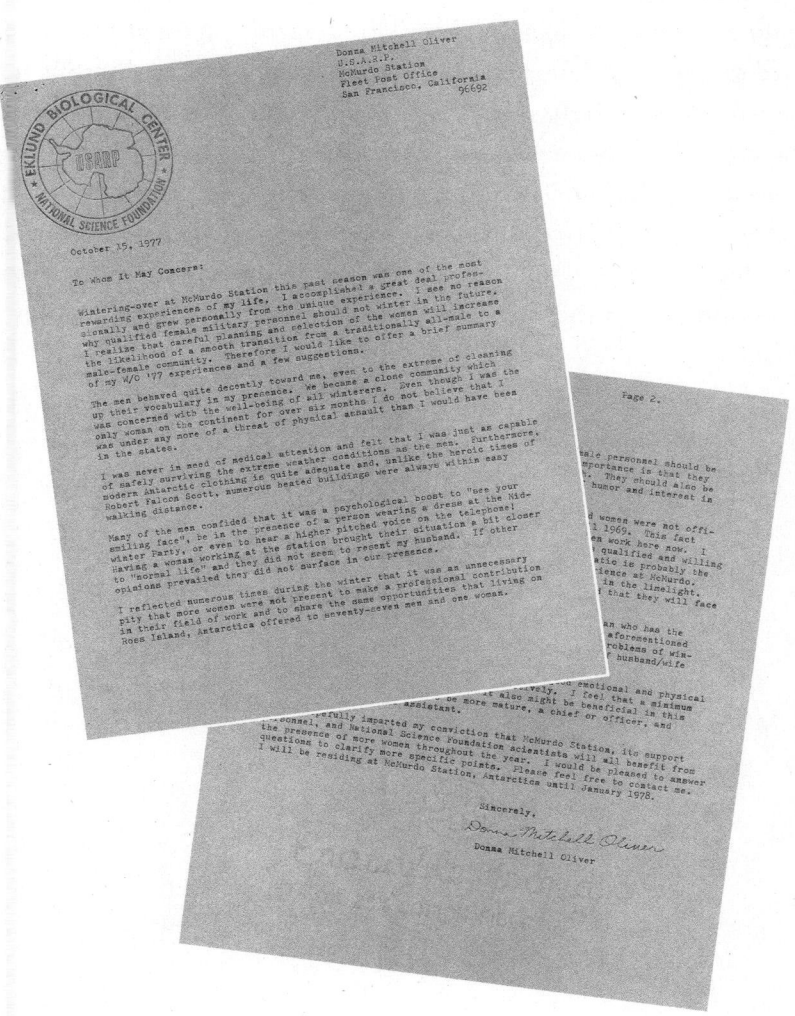

A few days later, the commander of Operation Deep Freeze wrote back with his reply.

He returned her letter. He wrote that her report was "not germane" to the issue of women wintering in Antarctica, and it would not be included in his recommendation to the top brass. (An assistant to the commander, at the risk of losing his job, told Oliver that he had been ordered "not to share this with anyone.")

But Oliver would not be dismissed so easily. The letter could be buried, but the proof of her wintering over could not. The following summer, in part thanks to Oliver's trailblazing, another woman applied to winter at Antarctica. Again the men protested. But this time the woman effectively said, "If you don't allow this I'll sue you, and thanks to the Supreme Court, I'll win."

So they let her in. Then they let more in. Oliver is now proud that each winter, in Antarctica, roughly a third of the scientists are women. And they often reach out to Oliver, now in her seventies, for advice and support—for she knows there's strength, beauty, and even growth in isolation.

2

The Edge of
Knowledge

The edge is not a simple concept. And it's not one-dimensional. Someone trying to find the North Pole is both at the edge of the known world and at the edge of knowledge . . . and likely also at the edge of survival and perhaps sanity. These categories are not mutually exclusive.

That said, many explorers—perhaps most explorers—are on a quest to push the edge of knowledge. Robert Peck has done this for decades, embedding himself with scientists and sending countless letters to tell their stories.

Or take Andrés Ruzo, a geoscientist who was inspired by a story from his grandfather to search for Peru's mythical "Boiling River" and then discovered microbes that could hold the key to fighting climate change. Jessica Glass, a geneticist, sought to understand the DNA of fish but instead found herself stuck in a "shit bridge." Martin Nweeia's search for knowledge was interrupted by a murder. To gather better data on volcanoes, Ben Jordan braved a deadly pool of lava. "Exploration is going into the unknown to seek new knowledge," says Trevor Wallace, who, along with Gino Caspari, pretended to be a criminal to explore the underground dark markets of antiques in Hong Kong.

Ultimately, the search for knowledge—and the desire to learn—is the quest of every explorer, dating back to our ancestors' question of "What's over the next hill?"

THE CHRONICLER OF THE EDGE

Robert Peck

WHAT MAKES A GOOD letter from the edge? This is something that Robert Peck has thought about for decades. Since the early 1980s, Peck has served as the official chronicler of expeditions for the Academy of Natural Sciences in Philadelphia, which has been sending scientists into the field since 1812. (It's one of the few such organizations that predates The Explorers Club.)

The Academy's roster includes 150 scientists, and then there's Peck, who thinks of himself as the "humanist on staff." His job is to tag along with the scientists as they hopscotch across the globe to conduct research. On every expedition he writes letters to capture the journey. He's sent countless letters to the Academy, to colleagues, to friends, and to his family to tell them he was okay.

Peck has learned that people wanted to hear the nitty-gritty of expeditions, and the grittier the better. "They love to hear how bad the food is, or how hard it is to pitch a tent that's at a forty-five-degree angle," he says. "How do you keep from getting parasites? How do you take the leeches off yourself? How do you stay out of quicksand?"

Here's how he describes the roads of Mongolia, for example:

> The road north from Hatgal . . . is considered [to] be one of the
> worst in Mongolia. That's saying a lot. In wet weather, it is a gooey
> mud track that can cling to cars and trucks like glue, or suck them
> down like quicksand. When the mud hardens, as it has in time for
> our drive, every rut, gully, hole, and mound created by a previous
> vehicle hardens into a cement-like obstacle course that must be
> navigated over, around or through . . .

Imagine the worst dirt road you have ever been on, multiply it by a factor of ten, sprinkle it with boulders, logs, and pools of mud as large as swimming pools, and you begin to approximate the surface of the road we were driving for a little over seven hours. . . .

When I finally climbed from the car tonight, I felt as though I had been traveling inside a mechanical bull. It is good to be out and walking again. Mongolia is really a country better suited for horse travel than cars. With luck, tomorrow's drive will be a bit better.

Just as most explorers have their trusty gear they bring on every expedition—a favorite beanie, a beloved compass—Peck always brings his preferred writing supplies: waterproof paper, envelopes, and always pencils instead of pens, as "they're durable, you can sharpen them, and you know they won't run out of ink."

He uses these pencils every night. Peck has developed a ritual with a two-step process: By the light of a lantern, while the scientists write up their notes and prepare their specimens, Peck first jots down notes in his field journal. Then he composes his letters. The journaling helps him clarify and organize his thoughts—informing the letters—and if he runs out of time to write his correspondence, he can mine his journal later for specific details.

Failing to keep a journal is a rookie mistake. As Peck says, ' The problem with writing a letter at the end of a trip is that you tend to summarize. You lose the details." A journal keeps the details fresh. Details, for example, like getting food poisoning from a goat, also in Mongolia:

After almost a month of visiting herding families and eating whatever I have been offered in cups, bowls, and plates of doubtful sanitation, it was inevitable that the risks of local eating would finally catch up with me.

We are staying with a very generous herding family a few hours south of Renchinlhumbe. This morning they killed one of their three hundred goats to cook a "horhog" for us. . . . The goat was butchered, river stones were heated in a fire and then combined with the animal's body parts, blood and a little water, in a large aluminum milk can and put on a fire to cook . . .

After a while, the horhog was declared finished and we were served the juice from the can. It was strong in flavor, but undeniably tasty. The internal organs and other miscellaneous parts were also good, though somewhat tougher than usual, suggesting they may not have been fully cooked.

As the day wore on, I began to regret eating with such gusto. In one delirious moment, my imagination saw the goat's glazed eye winking at me, as if to say that after having such an unpleasant morning, it was enjoying the last laugh. . . .

Whatever it is that has invaded my intestines has kept me on the ground most of the day. Since my tent temperature is well north of 100 degrees when the sun is on it, I found it cooler to be in the shadow of our vehicle, a spot I shared with a day-old lamb that seemed to enjoy my company. . . .

We had hoped to start our return drive this afternoon, but as I am in no condition to travel, we are going to wait another night. The setting is spectacularly beautiful, with an almost full moon hanging, Ansel Adams–like, above the Horidol Saridag mountains to our east. I am sure I will be up from time to time through the night. The only reward for a bad night stomach is the opportunity it provides for stargazing and admiring the moon.

Letters do more than just give facts and updates. They tell stories, they bring expeditions to life, and they even serve as the "first draft" of history.

Most of us take this for granted. But much of what we know of the United States' Revolutionary War era, for example, is gleaned not from the Declaration of Independence or the Constitution—a combined twenty pages—but from the 184,000 letters sent among the Founding Fathers. (There are 31,730 letters for George Washington alone.)

This is equally true for exploration, which is why explorers often write letters—or emails, texts, or videos—intended not just for the nominal recipient but for the sweeping eye of history. Peck knows that his letters from the field to the Academy of Natural Sciences are at times blown up and mounted in the museum. So he writes accordingly.

Writing letters, for Peck, even imbued him with a sneaky super-power. He often traveled with scientists into life-threatening situations, such as when a bounty was put on their heads while on expedition in Ecuador. ("We had to stay up at night with guns, and so on," Peck says nonchalantly.) Many in the expedition worried they would be killed. "There were all kinds of reasons why any of us might have died," says Peck. "But it never occurred to me that I would, because I was there as the chronicler, and I had to get the message out."

In other words, since someone needed to "live to tell the tale," the fact that Peck was telling the tale meant that he needed to live. (Peck chuckles; the shaky causality of the logic is not lost on him.) But the idea helped him psychologically. "I put myself in the role as the observer and chronicler," he says, "and not as the victim."

There is, we should admit, a certain paradox at the heart of the "letters from the edge" conceit: The closer you are to the edge the harder it is to send a letter. Peck deals with this conundrum all the time. For decades he has surveyed the field for the nearest post office—hoping to send his letters while on the expedition, if possible—but often he is forced to lug the letters until he returns to the nearest town. Sometimes he gets lucky and stumbles into a small, overlooked, one-person post office.

One such example was in Mongolia, which doesn't send a ton of outgoing international mail. Peck found they weren't even sure how much postage he should use, so he just slapped as many stamps as he could on the envelope and dropped the letter in the mailbox.

When Peck returned home, he discovered the recipient never received the letter. This wasn't particularly shocking. Then in an odd coincidence, one year later, Peck found himself back in Mongolia and back at the same tiny post office. He spoke to its lone employee.

"Do you ever mail anything from here?" Peck asked.

"Oh, there's a mailbox outside," the worker said.

Peck was confused. That very mailbox was where he dropped his letter, a year ago.

"Let's go look!" the worker said excitedly.

Peck and the postman went outside and opened the mailbox. And sure enough, there was Peck's letter, just where he'd left it, along with several others that had been languishing for years.

The letter was eventually sent by Peck, along with countless others from Gobi, the Himalayas, the Amazon, Siberia, and all across the globe for nearly half a century. Peck always returns home safely, because someone needed to live to tell the tale.

MYTHS, MICROBES,
AND A HIDDEN CITY OF GOLD

Andrés Ruzo

WHEN ANDRÉS RUZO was a little kid in Lima, Peru, his grand-father told him stories. In a whisper, his grandfather spoke of legends and myths from the Peruvian Amazon. He told Ruzo the story of a lost city of gold and spirits that haunted the greedy Spanish conquistadors.

In the 1500s, said his grandfather, after the Spanish conquistadors killed and butchered the Incas, they were hungry for more civilizations to loot. The Inca told the Spanish of a hidden city of gold, sparking quests deep into the Amazon. But when the conquistadors reached a mysterious part of the rainforest, they were stunned to find powerful shamans who somehow ordered the jungle to attack them.

The conquistadors were confused, scared, and lost. "They marched in perpetual darkness," his grandfather said in a whisper. "Mosquitos and biting flies left them drained of blood. The jungle drove them mad with green monotony. . . . Starvation, dehydration, and madness were their only companions. They told of snakes that swallowed men whole, spiders that ate birds—even of a river that boiled."

The legend of this boiling river stuck with Ruzo for years. When he grew up, he studied geothermal energy, and he worked with Google to help create heat flow maps of the United States to quantify the flow of thermal energy between Earth's interior and its surface. He also worked on a geothermal survey of Peru, a country that represents what he calls "one of the greatest volcanic mysteries in the world."

Peru happens to be a part of Earth's Ring of Fire—a ring of active volcanos looping around most of the Pacific Ocean associated with tectonic subduction zones where tectonic plates collide. Mysteriously, the volcanoes in most of Peru "turned off" roughly two million years ago—resulting in active subduction, but no active volcanism. Why?

While collaborating with the Peruvian government, Ruzo realized there were hot springs in the Peruvian Amazon. He remembered the old legend from his grandfather. If there were hot springs, could there also be a boiling river?

For two years he was obsessed with this question. He asked every expert he could find whether a boiling river could exist in the Amazon rainforest. Everyone said no. There was no boiling river on any maps. There was no boiling river in any survey. The Peruvian rainforest had been mapped extensively—including by oil companies since the 1920s—and if it existed, the world would know.

At the end of this two-year inquiry, Ruzo met with a mining company geologist and asked his usual question: "Do you know of the boiling river?"

The geologist told him, essentially, to stop asking stupid questions. "This 'legends' stuff, it's not professional," the geologist told him. Ruzo felt foolish. He even apologized to the geologist, and he was ready to finally abandon this quixotic study.

That very night, Ruzo happened to have a family dinner with his aunt and uncle. His aunt worked extensively with Amazonian people advocating for Indigenous rights.

She asked Ruzo how his work was going.

"I was really curious about this legendary boiling river," he told her, 'But it doesn't exist."

She looked at him. "No, Andrés, it's real. I've been there."

What?

His aunt told him that not only had she been to the boiling river, she had swum in it. (How could she swim in boiling water? Because a heavy rain had temporarily cooled it.) She said it was a sacred place, protected by a powerful shaman, who had invited her to see it. Ruzo found her report almost impossible to believe. *How could it be?* But his aunt was true to her word and told him that she would lead him through the jungle to the shaman.

It would be a full day of travel to reach the shaman's community on the banks of the boiling river. They took an airplane into the Amazon, then a four-wheel drive truck to a remote river-town where they would meet the shaman's apprentice, who would be their guide. The apprentice took them deeper into the jungle on a motorized canoe.

"There is the mouth of the boiling river," the shaman's apprentice said to Ruzo, pointing to a stream flowing into the larger Pachitea River. He signaled Ruzo to put his hand in the water. It was warm. Then, as they canoed closer to the boiling river, it became hot. Maybe the temperature of a hot bath, but it wasn't a scalding or boiling river like the legend promised.

Ruzo wasn't impressed. He had expected more, and he was concerned he came all this way to see a pleasantly warm stream. The shaman's apprentice was amused. "Just wait until we get deeper into the jungle," he said.

They hiked an hour farther into the jungle. Then, in the silence of the Amazon's sweltering heat, Ruzo heard something—a low surge coming from the valley below. He saw what looked like smoke and turned to the shaman's apprentice: "What is that?"

"The river. Go."

Ruzo raced down into the valley and what he saw would change his life forever—the surge was coming from powerful river rapids crashing over rocks. The "smoke" wasn't smoke at all, but vapor from the river's heat. The water was a beautiful transparent turquoise, stretching wider than a two-lane road and flowing for hundreds of yards before curving out of view into the jungle.

When Ruzo took a deep breath, he felt a hot, dense, sauna-like air going through his nose down through his throat and into his lungs. He felt real awe. *Could this actually be true?* The scientist in Ruzo remembered to measure the water; he was astonished to see that it was 187 degrees Fahrenheit. That's hot enough to cause a third-degree burn. That's hot enough to scare Spanish conquistadors who are greedy for gold.

The apprentice, smiling, then introduced Ruzo to the shaman. Ruzo soon became the first geoscientist to be granted the shamanic blessing to study the boiling river. And the shaman asked Ruzo to help responsibly share the boiling river's story with the world. In the face of increasing deforestation, said the shaman, "We can no longer conceal to protect."

The moment Ruzo returned from this edge of discovery, he sent a letter to his closest inner circle.

> Dear friends and family,
>
> As many of you know I am currently doing geothermal research in Peru for my PhD dissertation. With this email I wanted to give you all a sneak-peak into a major discovery.
>
> I have spent the past 2 days in the Amazon seeing if a legendary boiling river truly exists. I spent my time there coordinating future research with the shaman in charge of the area and collecting samples. Resulting in the first scientific documentation of a near-boiling river in the heart of the Peruvian Amazon, over 700 kms away from the nearest active volcano. . . .
>
> This is sensitive information for various reasons (documentary, study, working with Indigenous peoples . . .) and I would greatly appreciate keeping this in confidence. As close friends and family, I am really excited to share this with you, and hope you enjoy the stories, reports, and photos. . . .
>
> I went with a healthy scientific skepticism, expecting either exaggerated stories or in the worst-case scenario, that the source of the geothermal waters was an abandoned oil or gas well.

Ruzo was quite concerned, before he left, that the "boiling river" might be nothing more than a byproduct of recent oil exploration—a simple oil field accident. But his fears were unfounded.

After going, I could not be happier to report that this place is real, natural, and far more incredible than I imagined. At the risk of sounding cliché—what I saw moved me, on personal, spiritual, and technical levels. This is one of the most beautiful places I have ever seen.

Ruzo also felt a responsibility to do right by the shaman, to respect the knowledge and sovereignty of his community.

Given the highly sensitive issue of working at the sacred site of an Amazonian community, please keep this email in utmost confidence until I finish my study. The people have given me their trust, and are excited for me to organize an expedition to study their land. They are afraid of anyone coming that would disrespect their land, and have asked for my help with regard to keeping their sacred site safe, particularly from geothermal or any other industry expansion into their space. . . . With all this said, below are summaries of some of the things I saw.

Ruzo continued to gather samples and collect scientific data. Soon he began to piece together the puzzle of how this boiling river could possibly exist, even though it was 430 miles from the nearest volcano.

Geologically—The Mayantuyacu community and its geothermal river is on the northern end of large eroded geologic dome, that at its center is made up of sandstones that have been heavily faulted and fractured.

The faults likely allowed water to circulate to great depths, thereby heating up, and coming to the surface in the form of various thermal springs along the run of the river. The area is fossiliferous. The shaman, Maestro Juan Flores, actually gave me a very well-preserved oyster fossil as a protective talisman and gift.

Ruzo again thought of the legends from his grandfather, the tales that included giant snakes and powerful spirits. He began to find more clues, as he outlined in the letter:

> Where the river begins to heat up, and grow in volume, there is a sacred site the locals have named the "Yacumama," literally, "mother of the waters" (as in their legends it is a giant snake that births water). Here, the "Yacumama" is represented by a large sandstone boulder that looks strikingly like the head of a large constrictor snake. Beneath the boulder's "snake jaws," there is a fault-fed hot spring mixing with cold stream water—and in a sense bringing their legends to life.

As Ruzo explored the striking beauty of this river, he carefully inspected the surrounding ecosystem.

> Biologically—I have tremendous interest in the upper part of the river, particularly because there is a "thermal wall" of water cutting off the populations of fish, shrimps, and other life forms. There is a point where the water is too hot to support life, and I saw remains of a boiled frog, snake, various insects, and even the jaw of a fox-sized mammal. . . .
>
> With this in mind, the statistical potential should be very high for discovering a new species or subspecies trapped by the "thermal wall" isolating them from the rest of the Amazon fauna.

Over a decade has passed since Ruzo's first visit to the boiling river, and he regularly returns to the site to continue his work and honor his commitment to the shaman. The world now knows that the boiling river is more than a legend. The shaman and his community now legally own their land. The area has been put on the map of conservation and ecotourism initiatives in Peru. The scientific work has expanded to include dozens of fields of studies and nearly 100 collaborators seeking to understand the boiling river and its jungle, and how to best protect the area.

But apart from being a childhood fable sprung to life, why does this matter? What's the true significance? Locally, this is a culturally important area—with deep significance to many Indigenous and mestizo groups. It's also a critical ecosystem for local wildlife. And while it's true that there are other "boiling rivers" in the world, most are associated with active volcanoes. This is the largest documented thermal river in the world.

But there's something even deeper at play.

It dawned on Ruzo that the boiling river was not just a geothermal anomaly but potentially the key to solving a far bigger problem: How can we protect the planet as it keeps warming? How will plants and creatures survive? (Once again, knowledge from the edge can solve the problems at home.)

The world will get warmer, thanks to climate change. This much we know. And the way Ruzo and his collaborators see it, we have much more to learn about how plants, creatures, microbes, and the rest of the ecosystem will react to a hotter Amazon. But the boiling river can give us clues. "Because of the boiling river, you have a heating element in the valley," says Ruzo. "You have higher-than-normal temperatures, and some plants have adapted to, and are surviving in, this ecosystem."

The boiling river can act as a "natural laboratory," shedding light on which plant species will likely die, which will show significant stress, and which might even adapt and thrive.

We can also learn from the river's microbes, and the microbes could be the real treasure. "Geothermal conservation and protecting geothermal systems [like the boiling river] might be the most important conservation discussion we can be having right now," says Ruzo. He cites the example of PCR, or polymerase chain reaction, as in the PCR tests that most of us took to see if we had Covid. The only reason we have PCR, says Ruzo, is that scientists discovered a microbe that could thrive in the geothermal systems of Yellowstone. "These technologies have given us the modern world, saved billions of lives, and opened up multi-trillion dollar economies," says Ruzo.

So the boiling river's microbes, in a sense, are even more valuable than gold. But there is a question that remains: What about the lost city of gold? Ruzo asked the shaman about it.

"You mean you have missed it?" the shaman asked.

At first Ruzo didn't understand. Then he realized that, ancestrally, gold was often considered a symbol of life itself; meaning that a "city of gold" could also be a "city of life." Maybe Inca vengeance, in the end, was exacted on the Spanish through a play on words. "The Amazon is one of Earth's great celebrations of life," says Ruzo. "All around you creatures buzz, crawl, hop, and slither. It is very much a city of life."

Ultimately, Ruzo thinks we need to make a choice. "Can we recognize the true value of the Amazon's city of life," he asks, "Or are we destined to follow the ill-fated path of the Conquistadores, greedily chasing a mythical city of gold?"

FISHING FOR ANSWERS

Jessica Glass

THE REALITY IS that most expeditions *aren't* gripping tales of life and death. (If that were the case, The Explorers Club would be doing something very, very wrong.) And the day-to-day grind of field-work is something that usually gets overlooked, even if it's the back-bone of exploration.

Consider an expedition from Jessica Glass, a geneticist and evolutionary biologist who focuses on fish. "There are over thirty thousand species of fishes, more than any other type of vertebrate animal," Glass says with excitement in her voice. Her mission is to "figure out the fish tree of life."

Sometimes that work means analyzing DNA in a lab, but sometimes it involves something far more basic: catching fish. So, in 2017, to study the giant trevally (GT) fish, Glass traveled to Seychelles, South Africa, where this species is thought to be plentiful. Glass needed to study and tag some actual GT to "fill in the gaps of sampling," meaning that data models can only get you so far—she needed raw observations. This would help her understand the fish's diet, ecology, migrations, and how it fit into the larger genetic puzzle.

All of this is easier said than done. For starters, Glass was a PhD student at the time, and PhD students are not, typically, flush with cash. It cost 1,800 euros a day (just under $2,000) to charter a fishing boat, and her modest grants were already stretched thin.

Then there's the tricky nature of the GTs themselves. This isn't an easy fish to catch. (Luckily, as a child, Glass grew up fishing.) A GT can be more than three feet long, and they put up a fight. They're even something of a popular sporting fish—what Glass calls a "bro fish," as "so many guys want to catch the biggest GT they can find." Glass kept her sense of humor, kept her fishing rods at the ready, and kept a detailed journal of the expedition.

> I've skipped Days 1-5 of the 2017 Seychelles expedition, partly due to no time but mainly due to no fish (although not for lack of trying!). . . . My field assistant is leaving tomorrow back to Singapore and caught zero fish but provided substantial moral & financial support. . . . Much needed as Seychelles is tiny but makes up for it by charging exorbitant prices for everything on the island.

Each night Glass returned to her Airbnb exhausted and sweaty in dirty fishing clothes. People looked at her in confusion and said, "You've been fishing? But you're a woman."

> I dropped off (Field) assistant 4 hours early at the airport so I could . . . tag along with a man from Ukraine who is a hardcore GT fisherman. He speaks only Russian and brought along his "translator" aka young hot girlfriend/mistress? I don't ask questions, I just take samples and try to be helpful. They . . . are both very nice, and his assortment of rods and tackle are probably worth more than a year's worth of salary. Ok, that's not saying much, given that I am a PhD student.

There's something that her journal omits, given that it's such a natural part of the field researcher's day, as regular and unremarkable as brushing your teeth: the grind of real-life academia that still needs to chug along, somehow, even on expedition. Explorers are good multitaskers. Glass was also working on her thesis, writing grants, analyzing lab work, and teaching classes during or around the

Seychelles expedition. "All of these things have to happen in addition to fieldwork," she says.

> Monsoooon! So rainy today all fishing cancelled. . . . Needed to check emails so went to dreadful Eden Island, giving a ride to . . . former Turkish ambassador to Egypt and some other countries. I've met more ambassadors in two days than my entire life. Maybe will start introducing myself as the fish ambassador. . . . Overall a good day in spite of rain.

Her day started at 5 a.m. She'd fish for a few hours, then knock out some grant writing, then hop on a call with her thesis advisor, then do more grant writing, and then fish again in the early evening. "The historic naturalists of the 1800s were very wealthy gentlemen," says Glass. "They had fortunes that could allow them to go on these expeditions." Modern exploration is more of a hustle, and most explorers can relate to Glass's juggling act.

> Skunked again! What is the problem with these damn fish. Maybe this is why no one has studied them here . . . they are extremely evasive of scientists. The weather wasn't great—we had rain in the morning and the sea was pretty choppy—throwing those big poppers while trying to keep my balance was definitely some of the most challenging & exhausting fishing I have ever done. . . . Really worried about the fact that I didn't get the samples I need.

So . . . hopefully, it couldn't get any worse?

> New PhD low: fishing in the Seychelles Islands on a researcher's budget, i.e., casting under a bridge at 5:30 AM with no luck, as you stand under a sewage pipe that periodically reeks of shit and—best part—sprays sewer water on you. I need to get on a boat ASAP. No luck from shore the past 3 days. I just emailed every charter

operator on Mahe asking for help. Stephan said he'd make some calls. Suresh said he'll make a plan. We'll see if anything actually materializes. I'm getting (even more) worried. This god-damned island and its fish leaping just beyond where I can cast. . . . Spirits are low, if that wasn't apparent.

"I got really sick after that experience," Glass says with a laugh.

I got my car stuck in the mud! I was very, very close to having to call a tow, and by the time I got out of there it was past low tide! Morale reached an all-time low when I filled the car with petrol across from the airport but didn't have enough cash to pay for it and they didn't take cards (!) What gas station across from an airport doesn't take cards(!) So I had to promise them I'll come back tomorrow and pay the remaining 100 rupees. Then I went early to fish the bridge to Providence (I'm calling it the 'shit bridge') and I caught 3 little GTs (26-29 cm)! Finally! At least this trip was not completely wasted.

It turns out that Glass was saved, at last, by the "shit bridge"—a surprising destination for GTs.

2 big GTs today; Of course I didn't catch them because I'm apparently incapable of catching my study organism. Marvin pulled both of them up literally 5 minutes apart. . . . That man is a relentless fisherman, my god. . . . I discovered my new talent: catching sharks. I caught 3 white-tip reef sharks (decently sized) and nothing else.

How many fishers can say that on a "bad day" they were able to catch three sharks? Glass, in the end, managed to catch enough fish for her research, and she later published the world's first thorough study of the GT.

And her view of the edge?

Glass knew she wasn't dangling off a cliff or facing the edge of starvation, but that's rarely how field science works. She likes being on the cutting edge of knowledge and discovery. Every discovery invites and invokes new questions. "It's sort of awe-inspiring," Glass says, "to be pushing that body of knowledge forward."

TOO FEW WHALES, TOO MANY MURDERS

Martin Nweeia

EXPLORERS COME FROM many backgrounds. Dr. Martin Nweeia started as a dental surgeon. Eventually, his interests expanded to include dental anthropology—the study of how teeth offer clues to species' diets, health, and even evolution and migration.

Nweeia gave speeches around the world on dental anthropology, but there was one species that had him stumped. In fact, it had the entire world stumped. For more than five hundred years, scientists had been unable to figure out the purpose of the narwhal's tusk— a single tooth that can be up to nine feet long. These were mysterious and valuable. As *The New York Times* feature about Nweeia's work noted, "In the 16th century, Queen Elizabeth received a tusk valued at £10,000—the cost of a castle."

The scientists' best guess was that the tusk was a secondary sex characteristic, which basically meant they had no idea what it did. But Nweeia had a theory he wanted to test. So, after several research expeditions to the Arctic, he led a team that dissected and analyzed the narwhal's tusk, and they proved something astonishing: Far from being some dead organ, the tusk was a sensory rod that fed the whale information about its environment. As that same *New York Times* article reported, "The nerves can detect subtle changes of temperature, pressure, particle gradients and probably much else, giving the animal unique insights."

Nweeia's 2005 discovery went viral; it also set a record for "narwhal" on Google Trends.

But Nweeia wasn't finished. His 2005 report was a stunning break-through that solved a five-hundred-year-old mystery, but his insights had originated in the laboratory. Could he prove how the tusk works in the field itself? Could he go to the Arctic and analyze the whales in action?

He spent years preparing for the expedition. He applied for grants. He trained by testing novel equipment, such as field laboratories that could float on pontoons. And in 2008, he took The Explorers Club flag number 24 with him into the Arctic, a flag that had been in service since 1929 and had traveled from the Virunga Mountains to Kapingamarangi.

The result?

This is Nweeia's letter from the edge, sent to the president of The Explorers Club:

Dear Jon,

On almost every level of assessment, our expedition this year was a complete failure. . . . I have little to show for the effort. To make matters worse, we had about every tragedy an expedition could experience including a gruesome murder. . . .

After some reflection, I thought, "this story is exactly what people need to know about my work. These are the experiences I sludge through to get to 'the meaningful insights and results.'" When people ask, "What is it like to do whale research in the Arctic?" I will think of my expedition of 2008, and the Explorers Club Flag 24. . . .

On the first day of arrival into the small town of Repulse Bay, population 748, the lead hunter for the Hunters and Trappers Organization, whom we had met with only hours before to discuss plans and arrangements for our expedition site, was shot. His girlfriend had taken a 38 rifle to the back of his head and plastered most of its contents onto the kitchen wall.

Nweeia had met the hunter five hours before the murder. The hunter lived in a small Inuit community, where most people knew him. So, on the night after the murder, the town's streets were filled with anguished cries from the Inuit—wails of loss and pain. The murder scene was so gruesome and painful to process that the community simply burnt the house down.

The hunter was supposed to be Nweeia's main guide, and this happened on the very first day of the expedition. Should he keep going? He conferred with his team—including the local hunters, who welcomed the distraction—and decided they still had the resources, training, and motivation to push forward. Nweeia knew that despite this tragic first day, as long as they found some whales, he could still complete his objectives.

His letter continues:

> We located our expedition site about 20 km South of the town. For the first time in fourteen years, Repulse Bay did not have any large narwhal group migrate through its inlets near the town. . . . During our weeks there, we did not see one whale. By comparison, during the last two years, there were hundreds spotted. . . . All efforts were futile. We were merely spectators to the ways of nature.

Every day for three weeks, Nweeia woke up hoping to see a narwhal. Every night he went to bed disappointed. He held out hope until the very last day, as you never know when your luck can flip. But no whales came. "The Arctic is not there to make you happy," Nweeia says now. "It's going to do whatever it's going to do."

So, with the odds of accomplishing his mission vanishing, he turned his focus to safety and survival. What else could go wrong?

> Visits from polar bears were disturbingly common. Four times they came, twice by day and two times at night stalking the camp. The danger became great as darkness set in on the camp, making

it difficult to spot and follow the bear's path. The bear moved with great agility around the rock ledges that surrounded the camp. One bear managed to cleverly get in to the camp around 3 am.

"This is a great example of the difference between Inuit knowledge and qallunaaq knowledge," says Nweeia. "Qallunaaq" is an Inuit term referring to people from south of the Arctic. Nweeia often thinks of a prior expedition, on an ice floe, where he was on polar bear watch with an Inuit hunter. It was nighttime.

"Wake me up if a polar bear gets too close," the Inuit told him.

"How close is close?"

The hunter just looked at him. "You'll know."

So at three in the morning, Nweeia saw a polar bear crawl its way onto the ice floe. The bear prowled toward him. It got up on its hind legs as if to strike.

Martin knocked on the hunter's small tent. "Is that close enough?" he pointed to the oncoming bear.

"Oh yes." The hunter emerged with a gun.

He took aim but didn't shoot. He just waited. Patient. Calm He wanted to see what the bear would do.

And the polar bear simply walked by the campsite and then left. Nweeia, amazed, asked the hunter how he knew what to do.

"We recognize that the polar bear is king of this environment," said the hunter.

Flash forward to Nweeia's 2008 expedition. Two polar bears approached the camp. They weren't threatening. But immediately, without much consideration, one of the qallunaaq fired a warning shot. This scattered the polar bears, but they came back every night and tried to attack.

Nweeia's team survived the polar bears but faced one more surprise.

The final days of the expedition brought the worst. . . . An Arctic hurricane was forecast. With lingering hopes of spotting whales that could still be captured and released, we remained in camp to the last day before departure. We watched from a distance, as black smoke billowed in the sky. . . .

Persistent winds came first from the South . . . then switched with even colder winds coming from the North. In the midst of the storm was a full moon which created a tidal surge that largely destroyed the camp. Later, we would learn that steady winds were between 80-90 mph with 120 mph gusts. All of us piled into one wooden shack that was built as an outpost.

The hurricane violently pulled the tents from their stakes. The tent poles snapped. A Zodiac boat flipped and landed on a broken tent. In contrast, the Inuit hunters had built a small wooden shelter, and this survived. Nweeia's state-of-the-art "high-tech" tents didn't stand a chance. But there was one silver lining:

In the midst of tragedy came a small offering of knowledge from an unsuspecting source. I have always found that when we search for our deepest questions and inspiration, the answer and the messenger can quite often be right in front of us.

On expedition, the hunter who joined me on polar bear watch was relating a story from his grandfather who told him the telling sign of narwhal appearance. "My grandfather said, if the water does not show the reddish brown from young arctic cod, the narwhal will not come," he told me one night.

Pieces of a scientific puzzle sometimes come in odd forms and unexpected experiences. My work had already uncovered the ability of narwhal tusks to sense changes in water salinity. . . . The pieces began to fit. Why did narwhal brave the spring ice leads?

The expedition was a disaster by every objective standard, but Nweeia's conversation with the hunter stuck with him. It felt somehow important. He turned the words around in his head: "If the water does not show the reddish brown from young arctic cod, the narwhal will not come."

Nweeia eventually connected the dots between the Inuit's observation and his own research, field tests, and scientific theories. He realized that since the Inuit did not see the reddish brown, they could have predicted they would not find whales—an important data point he could weave into his analysis. "I like combining Inuit knowledge and science, to show people that science is not *the* way to think. it's *one* way to think," says Nweeia. And ultimately, this open-mindedness to Inuit knowledge moved the science forward.

And after the doomed expedition? Nweeia did not give up. He eventually returned to the Arctic, he found his narwhals, and once again he published a study that made front-page news. "I'm incredibly stubborn and obstinate," says Nweeia, channeling many members of The Explorers Club. "If you put up a wall, I'm climbing it. If you put up a moat, I'm swimming across it."

In a 2023 addendum to his letter, Nweeia wrote:

> This experience, carved in a sheet of ice, sits in my brain. Fifteen years later, it hasn't melted one drop.

LISTS AND LAVA

Ben Jordan

OFTEN AN EXPLORER'S "edge" is metaphorical. But in their quest for knowledge, sometimes the edge is quite literally an edge.

This is what Ben Jordan found when he journeyed to Mount Yasur, an active volcano on the archipelago of Vanuatu, just east of Australia, near the Pacific's Ring of Fire. When Yasur erupted in 2016 and spewed lava into the sky, most sensible people ran far away. Jordan hopped on a flight and got there as fast as he could.

He didn't do this for thrill seeking or an adrenaline rush; he did it to gather data and to test a new method of volcanic research. Jordan, a geologist and volcanist, knew that scientists struggled to obtain reliable insights, data, and photographs from actively erupting volcanos. The reason was simple: It's tough to snap pictures of something when it's blasting lava in your face. But what if he could send in a drone?

The overhead imagery captured by drones could help scientists learn, for example, if the vents in a volcano—impossible to see from the sides—are getting wider or narrower, which gives clues to the intensity and duration of the eruption. This could lead to better forecasts and models, which have pragmatic applications. Will a volcano erupt for days, weeks, or months? For many, the answer is the difference between life and death.

But sending a drone through a lava storm was easier said than done. Jordan didn't bring a crew or a safety team. He just brought his drone, his instincts, his carefully planned checklist, and his willingness to take some whopping risks.

Jordan emailed his wife, Michelle, from a bamboo hut just outside the volcano that miraculously had flickers of internet:

> It was spectacular hearing the deep roaring explosions and watching incandescent lava bombs surge up and then fall in parabolic arches.... I noticed that just before each large explosion there would be this massive increase in the amount of gasses coming out of the sides of the crater. Then there would be a big explosion with large bombs of lava thrown straight up to enormous heights overhead.

Jordan left for the volcano just after nightfall. He used a headlamp to see a few feet ahead in the darkness. He could hear the volcano before he saw it, a crackling roar as loud as thunder, and it rumbled through the ground like an earthquake, up his feet and into his chest. He could feel his heartrate spiking.

The volcano now sounded like booming firecrackers. The closer he moved to the center, the louder the explosions. The ground kept shaking.

Bombs of lava flew through the sky and landed in front of him, like in a war zone. He needed to get as close to the edge as possible. He saw a glow of red and orange and yellow, the pool of lava.

Meanwhile, the lava bombs continued to burst. A little voice in the back of his head told him, *You are crazy.* But another inner voice told him to ignore this. And that part of his brain remembered his checklists. "It really helps to do mental preparation beforehand," says Jordan. "So that when you get there, you're not making decisions in the moment. You've already made these decisions before."

Before he headed to the volcano, Jordan had created a plan for exactly how he would prepare, fly, and manage the drone. (He was partially inspired by the Apollo astronauts, who had detailed checklists for all the tasks they needed to do on the moon.) He took the drone out of its case, and as pellets of hot lava exploded nearby, Jordan methodically ticked every item off his list.

Fighting his fear with the calm of his checklist, Jordan sent the drone high in the sky and toward the eye of the volcano. The wind violently pushed it back. He tried to send it higher, like he was flying a kite in a storm.

The volcano emitted heat and lava in excess of one thousand degrees Fahrenheit that could easily melt the drone. Still, to Jordan, that was a risk worth taking. The entire point of the exercise was to test whether drones could gather data that humans could not. As he sees it, "I'd rather lose twelve thousand drones than lose one person."

Somehow the drone survived the wind, the lava, and the gasses, and it made it across the eye of the volcano. Then Jordan guided it back.

He had just unlocked a new tool for scientists. "This gives researchers and scientists the ability to go places and collect data in a safe way," says Jordan, who now gives a presentation to universities called "Drones and Volcanos—How to Get Data Without Getting Killed."

All of this moves the needle of scientific knowledge forward. And paradoxically, sometimes explorers like Jordan put themselves in danger to gain knowledge, tools, and systems to make a *less* deadly edge.

MELTING GLACIERS, MELTING HEARTS

Klaus Thymann

KLAUS THYMANN IS a climate change scientist. He has made several expeditions to the Rwenzori Mountains, aka the Mountains of the Moon, located near the border of Uganda and the Democratic Republic of the Congo.

Thymann had a two-pronged mission. First, he wanted to recreate an iconic photograph from 1906, by the explorer the Duke of the Abruzzi, that showed the gorgeous snowcapped peaks of Mount Baker. Thymann did indeed precisely recreate the shot . . . and it clearly showed that in 1906, the mountain was white; now it's brown and barren. The glacier was melting. Thymann knew simple side-by-side comparisons like that could do more to raise awareness of global warming—to rally people to climate change activism—than charts filled with data.

But the data also matters, and that brought Thymann to his second mission. He believes that climate change "awareness" is no longer sufficient. Now is the time for action. And action requires data. So Thymann planned an expedition in 2020 to gather data that could help local communities better plan for the melting of the glaciers, which feeds into the river system. "Five million people are depending on this water," says Thymann. "When the ice stops melting, the river runs dry." But no one knew how much time the local communities had. As Thymann puts it, "Data allows planning. Planning allows survival."

Thymann knew these trips were never easy. On one prior expedition, he fell through a poorly built wooden bridge. He had internal bleeding in his legs, but he just tied his boots tighter and continued the mission; he would get the photos and the data.

But besides the typical risks in any such expedition, the mission in 2020 had one additional drawback: He had just started a serious relationship with a woman he was smitten by, Allison, and in an ideal world he wouldn't be away and off the grid—the trip would mean thirteen days with no contact whatsoever.

Allison worked for CNN, and they met while he was on assignment doing fieldwork. He would report from Brazil about deforestation, and the two would have long conversations about the assignment and then about life. He enjoyed talking to her. They spoke on the phone for countless hours—for more than a year—before they met in person. "I kind of fell in love with her voice and her words," says Thymann. "She can express herself elegantly."

So, for long stretches of time, it was normal for Allison and Thymann to communicate over WhatsApp, texting and talking. Maybe, while he was gone, he could somehow recreate that experience.

Then he had an idea. Maybe it was a silly idea, but it was better than nothing. He could prerecord a series of voicemails for her to listen to, one a day, throughout the thirteen-day expedition. He almost thought of it like an advent calendar. He asked her to do him a favor and listen to only one a day—to never skip ahead.

When Thymann arrived in Uganda, he recorded a series of voice memos as close to the frontier (where he'd lose cell service) as possible. Because he recorded them while riding on a bumpy dirt road in a four-by-four, he wasn't even sure if Allison would be able to make out his voice.

These are the voice memos, recorded all at one time.

FEBRUARY 5, 2020

Hey, little Allison, this is just me, getting to the gate, and there will be another few messages. This is for the fifth.

FEBRUARY 6

Hey, Allison; it might seem like a long time until we'll speak again, but patience is a good thing, so we can long after each other and be very happy when we finally meet again.

FEBRUARY 7

I was thinking my brother doesn't have your contact details in case something happens to me, and that's a mistake, so maybe I will give the trekking company your details, but I hope you don't hear from anyone from Uganda today, and I hope you're having a good day.

FEBRUARY 8

I should be way up the mountains now. I am in the mountains, and I'm enjoying that it's not too hot. I have walked through a lot of vegetation with my little camera backpack. If you wanted to do that in a similar way, you can wear some nerdy stuff and walk around Brooklyn and feel a little bit like we did it together, some-how, in an odd connected way. Or you can just think of me when you go for a run next time.

FEBRUARY 9

This is actually Sunday, so you're probably doing Pilates and ev-erything else in between, and I am just trekking and trekking and trekking as I do, and I look very forward to just having a lazy Sun-day with you.

FEBRUARY 10

It's actually Monday. You don't know this because I'm not sure I've told you, but Monday is my favorite day. I love the week when it starts because there's a whole week left to do stuff, and do things that make me happy, and now there's a new week starting for you, which could be very exciting. I hope things at the kebab shop are going fine and you're having fun and all the programs have been good.

FEBRUARY 10 (BONUS)

You're probably listening to this on the eleventh, but this is actually bonus for Monday, because Mondays are fantastic, so this would be a little extra . . . I probably miss you a hell of a lot, but [audio hard to hear] I miss you.

FEBRUARY 11

[Audio hard to hear.] So this is the second part of . . . by now I should be well up the mountains . . . about [inaudible] meters . . . and my plan is get up very very early in the mornings and shoot at dawn . . . so I . . . get . . . the light [audio hard to hear].

FEBRUARY 12

I've probably told you about my mutation with my back . . . and . . . that's why I swim obsessively . . . I think I've read that, on average, a person has about three mutations . . . and if you don't know what yours are . . . it's a good thing to investigate . . . so it's Wednesday the twelfth, and I think you really should find out what your mutations are.

FEBRUARY 13

Allison Brown, it is Thursday the thirteenth, and by now I haven't showered [beeping alarm] . . . and anyway, when you think, "Oh it would be nice to see Klaus soon," . . . I haven't showered . . . I think that should [audio hard to hear].

FEBRUARY 14

Hey, it's Valentine's Day, I guess. In Denmark, at least I thought we don't really celebrate Valentine's, and I had a girlfriend and I broke up with her and it happened to be on Valentine's, and I should have known that but that's not what I'm doing here; I don't know how much you celebrate Valentine's, but I'm very [audio hard to hear] today . . . buy roses.

FEBRUARY 15

This expedition is sort of coming to an end and we'll be heading out and down soon. The thing is, last time I walked really really fast on the way out, so what was to take two days took me just one day, but now I know that, so I'm probably spending more time on Mount Baker . . . It's a very very cool place . . . It's the one that allows you to see the glacier all the way down, it has that 1906 historic picture . . . and that's the one I made a comparison from last time . . . and probably do that [audio hard to hear] and actually see what I'm doing.

FEBRUARY 16

There's a little spot . . . where I can walk out of the jungle where there's a phone signal, but I'm not sure if I brought my phone charger to the mountain . . . but if I have I might call you . . . but if not [audio hard to hear] on the seventeenth . . . so I'll probably give you a call.

FEBRUARY 17

The seventeenth . . . Allison, this is really good message because you should probably hear from me today, and if you haven't, by tomorrow, but don't worry I will call as soon as I have a signal. I hope you are well and I can't wait to hear from you. Very exciting, very exciting.

. . .

AND ON FEBRUARY 17, as promised, Thymann emerged from the mountains and from the jungle. He found a patch of cell service. From Allison's perspective she had been "hearing from" Thymann every day, but from Thymann's, he hadn't heard her voice in two weeks. He missed her. So when the bars of service flickered back to life he gave Allison a call . . .

And it went straight to voicemail. He just laughed.

She missed the call, and she missed him, but of course they eventually connected. She had reflected on the voicemails every day in a diary, and she later emailed him to share these thoughts. "I was delighted to see a little row of voice memos on my phone screen, so curious about what would be behind each tiny play button," she wrote in her email to Thymann. "I listened to them dutifully, one a day, careful not to skip ahead."

Since Thymann recorded the messages while rumbling on a four-by-four, sometimes the audio was so patchy that she pressed her earphones into her ears as tight as possible and listened to them again and again. The background noise was so loud that she thought he might be on a plane, although, as she wrote to him, "I heard enough to understand the idea."

She particularly enjoyed the visual of her wearing a "nerdy backpack" and hiking through Brooklyn as if on expedition. "Sometimes you sounded so excited as you spoke about what was to come," she wrote, "it was as if the message was coming in real time rather than recorded in advance."

Allison listened to the messages repeatedly. And she reflected on what they—and Thymann's mission—truly meant, both to them as a couple and with a wider lens. From Allison's email:

> Knowing what I know now about your experiences with these mountains and the glacial retreat, the description you shared about your favorite vantage point from Mt Baker is more poignant.

For me, the mountains have become characters in a dramatic story of interconnectivity and loss. As though the glaciers on Mt Baker, Mt Speke, and Mt Stanley are elders waning in life, with a community below that depends on them. I am inferring too much. I wonder what you will find when you return again.

UNDERCOVER TOMB RAIDERS

Gino Caspari and Trevor Wallace

TWO A.M., A SKETCHY BAR on the outskirts of Hong Kong. A guy known only as Jeffrey—skinny, tattooed, twitchy—pulled out a bag of crystal meth and plopped it on the table.

"I'm not scared of the cops!" Jeffrey said in his rapid-fire voice, gesturing wildly with his hands. "I'm scared of my mom, she's the scary one."

Jeffrey bragged that he could smuggle crystal meth from mainland China into Hong Kong. He could smuggle weapons. He could smuggle counterfeit goods. He hinted that he could smuggle humans. He could smuggle just about anything, including historic artifacts that were looted from tombs.

And historic artifacts were what interested Gino Caspari, an archeologist, and Trevor Wallace, an expedition filmmaker. They sat drinking beers with Jeffrey. They tried to keep up with his Cantonese-English as he kept firing off wild ideas, always gesturing with his hands.

"Be careful!" Jeffrey would say as he looked to the corners of the room, manic. "If they catch you moving anything out of China, they'll kill you."

Caspari and Wallace looked at each other. Did he just say that?

When they first met Jeffrey, the two explorers wondered if he was part of the Triad, the organized crime syndicate. This was plausible. Jeffrey told them he was a drug addict and had just gotten out of jail. In their first encounter he told them that, in fact, he'd spent "half my time in jail" and that "I can hook you up with whatever you want."

Wallace and Caspari, of course, were not looking for drugs or weapons, and they weren't looking to get killed. They had traveled to the edge of the dark markets for ancient artifacts, hoping to solve—or at least understand and document—one of the greatest problems facing archeology.

. . .

SINCE CASPARI'S FIRST EXCAVATION, in Rome, he'd been aware of the problem of looting. "Tomb Raider" isn't just a movie or a video game—it's a real issue. Countless historic artifacts are being plundered from tombs and excavation sites; and then, somehow, they're traded on underground markets, and sometimes they even make their way back to the world of legitimate art houses, like Sotheby's.

Could Caspari and Wallace find proof of this? And how did the crooked system work?

So they hatched a daring plan: They would go undercover to infiltrate the dark markets of stolen antiquities, chronicling every step of the journey.

"We're these two western white dudes in the middle of nowhere, and we really stick out," says Wallace. "So we thought, 'How could we use who we are to do something useful? How can we use how we appear to expose something about this art market?'"

Their goal wasn't to demonize or punish the people at the bottom of the supply chain, who are often poor and just trying to feed their families. Instead, they aimed to follow the supply chain as high up as they could—from the local trader all the way to the kingpins. They wanted to see how the system worked, expose any illicit activity, and hopefully spark changes in policies that would curb future looting.

At first they thought about creating elaborate characters and code names. They'd quiz each other to get their lies straight, like something out of a spy movie. Then they realized it was better to keep it simple. As Caspari says, "It's always smart to stick as close to the truth as possible."

So they each played a version of themselves. Caspari told the (partial) truth about his background as an archeologist, but then he added a crucial lie: that he was working on behalf of a billionaire client who was eager to get his hands on rare and treasured artifacts—the hotter and more expensive, the better. Wallace played the part of his business partner. "My responsibility was not seeming conspicuous, and knowing when to shut up and when to laugh," says Wallace. "I was playing the dumb American. Which is not that hard to do."

As part of their cover story, they needed to concoct this billionaire client who coveted rare artifacts. The duo soon realized that the less they said about this shadowy billionaire client, the better. Caspari found that "it added to the intrigue of our personas."

Caspari and Wallace began their journey in Xinzheng, at the heart of the ancient Silk Roads. At first, they just chatted with merchants in antique shops. (Caspari is fluent in Mandarin.) They went to dozens of stores. They told people they were only interested in artifacts that sold for at least $20,000, and that led to more serious conversations.

"People were excited to meet us," says Wallace.

It helped that they were foreigners, as the local merchants felt, in a sense, that they had the upper hand. "They perceived us as somewhat dumb, but generally benevolent," says Caspari. "They knew we weren't going to run to the police."

And the police were frequently on Caspari and Wallace's mind. Even back in 2017, at the time of this mission, they felt the slow-burn anxiety of constant surveillance by the Chinese government. Whenever they checked into a hotel, changed locations, or bought bus tickets, their actions would be reported to the police. Copies of their passports were routinely fed to local police stations. They often had tails. At one point, they stayed on a small island near Hong Kong, largely so they could lose their tail via ferry. They hitchhiked, vanishing off the radar for two weeks, and when they returned, the police approached them and asked where they'd been. "It was almost cute," says Caspari, "how upfront about the surveillance they were."

Wallace and Caspari set up several meetings with traders and art dealers. Wallace surreptitiously filmed as much as he could with a mirrorless camera slung around his neck. Sometimes he'd even be able to take shots "in character," with the excuse that their billionaire client demanded photos of the goods.

Soon they had plenty of proof that illicit artifacts were indeed traded at these markets. But that was only part of the objective. They wanted to move up the supply chain to see how it all worked. How could an antique figurine get stolen from a tomb and then end up in the hallowed halls of Sotheby's?

They met more middlemen, and then they were introduced to Jeffrey. This skinny, tattooed character seemed to know all the angles of how you can get "anything" across the borders. They began a lengthy (if borderline incomprehensible) exchange of WhatsApp messages with Jeffrey to coordinate meetups, which often happened at 2 a.m. Jeffrey was usually late, or he'd no-show completely.

Jeffrey's messages looked like this:

Hey Jeffrey- its Trevor- getting couple beers before leaving HK-you in YSW?

For?after we meet, i think we both make understand, for mesure can do anytime, and I really had start my job to hangout with someone too, maybe my English really fuck up la so u guys still not clear yet,,, if like this I don't want spend anymore time to that,, only a piece of cake easy job,y need i keep talked keep explain?No price, no pay for me help looking people and job only keep want meeting, what can I do like this???That really so easy job when I said can help to do with u guys, I said if the price match just choose the day to me can go right?me this way people also need money keep ask me, only u guys not trust or not make understand, is OK la, even can't deal,I also hope u guys can lucky la,,, take care la

Around this time, they realized that they needed to up their game and change locations. The middlemen told them that when a treasured artifact is looted, "things get sent to Hong Kong. That's the major hub."

●   ●   ●

AS THE DUO shifted their focus to Hong Kong, they changed their tactics—and their story. When they started, they had claimed to be the associates of a billionaire looking to buy coveted treasures. Now they said their client was a billionaire who was looking to move stolen artifacts from one country to another. This brought them closer to the world of crime syndicates, government corruption, and the trafficking of drugs and weapons and even humans.

The stakes had been raised. Wallace told Caspari, "You can't wear your tank top. We've got to get button-down shirts."

They upgraded their clothes and their gear. In phase one of their operation, Wallace stealthily filmed their meetups using his mirrorless camera, but that had certain drawbacks. Sometimes it was awkward to get the shot. Often, the battery died. So they found a spy shop in Hong Kong that sold all kinds of clever surveillance tools—think Q from James Bond.

The shop sold a power bank, for example, that was actually a disguised camera. So Wallace tried using that. During a meetup with traders, he set the power bank on a shelf, then awkwardly fiddled with it to get the composition right. This attracted attention, and the plan comically backfired, as the trader asked what it was—instantly suspicious and potentially hostile. The fake power bank wasn't the answer.

Then, through a spy gear specialist, Wallace found something ingenious: a button. He discovered a wide-angle camera that was so tiny it was disguised as a button, and the button was affixed to the center of a vest. Wallace could wear the vest, and the camera pointed to wherever he was facing. It was perfect. It also synced to the screen of Wallace's burner phone, so he could pretend to be checking texts while actually adjusting the video's composition. But the camera had hidden wires that connected to a battery pack. The wires and battery got hot, which meant that Wallace walked around for hours with his chest and back on fire.

So now Wallace was sweating, both literally and figuratively. The spy gear upped the stakes and upped the risk. When he was just filming with his regular camera, if caught, he could feign ignorance and say the camera was on by mistake. But if someone noticed the button camera and hidden battery? "At that point, we realized this was real," says Wallace. They were now headed to three-in-the-morning meetings with people who might be in crime syndicates. Crime bosses, as a general rule, don't react kindly when they discover deception.

They brought this spy gear to meetings with Jeffrey, and Jeffrey introduced them to more players. Their goal had always been to get conclusive proof that the artifacts were both authentic and illegally trafficked, and they wanted to find out how it was being done. They soon found two juicy bits of evidence.

Exhibit A was a set of burnt and blacked clay figurines. These were part of a mystery in the art world that stretched back to 2001. More than twenty years ago, a set of figurines were stolen from an imperial tomb and then somehow found their way to Sotheby's. The looters were caught, and the other figurines were red-listed as stolen. But an open question remained. The archeologists knew there were thirty-two figurines in the set, but only six were accounted for.

Where were the other twenty-six?

In one of Caspari and Wallace's many conversations with merchants and traders, a woman told them that she happened to have some figurines from the Han dynasty, and that these were special, not like the rest. They were blackened and burned. They were female, which made them especially rare. She seemed agitated when she mentioned these figurines, and she asked them to come back to the shop tomorrow.

The next day they returned, and she showed them a figurine. Caspari carefully unwrapped and inspected it. After doing a bit of research, he was convinced this figurine was part of the set that went missing decades ago. Did this woman have the others?

Caspari later went back to the trader and said, "We talked to our guy," referring to their elusive and nonexistent billionaire client. "He's potentially interested, but he has this nice open fireplace in his living room. For symmetry reasons, it would be nice for him to decorate it with four or five of them."

And the trader did indeed have multiple figurines for this "fireplace." Caspari and Wallace had cracked a decades-long mystery.

Their second piece of conclusive proof—exhibit B—was made of gold.

Toward the end of their undercover operation, the duo met a trader named Baldy, who quickly took a shine to Caspari and happily shared his life story. Baldy was an orphan who came from humble roots. He started as a drug mule and worked his way up to partner with some of the world's most prestigious artifact dealers. "We loved hanging out with Baldy," says Wallace, "but we weren't sure if he was complete BS."

They met at one of the many trinket-and-antique shops on Hong Kong's Hollywood Road, and Baldy proudly showed them his wares. Baldy liked Caspari and wanted to impress him. He presented artifact after artifact, showing increasingly more valuable items. "That's not even nice," Baldy would say, dismissing what was inside the display case. "Here, let me show you this!"

Baldy stepped out of the room and returned with a large gold mask. The mask looked too flashy to be real, like something from a movie. It had an almost alien-looking face and seemed to be made of pure gold.

Caspari felt a jolt. *Could that be what he thought it was?*

If his instincts were correct, and if that mask was somehow legitimate, it had absolutely no business being in this random trinket shop on a tourist street. He suspected the mask was from Sanxingdui, a

Bronze Age culture that was discovered in a famous excavation in the 1980s. There were only two excavations of the Sanxingdui sites in the entire history of archeology. Because of this, any objects from the tombs were unfathomably valuable. *There's no way*, Caspari thought. *This must be a copy.*

Wallace and Caspari had multiple encounters with Baldy, and Caspari kept thinking about that alien-looking gold mask. If it was legitimate, Caspari guessed it would be worth at least "double-digit millions." But it was just as likely that Baldy was hawking a fake.

Caspari and Wallace had another reason, more important than $10 million valuations, for ascertaining the mask's origins. The entire point of their mission, at heart, was to prevent future lootings and to protect excavation sites. Artifacts from Sanxingdui culture were extraordinarily rare. If it turned out this golden mask was the real deal, they hoped to find out where it came from and ensure that the rest of the excavation's treasures were safeguarded. Then Caspari had a wild idea.

"Baldy," Caspari said. "Could we see that very nice mask one more time?"

Baldy was eager to please, and again he trotted out the golden mask.

Caspari held it in his hand. On a prior visit, he had noticed there was a tiny piece of loose gold inside the mask. If he could run an analysis on that piece, he could determine the gold's composition. If the mask was a fake, the gold would be modern, and therefore, ironically, more pure. Something from the Bronze Age would have a more unique mixture of elements.

The problem, of course, was that Baldy wouldn't let the mask out of his sight. So Caspari held the mask in his hands and pretended to inspect it, and meanwhile he slowly loosened the tiny piece. Looser, looser, looser . . . then he removed the tiny piece entirely.

Then Caspari pretended to sneeze.

"May I have a tissue?"

Baldy happily gave Caspari a tissue, into which Caspari slipped the little gold piece. He tucked the tissue into his pocket, brought it back to Switzerland, and ran an analysis in the laboratory.

The results? This was almost certainly ancient gold. Baldy was sitting on a fortune. They now had emphatic proof of their thesis—that authentic artifacts were being traded and sold in illicit markets. And now the authorities, in theory, could track and trace the golden mask to its original excavation, preventing future lootings. (Whether the authorities would take action is another question and another story.)

When all the dust settled, Caspari and Wallace were surprised at how easy it was for thieves to rob graves and then legitimize the loot, even crossing borders without the government noticing or caring. "Even for two outsiders in Hong Kong who were only there for a couple of weeks, we could have located national treasures, exported them from mainland China, and sent them to anywhere in the world," says Caspari. "It's that easy. And while doing that, we could acquire a paper trail that makes them legitimate and give them an insanely high value on an international art market. That's the main takeaway."

3

The Edge of Survival

Almost all exploration contains risks. "If you want to be safe, you're going to stay on your couch, and even then, you might die of a heart attack," says Richie Kohler, the legendary diver of shipwrecks like the *Titanic* and the *Britannic,* who knows all too well the life-and-death stakes.

Ellen Pikitch, a marine biologist, was shocked when a routine submersible plunge became a fight for her colleague's survival. One explorer was kidnapped in Zaire. Others fought for survival in plane crashes and hurricanes, on Everest summits, coral reefs, and oil rigs.

Some live to tell the tale. Some don't.

BETWEEN TRIUMPH AND TRAGEDY

Paul Niel

MOUNTAINEERS WARN OF "summit fever." And now Paul Niel felt it.

He had been training to climb Everest for months and acclimating at base camp for weeks. The forecast had been good, or at least good enough to make the final push. And he and his team were tantalizingly close. They had left at 9 p.m. the night before, climbed through a cold and windy night, and were almost out of food. Now, at 8,500 meters' elevation, just before the summit, they heard from the radio that a storm was approaching and they would have to turn back.

When you have summit fever, it's hard to get that call on the radio. You get tunnel vision. Turning around could mean delay or defeat, and it's hard to remember that marching forward could mean death. But Niel turned around. Bitter and frustrated, he headed back down the mountain as the wind whipped his face, and he tried to block out the biting cold. Not everyone followed the warning. Others attempted to summit that morning, and they paid the price in fingers; the frostbite had no mercy.

Niel returned to his tent. It was so cold he dove straight into his sleeping bag for warmth, shivering, and thought about what to do next. He soon learned that another team had said, "Screw this," packed up their kits, and retreated to base camp.

Should Niel do the same? He agonized over the choice. He'd always been an analytical person, so inside that tent, in his field journal, he jotted down charts and decision trees to help inform his decision. He considered factors like how much oxygen he had remaining and how long he had been in the "death zone."

The death zone is exactly what it sounds like. It's the altitude where if you stay too long, the lack of oxygen can cause death. On a normal Everest climb, you are in the death zone for between eighteen and twenty-four hours. Twenty-four hours is the maximum recommended. Beyond that, it becomes dangerous, and Niel was already pushing twenty. His tent was in the lower part of the death zone, and if he attempted Everest the next morning the clock would keep running.

Niel factored all of this into his decision tree. The actual chart was fairly simple, but in that frenzied state, he felt like he had just solved some complicated puzzle worthy of a Nobel Prize.

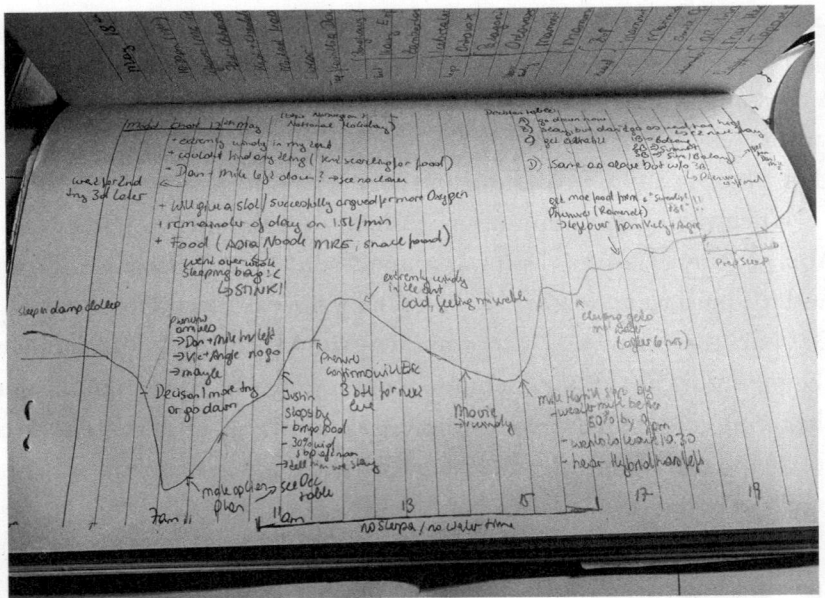

Ultimately, this analysis led to a clear decision: He would rest and try again tomorrow. The extra unplanned day meant he was running low on food; their rations were so meager that when Niel dropped a noodle from his Chinese noodle soup, he scraped it off the ground and hungrily scarfed it down. But no matter. Niel knew that at such a high altitude you really don't get *that* hungry on the final assault, and he suspected that adrenaline would push him through.

He was right. The next day, the skies cleared and the conditions were perfect. Niel was exhausted, but he reached the top of Everest on May 18, 2013—almost sixty years to the day after the first summiteers Hillary and Norgay—and then, instead of elation or euphoria, he focused on one thing: chores.

Niel had only twenty minutes at the top. And unlike most summiteers, he had two extra things to think about. The first was that he owed a litany of photographs and selfies to sponsors, so he took shot after shot on his punch list. There was little time to celebrate. It was stressful. It even felt stupid. He had even promised someone he would solve a Rubik's Cube on top of Everest without his oxygen mask, so he broke out the toy, and his freezing hands fiddled with the cube.

The second thing he had to worry about: His climb wasn't done. Really, he was only at the halfway point. For months, Niel had been training not just to climb Everest—now table stakes for premiere mountaineers—but also to summit nearby Lhotse, also at 8,000 meters' elevation (and the world's fourth highest peak), *within the same twenty-four hours*. This would be like finishing a marathon and then immediately running another marathon.

As Niel descended Everest, he realized he was tired and nearly spent. He rested at camp. Then, at midnight, he began the second push. Or really the third push, since he had climbed Everest the day before.

Few people climb Lhotse. Niel considered it a forgotten stepchild compared to Everest, which was one reason he was drawn to it. The climb was uncomplicated but demanding—a narrow, steep snow and ice shute that shot straight up. He was depleted. At every step, he needed to bully his body into moving forward. From the side of Lhotse, he had a clear view of Everest and the many people who were climbing it. Comparing that image to him on Lhotse—alone, on this steep narrow path, away from the crowds—felt somehow satisfying.

But near the peak of Lhotse, he witnessed a sobering reminder of how high the stakes are when climbing a mountain. Something was lodged in the ice: a dead body, hanging on the climbing ropes. He realized the body was still there because there was no realistic way to bring it down the mountain; the path was too narrow and steep, and it was too dangerous to send a helicopter. There was nothing for Niel to do but step over the corpse and continue to the top of Lhotse—no time to dwell on this death or contemplate how it happened or who this was; the risk of dying is real, and this is something every mountaineer knows.

A few more steps and then, finally, he reached the peak. And now he could feel the euphoria.

Suddenly, he had nothing to do. No photos, no sponsor duties, no checklists. Whereas Everest had a large ledge that enabled proper photography, Lhotse was a literal peak, with no room to maneuver. So Niel could only stand in one place and contemplate the moment. He spent twenty minutes just admiring the view. He felt at peace. Niel had just pulled off a great feat of endurance. And he descended Lhotse on a high, even if he was almost knocked over by the rocks that slid down the trail.

So Niel returned to his tent, ecstatic, and soon learned that something was very wrong. There were other tents nearby, and a sherpa was standing outside of one of them, a grave expression on his face. Niel peered inside, but before he could see anything, he was assaulted by a smell. The tent smelled of urine and feces.

And now he could see that someone—another climber—was in a sleeping bag. He seemed to be barely conscious, moaning, clinging to life. Clearly the climber needed help. He appeared to be Chinese. Niel, who lived in Hong Kong at the time and knew a bit of Mandarin, tried to wake him up. Niel and others tried to radio base camp to identify the climber and get him help, but no one knew who he was. Niel—himself beyond exhaustion—attempted to give him medical assistance. Niel checked his pulse.

They radioed for a helicopter, but at the time (2013), no rescue helicopter had ever reached an elevation of 26,000 feet. A helicopter circled the valley below, but it was physically impossible to reach them, and the chopper backed off. Niel wrapped the climber in his own sleeping bag. He gave him medication. He wondered what else he could do.

Then the manager of the base camp called Niel by radio. "I know this is going to be tough for you," he said, "but now you need to leave."

Niel protested.

"There's another mountain guy coming. You need to leave."

Niel didn't want to leave. But the base manager knew what Niel refused to accept: that Niel had now been in the death zone for eighty hours, which was far too long. "It's bad enough to have one casualty," said the manager. "We don't want two." He told Niel to look below, and Niel could clearly see that, yes, as promised, another mountaineer was on his way up and just about to reach them. "See, you're not abandoning him," the manager said.

Finally, Niel nodded, packed his gear, and descended toward base camp. His body felt on fire even though it was snowing. He survived, but he was wiped.

In the coming days, Niel would celebrate his mountaineering achievement. But he also learned that the other climber perished.

Now the triumph is laced with tragedy, underscoring for Niel how thin the edge is, as he says, "between success and failure."

MAYDAY, MAYDAY!

Ellen Pikitch

ELLEN PIKITCH WASN'T worried about survival. She just had a simple question: Where were the baby fish?

In 1987, that was the question that haunted Pikitch, a marine biologist. Her research had already led to improvements in fishery management. Her fieldwork showed, for instance, that rockfish, which were thought to live for only twenty years, could actually live to be more than two hundred years old—meaning that there are fish in the ocean that have been alive since the days of Ludwig van Beethoven. Now Pikitch was obsessed with the mystery of where the rockfish were spawning. The answer to that question was important, because it would help scientists better understand the complex ecosystem of rockfish and other lesser-known families. Pikitch had a hunch that the baby fish (here, "baby" is a relative term) were in the Heceta Bank, off the coast of Oregon. But that was tricky to prove. Given its rocky topography, the region was not trawlable, meaning that researchers would need to explore it in a small submersible, which could only accommodate a pilot and two scientists.

So, in August of 1987, Pikitch joined a team of five other scientists on a research cruise to explore the depths of the Heceta Bank. This was a close-knit group. They all conducted research in a small town in Oregon where they celebrated one another's birthdays, made potluck dinners, and helped one another move apartments, forming a human chain to pass along the boxes and chairs. They were friends as well as colleagues.

Because the ship's submersible could only fit two scientists at a time, they would be taking turns, in three different shifts. When the pilot gave them a safety briefing, Pikitch paid attention, of course, but she was also thinking along the lines of *Yeah, yeah, yeah. Let's get this show on the road*. The pilot explained that the sub had multiple fail-safe mechanisms, such as dropping an emergency weight that would propel the vessel to the surface. As the pilot described each of the safety protocols, it almost felt to Pikitch like when a flight attendant gives the safety speech on an airplane: important information, sure, but something you'll probably never need to use.

The first few dives in the submersible were magnificent. She saw more species of fish than she could have dreamed of, in almost psychedelic patterns of pink and red and yellow and orange. It was beautiful, and it supported her theory that the Heceta Bank was a crucial nursery for rockfish, which would mean that it should be protected. No one had known this before. Each dive brought more evidence of the rockfish nursery's existence. The scientists were delighted. The mood was festive, and they played cards at night (when they couldn't dive) and punched data into their computers.

A few days into the mission, Pikitch was relaxing on the research ship's bridge and chatting with the captain while two of her friends, Dave Stein and Mark Hixon, were underwater in the submersible, taking their normal shift. Pikitch remembers Stein as the group's biggest "character." He was always cracking a joke. He came awfully close to the line of being annoying but never quite crossed it. (Or as Pikitch put it, "He talked too much.") Mark Hixon was a handsome guy with movie-star looks. Smart and friendly. As Pikitch remembers, he was "the kind of guy who would ride away on a horse in a cowboy hat." Hixon and Stein were close, and they loved to chitchat.

But on that sunny morning in August 1987, on the bridge of the ship, Pikitch wasn't thinking about the characters or merits of her friends. She was just killing time with the captain. So she was startled to hear the captain's radio blast, "Mayday, Mayday! Fire in the sub!"

The captain looked at Pikitch. She looked at him. Did they really hear that?

The radio again crackled, "MAYDAY, MAYDAY! Fire in the sub! Fire in the sub!" And then again, "MAYDAY, MAYDAY! Fire in the sub!"

Before the captain could learn anything more, the fire knocked out communications. Pikitch tried not to panic. She remembered that the pilot had at least three fail-safe mechanisms in the event of an emergency. There were multiple ways the sub could resurface. Even if the instruments were burnt by the fire and unusable, the pilot could dislodge the weight so the sub would pop up. But how bad was the fire? Pikitch thought back to the safety briefing she had only casually paid attention to. In the case of a fire, would she remember where to get the mask for an alternative air supply? Would Stein? Would Hixon?

Pikitch and the captain strained their eyes to scan the ocean and look for any signs of the sub. They saw nothing.

A few agonizing minutes ticked by. Still nothing. Even with her rudimentary understanding of the safety protocols, Pikitch knew the sub should have climbed to the surface by now. And still they saw nothing. The captain suggested that the sub might have been pulled in a different direction by the waves, so he steered the ship in a search pattern. Still nothing. It now felt like the sub had been under for an eternity. Pikitch had the gnawing feeling that Stein, Hixon, and the pilot were dead. The captain continued to search in vain, even though they both suspected it was at the bottom of the ocean.

They had nearly let go of hope when finally, in the distance the submersible rose to the surface. Immediately the captain sped toward it, but Pikitch was heartsick. She had a gut feeling. The prolonged fire—with no radio contact—meant she was looking at a floating coffin. The captain and Pikitch approached the submersible, which could only be opened by a screw-off lid from the outside. He put his hands on the lid and gave it a fierce tug. He kept turning it. And when the lid opened . . . billows of dark gray ash filled the sky, darkening it with smoke.

Pikitch's heart sank, and she broke into tears. She knew they were dead—there was no way they could have survived a fire and smoke that thick.

She broke down in tears. She looked at the captain, he looked at her, and they each began to think about what would happen next and what they should do. She thought about the safety briefing. She thought about how quickly this had flipped from pleasant discovery to tragic loss.

Then the shape of the smoke began to change. She saw movement. Just the hint of an object began to emerge from the sub, silhouetted by the smoke. It moved slowly. Was it more smoke? Some kind of second gasp of an explosion? The object became clearer, and Pikitch realized that it was a head—a human head. In fact, it was the head of Dave Stein, wearing a mask, and he was very much alive. So was Hixon. So was the pilot.

Somehow, all three had survived.

Pikitch, barely able to believe this miracle, rushed to her friends. She learned that, thanks to the quick and decisive actions of the pilot, all three had grabbed their masks and protected themselves from the fire. Then they'd snuffed the flames with an extinguisher. They were able to keep breathing with the alternate air supply.

"There's still a mystery of why, exactly, it took so long for them to come up," Pikitch says now, raw emotion in her voice. "We didn't talk about it with other people for a long time. We kept it to ourselves." She added that there was concern that "if people knew, they would kill the research program."

Sometimes the letter from the edge is a handwritten note that pulls the heartstrings, but sometimes—perhaps far more often—it's an academic paper that fuels scientific knowledge. These papers stick to the facts and rarely share the human story of how the mission was accomplished. This harrowing near-death experience of Pikitch's colleagues was not covered in the newspapers. It was not featured on the local news, and it did not even make in into the academic paper itself. The authors simply note, "We dove 16 times in the vicinity of Heceta Bank."

Submersible Observations of Deep-Reef Fishes of Heceta Bank, Oregon

W. G. Pearcy, D. L. Stein, M. A. Hixon, E. K. Pikitch,
W. H. Barss, and R. M. Starr

ABSTRACT: Rockfishes, *Sebastes* spp., were the most numerous and speciose fishes seen during 16 submersible dives from 64 to 305 m depth in the vicinity of Heceta Bank off the coast of Oregon. Dense schools of juvenile rockfishes and large yellowtail rockfish, *S. flavidus*, were observed only over rocky, high relief areas near the top of the bank, and highest densities of small benthic rockfishes (up to 5–10/m^2) on the flanks of the bank. These observations suggest that shallow, rocky portions of Heceta Bank are a nursery area for juvenile rockfishes. Two species groups of nonschooling fishes were identified based on transects over the diverse seafloor habitats around the bank: one comprised primarily of rockfishes in shallow water on rock and cobble, and the other comprised of flatfishes, agonids, sablefish, and some rockfishes in deep water over mud and cobble. Species composition of fishes observed from submersible dives differed from species composition of fishes taken from trawl catches in the same general areas.

Prominent offshore submarine banks of exposed bedrock, formed by subduction of oceanic plates, occur along the continental shelf of western North America (Kulm and Fowler 1974), providing a specialized habitat for marine fauna. Large aggregations of rockfishes (Scorpaenidae: *Sebastes*) and other fishes are often associated with these banks (Isaacs and Schwartzlose 1965), just as concentrations of fishes are found on or over seamounts in the North Pacific Ocean (Uda and Ishino 1958; Uchida and Tagami 1985; Uchida et al. 1986).

Heceta Bank, located about 55 km off the central Oregon coast, rises abruptly from depths of over 1,000 m on its seaward face to depths of <60 m (Figs. 1, 2). Trawlable areas around Heceta Bank support a large portion of Oregon's commercial fishery production. The bank itself is thought to be a nursery for juvenile fishes. Several surveys of near-bottom fishery resources of the region have been attempted using bottom trawls (Gunderson and Sample 1980; Barss et al. 1982; Weinberg et al. 1984). However much of the bank is too rugged for bottom trawling, and until our study, no submersible surveys of this area had been made. Thus, species composition, abundances, and distributions of fishes on Heceta Bank itself are largely unknown.

We used a manned submersible to conduct surveys of fishes on and around Heceta Bank. Our goals were to assess visually the abundances of fishes on Heceta Bank, to relate distributions and species assemblages with habitat type and depth, and to evaluate the importance of the bank as a nursery and refugium for commercially important fishes.

METHODS

We dove 16 times in the vicinity of Heceta Bank (Fig. 2) during daylight on 23–31 August 1987, using the submersible *Mermaid II*. Bottom depths ranged from 64 to 305 m. Usually two or three visual belt transects were made during each dive. During each transect the position of the submersible and the distance traversed in 30 minutes at speeds of 1.5–2.0 km/h were determined from Loran C fixes by the surface vessel *Aloha* as it followed a surface buoy towed by the submersible. In this paper we report on 21 transects from 10 dives in which the submersible attempted to follow a compass course parallel to isobaths. Two scientists and a pilot were on each dive. Scientists switched positions from the bow window to a stern jump seat between 30 min transects. Seven scientists made dives.

All fishes seen between two fixed points on the submersible's bumper (a path about 3.5 m wide

W. G. Pearcy and D. L. Stein, College of Oceanography, Oregon State University, Corvallis, OR 97331.
M. A. Hixon, College of Oceanography and Department of Zoology, Oregon State University, Corvallis, OR 97331.
E. K. Pikitch, Department of Fisheries and Wildlife, Oregon State University, Corvallis, OR 97331; present address: Fisheries Research Institute, University of Washington, Seattle, WA 98195.
W. H. Barss and R. M. Starr, Oregon Department of Fish and Wildlife, Hatfield Marine Science Center, Newport, OR 97365.

Manuscript accepted February 1989.
Fishery Bulletin, U.S. 87:955-965.

Not every life-and-death expedition involves a scientific study, but perhaps more scientific studies than you know—than any of us know—involve untold stories of survival.

UNDERSTANDING THE DEPTHS

Richie Kohler

THE PHONE RANG. It was Carl Spencer.

"Hey, mate," Spencer said. "I'm heading up a dive team back to *Britannic* in 2009. You in?"

Hell yeah, he was in. When Richie Kohler received that call from Spencer, he knew nothing would keep him from that dive.

Kohler and Spencer were good friends. They were both experienced divers—even legendary divers. Kohler hosted diving shows like the History Channel's *Deep Sea Detectives* and Spencer worked with director James Cameron on dives to the *Titanic*. They also shared something of a hot take: that the best shipwreck dive on the planet was not the *Titanic* but her less famous "sister" ship, HMHS *Britannic*. The *Titanic* gets all the glory. But the *Britannic,* in many ways, held even more mystery.

The *Britannic* was originally intended as a passenger liner. It had a similar design as the *Titanic* (and was built by the same company), but then, while still under construction, two things happened: (1) The unsinkable *Titanic* sunk; (2) World War I broke out.

So the *Britannic* was converted to a hospital ship to help the war effort. And in the wake of the *Titanic*'s sinking, engineers tweaked her design to make her safer. Supposedly, she was three times as strong as the *Titanic,* hardened with a double hull. If the *Titanic* was unsinkable, the *Britannic* was truly and certainly and undeniably unsinkable. Then in 1916, while off the coast of a Greek island, she hit a German naval mine and sunk, joining her older sister at the bottom of the ocean, albeit with far less loss of life (only 30 dead compared to 1,517 on the *Titanic*).

The accident baffled the experts: The mine shouldn't have felled the ship. And the *Britannic* was "three times as strong" as the *Titanic,* but it sunk three times as fast. Why? What happened? Decades earlier, the legendary Jacques Cousteau had discovered the *Britannic* under the sea but was perplexed by the cause of its sinking. It remained a mystery.

Both Spencer and Kohler kept diving to find the answers. They knew deep-sea diving contained risks, but the risks were manageable. Safety procedures were in place. "I am not reckless," Spencer once said. "My wife and kids are the most important things in the world to me. But I do get a kick out of knowing I'm putting myself at the edge."

So, in 2009, Spencer took The Explorers Club's flag number 68 (which, since 1937, had journeyed from Siberia to outer space) on a deep dive to investigate the *Britannic.* Spencer led a National Geographic film crew and a top-notch diving team. "The preparation for this expedition was as good as it gets," Kohler later wrote. "The team Carl assembled included some of the best technical divers and underwater cameramen in the world."

Spencer and Kohler hoped to explore the sunken vessel's Turkish baths, first-class dining areas, and boiler rooms. None of these had been seen before. They were particularly curious about whether the boiler room's massive doors were open or closed. The conventional wisdom was that the doors would be closed due to security protocol. But if they were open, it would suggest some kind of panic has set in (the men opening the doors to dash for safety), water flooded through the vessel, and that was how it had plummeted so quickly. These were questions that needed answers.

Kohler, Spencer, and a larger crew wiggled into their suits and strapped themselves into their rebreathers (breathing devices), like they'd done so many times before. They plunged into the water, cove more than three hundred feet, and took in the sight of the *Britannic.* The water was bright and blue. Peaceful.

This was in sharp contrast to their earlier dives to the *Titanic.* On

Kohler's first *Titanic* expedition, years before, he was awed by the iconic ship. This was the holy grail of shipwrecks. But after several hours of trawling the ruins, the euphoria faded when it truly hit Kohler—he was visiting a graveyard. As he dove deeper, he felt a chill in his bones—literal and figurative. "It became apparent to me that this was the grave of 1,500 people," says Kohler. "The *Titanic* left me with this dark feeling."

The *Britannic* felt different. In the warm and clear Aegean water, Spencer and Kohler could see many signs of life—colorful fish, soft corals, sunlight.

The two friends split up. Kohler headed for the boiler room, and Spencer had science experiments to conduct. Kohler swam deeper and began to inspect the *Britannic,* and, as always, one corner of his brain kept track of his oxygen. This isn't as simple as it sounds. As every deep diver knows, there's a strange paradox when it comes to how our bodies interact with oxygen. "What supports life at the surface will kill you at four hundred feet," says Kohler. The deeper someone swims, the higher the water pressure gets, and at a certain point, the oxygen becomes toxic. Too much oxygen can cause nausea, dizziness seizures, and death.

Divers have known this for decades. The workaround is to essentially "dilute" the oxygen with helium, and the deeper you swim the more you dilute. The proper ratio of oxygen and helium is always changing. This used to be quite complicated. Generations ago, divers swam with multiple tanks, each with varying mixes of oxygen and helium, and then they manually tweaked their percentages as they dove deeper—at 200 feet, maybe 18 percent oxygen and 82 percent helium; at 300 feet it would be 8 percent oxygen and 92 percent helium, and so on. Prior to the 1990s, says Kohler, any human error could result in death—and this happened plenty. "We were killing divers." (Recreational scuba diving is generally limited to 130 feet, where oxygen toxicity is not an issue.)

Over time, better tech allowed for the constant, automatic calculation of the ideal mix of oxygen and helium—and sometimes oxygen and helium and nitrogen, or "trimix." This allowed divers to go deeper and more safely. Modern tools, like the "rebreather," let divers focus on the task at hand.

As Kohler dove to the doomed *Britannic* 360 feet below the surface, the rebreather allowed him to spend his time searching for the boiler doors instead of fiddling with gas tanks. Kohler swam with a camera in front of him. At one point, his guideline became stuck on a pipe, and he was worried he'd become trapped. It was hard to see in the milky-brown water.

He focused on the one thing he could see clearly: the three beautiful lights of his heads-up display, which told him his rebreather was working properly. That's one of Kohler's diving mantras: "If you're breathing, everything is okay, so just focus on the problem at hand, fix it completely, and move on." Kohler untangled himself and kept exploring.

Meanwhile, Spencer swam through an entirely different part of the ship. Since he was the leader of this National Geographic expedition, a Nat Geo cameraman followed him and filmed his every move. The cameraman, incidentally, was Evan Kovacs, a close friend and diving legend in his own right. Kovacs was getting some good footage. He describes the scene as a stunning black-and-white underwater photo, but deep blue instead of black. Sometimes it was so dark that he needed to use his hands to trace the walls of the ship for guidance.

And then, with no warning, Kovacs saw Spencer switch from his rebreather to one of his emergency tanks. *Shit.* Kovacs knew this was serious. At a depth of 360 feet, a diver switching to an emergency tank was like a parachuter cutting their main chute and using their backup—there was no margin for error.

Spencer, aware of the danger, immediately swam for the anchor line, where the team had clipped emergency tanks of trimix. But now the math got tricky. He was no longer using the rebreather, which automatically made all the tedious but life-and-death calculations of oxygen-to-helium ratios. So, as he swam upward toward the surface, he would need to carefully switch trimix tanks several times. You have to "decompress" the gas bit by bit; if it happens too fast, this can cause decompression sickness, aka "the bends," which can be deadly. So divers need to take their time swimming up, pausing for decompression breaks throughout the journey.

Spencer left the *Britannic* at 360 feet. At 280 feet he paused—following protocol—and waited one minute for decompression. At 270 feet he waited another minute. Kovacs stuck with him the entire way. They kept this up for several stops on the way up, and then stopped again at 190 feet. Now they were close enough that other crew members dove down to assist. And Spencer grabbed another bottle of breathing gas—an emergency-yellow bottle that was tied to a safety line. As Kovacs would later write:

> Carl then tried to clip on the yellow bottle from the shot line to himself. Walter helped him clip it on because he could not do it himself. Right after he clipped it on, Carl seized the shot line, shook it violently, hit himself in the head (almost as if he were cursing himself), and seemed to fumble with the line he had tied himself to the shot line with. I followed his hands to the line, and when I looked up, Carl was starting to convulse. The regulator was out of his mouth.
>
> I grabbed the regulator and tried to put it in his mouth while purging it. Pete tried to inflate his BCD, but Carl's diluent tank was empty. I didn't know the tank was empty, so I tried to inflate the BCD unsuccessfully.

Kovacs was confused. When Spencer banged his own head with his hand, this could have meant he had a bad headache, or that he'd made a dumb mistake. Either possibility could be explained by too much carbon dioxide in his blood.

Now Kovacs had to make an agonizing choice.

At this point in the dive, Spencer had a "decompression obligation" of at least three hours, meaning it should take him that much time to safely get to the surface, incrementally, gradually tweaking his oxygen along the way. If they surfaced too quickly, Spencer could get the bends. That was potentially lethal, but it was not certain death—with luck, decompression sickness can be treated. But if Spencer remained below? He was about to drown, and drowning meant instant death.

So Kovacs made the only call he could. He needed to get Spencer to the surface.

. . .

RICHIE KOHLER, MEANWHILE, was still diving under the *Britannic,* still exploring the boiler-room doors, and still oblivious to all this.

He finished and then swam up—decompressing along the way, came to the side of the research ship, and climbed aboard the deck. Immediately he sensed something was wrong. Normally there would be a crowd, celebrations, fist bumps. Here there was no crowd. Just a couple of deckhands to help him climb up.

What the hell? Kohler, frantic, tried to figure out what was happening. Finally, someone told him, "He didn't make it."

Kohler was still strapped into his rebreather. He yanked it out and said, "What are you talking about?"

"Carl didn't make it."

Kohler had no words. He had just spoken to Spencer eight hours earlier. Everything had been fine. In that moment, as he remembers now, "my heart felt like a black hole." He was torn between asking a million questions and respecting the gravity of the situation. But the main thing he thought at the time was *What the fuck?*

. . .

KOHLER, KOVACS, AND THE TEAM inspected Spencer's death from every angle. They agonized over it for hours. Then days. Then weeks. Then years. Kohler thought about it every day.

Why did Spencer bail out of his rebreather, which triggered the devastating chain of events? More than fifteen years later, this is still a mystery. "The Greek police confiscated his equipment," says Kohler, so there was never a proper forensic exam.

A few years later, when leading another dive team, Kohler was asked point-blank, "What would you do differently in light of Carl's accident?"

Kohler had thought about that question a million times. The irony is that Spencer was fastidiously devoted to safety. But it was also true that on the 2009 *Britannic* dive—which was doubling as a National Geographic special—Spencer had a dizzying amount of nondiving responsibilities. "Carl had worn too many hats as team leader," Kohler later wrote, "herding all the cats, as a coproducer working on shot lists, project goals with each team, as onscreen talent being interviewed, and having the camera in his face or over his shoulder all the time, and then as a working diver on a difficult dive."

In the wake of the tragedy, Kohler developed new safety protocols that would mitigate risk in the future, such as a dedicated *nondiving* dive marshall "who could flag [call out for safety] a dive or diver without being second-guessed by anyone."

In the final analysis, for Kohler, the cause of Spencer's death is as simple as it is confounding. "We all failed Carl Spencer," says Kohler. "We are our brother's keepers." Spencer wasn't the first of Kohler's friends to be killed in a diving accident, but his death hit him "as hard, if not more, than any other." But despite the risk and the grief and the loss, before too long, Kohler once again suited up, grabbed a rebreather, and plunged himself back underwater. Or maybe it was partly *because* of the risk and the grief and the loss—he knew Spencer would want to see him exploring. Over the next six years, Kohler made 228 dives, including an epic search for U-550, a World War II German U-boat.

Then, in 2015, it was time. Kohler filled out an application to check out an Explorers Club flag for a special expedition. The request was granted. Kohler and Evan Kovacs's mission: return to the *Britannic*.

They would find conclusive proof that the boiler doors were open, which could at last solve the mystery of how the *Britannic* sunk. They would finish the work their friend Carl Spencer had started.

Kohler kept detailed field notes throughout the expedition. Some excerpts:

> My eyes hadn't fully adjusted yet to the dimming light; the water was wonderfully clear but darkening with each foot I descended . . .
>
> The side of the hull is at 300 feet, and it was here I made final adjustments to my rebreather . . .
>
> We were finally here, on the wreck for the first time since Carl's accident. Our lives had been impacted in a way we would never forget. For Britannic, resting in her grave, had six years brought noticeable changes? . . .
>
> I was transported back to the 2009 dive, every movement we made indelibly etched into my mind. . . . In looking at Britannic's vastness again, in melding past with present, I felt like Carl would think we had waited long enough. It was time to share our stories about the open doors. Then, in what seemed the blink of an eye, our allotted minutes for the dive were over.

From this dive, Kohler and Kovacs now had the proof that they and Spencer had been seeking: The boiler-room doors were open, which would have allowed water to gush from compartment to compartment. They documented and videoed the evidence, finally revealing how the *Britannic* sunk—an open question since the days of Jacques Cousteau.

Even now, knowing the life-and-death stakes like few others, Kohler insists the rewards of exploration are worth the risk. He still feels that childlike wonder. "I love the sense of adventure," he says. "There is nothing in this world more exciting to me than pulling myself down an anchor line in blue water, not knowing what lies at the other end of that line."

On that 2015 trip to the *Britannic*, Kohler jotted one last note in his dispatch from the edge:

> At around 220 feet, I looked down from the bell and could see nearly one-fifth of Britannic lying beneath me. I kneeled down on the floor of the bell and waved goodbye—to the wreck and to Carl. I thanked him for watching over us.

THE STORM CHASER

Jaclyn Whittal

THE EDGE CAN be a moving target. The edge can change thousands of times per second. This is the case for Jaclyn Whittal, a storm chaser, who races toward one-hundred-miles-per-hour hurricanes while everyone else runs away. Whittal is a meteorologist. She literally throws herself into storms so we can better understand how they operate, determine whether the forecasting models are accurate, and tell the stories of loss and survival, devastation and hope.

And sometimes a storm can bring the unexpected.

While working for The Weather Network (Canada's version of The Weather Channel), Whittal hopped on a flight to Florida to chase Hurricane Michael, which ravaged the Gulf of Mexico in 2018. When she boarded the flight, it was a Category 1 hurricane. By the time she landed in Florida, it was Category 4. It would eventually swell to Category 5 and is now regarded as one of the most devastating hurricanes ever recorded.

Winds topped 160 miles per hour, although speed is only part of the equation. Whittal often thinks of the folksy meteorological saying, "It's not how fast the winds are going, it's what the winds are throwing." In the crucible of Hurricane Michael, she saw glass blown from windows and steel flying off buildings. Chunks of wood shot through the air like bullets. It felt more like a war than weather.

During the most violent stretch of Hurricane Michael, Whittal and her TV crew worked from a parking garage—their usual playbook—which let them shoot footage and broadcast stories from a place of relative shelter. Once the winds became less punishing, they used Twitter to track which neighborhoods endured the most damage. They followed that digital trail and headed east, toward the coast, to a small town called Mexico Beach.

She arrived to find a wasteland. Homes were leveled. Trees were snapped. Emergency vehicles zoomed into town with sirens blaring. People frantically searched for loved ones in the piles of wreckage. Even for Whittal, a thirteen-year-veteran storm chaser, this was almost unthinkably awful. But there was nothing she could do except get the story out; it was the best way to honor those who had lost.

As she walked through the rubble, she could see grim reminders of the lives that were wrecked. A vacuum cleaner. A toaster. A Barbie doll. Then she saw something else: a glimpse of jewelry. It was a small box. A burgundy ring box. Should she pick it up? What were the ethics here?

She decided to pick up the box. She opened it . . . and the box contained two rings: clearly a wedding and engagement ring set. A jolt of energy passed through her. Her first instinct was to give the ring to someone immediately, and her second was to locate the owner.

She gave the rings to the local sheriff, but before that, she snapped a photo and posted the image to Twitter. Via social media, she sent this letter from the edge of Hurricane Michael's destruction:

> I found a wedding and engagement ring in the debris path in
> Mexico Beach. We gave to a local sheriff. If you live on 41st
> and are missing this—it was in the storm surge damage—claim
> it by contacting the local sheriffs department—PLEASE
> RETWEET.

The tweet got a like. A second like. A retweet. While it's true that some internet trolls acted like trolls ("How do you know this isn't unpaid for from a ruined jewelry shop?"), the bulk of the replies were supportive and helped spread the message. Whittal's tweet went viral. A company called Firsthand Weather posted the tweet on a Facebook group, and before long, amazingly, they reached out to say that the owner had been located.

Whittal arranged a call with the owner, a woman named Terri Hays. Hays told her that when the storm barreled toward the town, she was forced to abandon her home as quickly as possible. She frantically looked for the rings but couldn't find them. They were more important to Hays than Whittal, the sheriff, or anyone could have imagined. Her husband had passed away. The rings, in a sense, were the last physical link to his memory.

"I had not cried until that text," Hays told Whittal, her voice thick with emotion, referring to the text saying that the rings had been found. "And I went down on the asphalt and broke down." Hays said the found rings were "a sign to me that my husband is still taking care of me."

Whittal now thinks of this story as the "diamond in the debris." And while she is, at heart, a rational scientist, she was moved by the astonishing odds of the rings' survival and discovery. "While Mother Nature is usually in charge," says Whittal, "sometimes fate has a way of overcoming even her power."

CRASH LANDINGS

Peter McMillan

PETER MCMILLAN'S DISPATCH was too urgent to send as a letter. He needed help, and he needed it now. His co-pilot barked into
the plane's radio:

> Mayday, Mayday, Mayday! Vimy One, Vimy One, Vimy One. We've
> had an engine failure. We're making an emergency landing.

The date was October 9, 1994. But McMillan wasn't flying a plane
designed in the 1990s. Or even in the '80s or '70s or '60s or '50s.
McMillan was flying an exact replica of a Vickers Vimy, the legendary open-cockpit World War I bomber.

In 1919, a young pilot had pulled off one of the most daring stunts
in aviation history, flying a Vimy 11,000 miles over twenty-eight days
from London to Australia. McMillan had sacrificed his job, his career and his life savings to recreate this historic flight, meticulously
constructing the replica Vimy using only parts and technology available in 1919. Along with a National Geographic film crew (who
planned to make this into a book and a movie), McMillan had been
flying close to the ground—the wind whipping his face—for thousands of miles.

The apparent purpose of the expedition was to rekindle the
world's sense of adventure and risk-taking, but McMillan had a
deeper motivation. While The Explorers Club puts a premium on
scientific knowledge and discovery, many members are drawn to exploration and all its challenges as a way of overcoming their own

self-doubts or inner barriers. Few are brave enough to admit this. McMillan has the guts to come clean.

"The whole point of it for me personally was that I knew deep down that I was a coward," says McMillan. "I'd read all these books about heroes, and I wanted a way to prove that I could be one of them. I was going to sit in this seat in a plane and fly around the world."

That was his dream. And now, over the Indonesian island of Sumatra, it was all, quite literally, going up in flames.

The prior two hours had been the most terrifying of McMillan's life. Earlier in the day's flight, McMillan had noticed what he thought were mist and clouds. It was smoke. McMillan couldn't see through the smoke, so he'd tried to fly under it, which meant he descended to 200 feet above the ground. The smoke was so thick he could barely see the tail of his aircraft. Flying into the wind, closer to the Java Sea, allowed them to gain altitude—up to around 1,800 feet—but the right engine sounded like a death rattle. Like it was about to go kaput.

And then it did. He lost his engine.

The plane would crash. This was now certain.

McMillan did some quick math. He knew that at an altitude of 1,800 feet, he could still control the plane with only the left engine for roughly seven minutes. (This was why he'd climbed so high in the first place.) At that altitude he could find some type of clearing amidst the jungle so the plane wouldn't flip on its back or spear into the canopy . . . with four hundred gallons of fuel on board. So he tried to stay calm and looked for places to land. Beneath him was a road but it was too narrow, with deep ditches on either side. Some kids were riding bicycles on the road, and the plane was flying so low that they panicked and drove their bikes into a ditch.

The Vimy kept drifting lower. He had to make a call.

He saw a farm and a field. The field wasn't ideal—there were small fences and walls that the plane might hit—but he no longer had a choice. He wrestled with the wheel, and the plane kept sinking but he prevented it from flipping. Lower, lower, lower, until finally, he smashed into the ground. The Vimy crashed into the field, and McMillan crashed into an earthen wall—then another, then another, and then another. The plane's axels shattered, but it stayed upright. McMillan's co-pilot and his photographer (Nat Geo icon Jim Stanfield) were alive and safe. So was McMillan.

But the wounded plane—lying in a smoldering rice field—left McMillan thinking that the entire expedition, three years in the making, was doomed. McMillan's co-pilot, Lang Kidby, had other ideas.

"This is going to be fine," said Kidby, incredibly unconcerned, and after only an hour on the ground, they were somehow on the back of a truck making a four-hour trip to the nearest town.

The plane weighed twelve thousand pounds and was stuck in the dirt so they used logs as levers to dig it out. With help from the local farmers, they built a makeshift runway. The trailing camera plane arrived with a backup engine, and that plus some landing-gear repairs brought the Vimy back from the dead. Within six days of the crash, they took off and resumed the epic journey.

In the end, just as he'd planned, McMillan completed his quest to recreate the 1919 flight of the Vimy. The *National Geographic* cover story, documentary, and book were a success, inspiring in many a zest for aviation. And he'd proved to himself what he needed to prove.

But he often thinks about that ride after the crash.

As the plane was burning in a field and stuck in the mud, McMillan rode on the back of a truck with several Indonesian villagers. He was devastated, nearly in tears, and sitting next to him was a fifteen-year-old boy named Heno. The boy handed McMillan a St. Christopher medal and said, "Mr. Peter, this will help you."

McMillan felt a wave of relief. And to this day, he's still in touch with the boy.

THE INFERNO

Ed Punchard

ED PUNCHARD'S LETTER from the edge is clearly a product of
the 1980s. Consider how it was printed:

> I thought I'd touch base as I have a computer with me on the plat-
> form and it has a nice little dot matrix printer that comes with it.
> So here I am writing a letter on it. . . .
>
> There was quite a smell of gas the other day which was odd. I
> think it was to do with the excessive flaring going on at the mo-
> ment. . . . The flame . . . is huge, much bigger than normal.

Punchard wrote this from Piper Alpha, an oil-drilling platform on
the North Sea around 120 miles north of Scotland. Punchard, a diving expert, worked on the platform alongside 225 others. In this letter, he noted the smell of gas, a flame, and a boom that was "much
bigger than normal." Perhaps he thought of this letter a few weeks
later, on July 6, 1988.

. . .

PUNCHARD DIDN'T JUST hear the explosion, he felt it. A shock-
wave reverberated in his chest. Then he saw only darkness.

Punchard knew that something had gone very, very wrong. He was
the Inspection Controller for the dive team, whose job was to inspect
the rig's underwater integrity. Punchard sought the dive team's escape
route, so he bolted from his office—sometimes barely able to see and

with all routes blocked by flames. Soon he was joined by the dive team.

Now he could see the bright lights of terror that cut through the darkness—an oil fire. There was nothing more dangerous than an oil fire on an oil rig. They had to act, and they had to act now.

Punchard and his team stood on a platform on the rig's edge, about seventy feet above the water. He knew the rest of the hundreds of workers would be trying to escape. His team needed to do the same. He looked around the platform—flames all around him—for a means of getting to safety.

They tried to deploy the inflatable life rafts, but they were defective and wouldn't inflate. Punchard surveyed the flames and his options. He needed to move fast. He found the escape rope for the life rafts; that would have to do. As balls of flames swirled above him, he tied the rope to the railing, and a diver chucked the rest overboard.

Punchard lowered himself off the edge of the platform and began climbing down the rope. Instantly, he fell. He plunged toward the water in a free fall. At this height, that meant death. But the rope caught, somehow, miraculously. Punchard realized, belatedly, he had made a mistake tying the knot, and it had slipped, dropping him ten feet. But now it held. Hopefully it would keep holding.

He slithered down the rope, using his feet and legs. Above him he could see the smoke and the giant ball of flame that would eventually become a thousand-foot inferno. Now the other divers joined him on the rope. Around him, fireballs the size of cars pelted into the ocean. As he climbed lower and dangled from the rope, he was reminded of going to the movies as a kid and seeing balls of fire flying through the sky in *Jason and the Argonauts*.

Punchard finally landed on a lower deck at the base of the platform. The momentum from his fall had almost knocked him off the rope, but he caught his boot on the railing and managed to drag himself over. He checked and confirmed that the rest of his diving team, somehow, was following him.

In the distance, Punchard could see an inflatable rescue boat headed in his direction. As it got closer, he waved it toward a ladder that reached into the ocean. Flames continued to rain all around him.

Above them on the rig, the raging fire expanded, growing so large it threatened to consume Punchard and his team. Eventually, the rig's white hot legs would buckle and 80 percent would sink. Piper Alpha would go down in history as one of the most devastating nonnuclear explosions of all time. Only 61 would live; 165 workers would die.

Punchard didn't know the extent of the disaster as he saw the rescue boat approaching. All he could do was try to get his team to safety. When the vessel approached, the divers quickly scrambled aboard. Punchard was the last to hop off the ladder. The inferno reached over the vessel and everyone ducked for cover. Punchard went overboard to escape the heat, and just then the boat's skipper gunned it, trying to get them away.

As the rescue boat pulled away from the explosions, Punchard was just barely able to grab a rope hanging off the side and cling to it. The skipper sped the ship up—desperate to elude the flames—and Punchard's legs dangled in the water and pulled him under. His hands ached. His body flooded with pain. Since Punchard was a veteran diver, he had experience controlling his breathing, so he did that now to remain calm. He also knew that if he slipped off into the dark water, no one would know he was missing. And he was wearing heavy work boots from the oil rig; those were like anchors. If he let go of the rope, he'd be dead. He thought of his baby daughter.

Eventually, a diver spotted Punchard and called for the skipper to stop.

Punchard, exhausted and on the brink of death, calmly and politely asked the skipper, "Would you be so kind as to help me up?"

· · ·

ED PUNCHARD WOULD think of Piper Alpha many times over the next thirty years. He wrote a book about it. He made a film about it.

He gave extensive testimony about the system failures in safety protocols that led to the tragedy, and what should be done to ensure it never happened again. He was instrumental in pushing for change. He also used this near-death experience as a springboard for filling the next chapter of his life with exploration. This started with a letter that he sent, via fax, as part of a job application:

> Having survived the Piper Alpha disaster I now need something new to do. I have a second class honours degree in Political Theory from the University of Wales, and close to eight years experience as a Professional diver, do I qualify?

Five minutes later the fax machine chimed with a return message:

> You are in.

Since then, Punchard's film production company has made more than three hundred documentaries, many about exploration. He has dived to explore the oceans and helped discover shipwrecks. In some ways, Piper Alpha kickstarted it all. "I couldn't waste my life," he says. "In the background of my psyche, there's always been this notion that there's all these dead people that don't have lives. It falls on me to do two things: Do something to make sure that those people are remembered, and so something like this can never happen again; and two, have a good life yourself."

Ultimately, says Punchard, "Nobody is going to fix your life but yourself." When people hear about Punchard's story, they often assume he has a case of "survivor's guilt." He hates that expression. "It evokes the notion of some poor chap sitting with his head in his hands, worrying," says Punchard, who might be speaking for all explorers who have lived when their compatriots have died, from Ada Blackjack to Paul Niel to Richie Kohler. "For me it wasn't like that at all," he says. "It was, pick up the ball and run."

GHOSTS OF THE *TITANIC*

Charlie Pellegrino

THINK OF YOUR FAVORITE blockbuster movie.

Whatever it is, there's a good chance that it was somehow influenced by Charlie Pellegrino, a polymath whose expertise includes—and this is just a small sample—nuclear propulsion, astrobiology, archeology, writing science fiction novels, magnetic levitation systems, space rockets, and the *Titanic*.

Pellegrino literally wrote the books on the subject, including *Her Name, Titanic* and *The Ghosts of the Titanic,* which Jim Cameron loved and used as source material. Pellegrino's writings on dinosaurs and DNA inspired Michael Crichton to write *Jurassic Park*.

Pellegrino and Cameron, both members of The Explorers Club, were friends. In 2001, Cameron asked Pellegrino a question: "Are you ready to go back to the *Titanic*?"

This was not a hard question to answer.

The expedition, launched in August of 2001, would evolve into Cameron's documentary *Ghosts of the Abyss*. Signing on as a scientific advisor, Pellegrino joined Cameron, Bill Paxton, teams of American and Russian scientists, and a larger crew of more than one hundred to once again explore the unsinkable. They used newly invented robotics to explore parts of the ship that had never been seen before. They also studied "rusticles"—deep underwater rust accumulations that look like icicles—to learn about the possible medical uses of their chemical properties.

Just before the trip, Pellegrino wrote an email to his longtime friend and fellow science fiction author Arthur C. Clarke. The wrote gives a sense of Pellegrino's excitement and an appreciation of how lucky he felt to be exploring:

> Dear Arthur: I'm off to New Foundland [for the *Titanic* expedition]. . . . Upon return, I'll have to plan a "real" holiday with Mary. I haven't done so in two years, but it's difficult to notice because isn't what lucky SOB's like you and I do for a living a lifelong holiday of discovery in the first place—from which we never, ever wish to retire?
>
> Cheers,
> Charlie P

Pellegrino and Cameron had planned, as usual, to stay in touch with friends and family over email. Then the team lost access to the internet. Thanks to a satellite phone, they had a tenuous connection to the outside world, but they were unable to send email. But that didn't stop Pellegrino from sending letters.

Each morning, while floating above the *Titanic* aboard the research vessel *Keldysh*, Pellegrino used a pencil to write notes in his expedition log. Then he would photocopy the entry, along with the coordinates of their location on a map, and send these entries as letters.

Without email or postal service, how did he send these letters? Pellegrino went old school, harkening back to a much earlier time. He sent letters in a bottle.

Pellegrino literally printed out physical letters and inserted each one into a bottle, then tossed the bottle overboard. He would send up to six bottles per day. Each message included the address of Pellegrino's recipient, with a request to forward it along if possible.

Pellegrino wrote his very first message in a bottle to his three children, Ashley, Kyle, and Kelly, and to his girlfriend, Mary. He would write to his family many times.

August 18, 2001

Dear Ashley, Kyle, Kelly—and Mary too.

This is the first time that I have ever written an expedition log as anything except notes to myself. I don't know what that says about me at this point in time, or if it means anything at all. It just feels right.

But you'll please forgive me if I sometimes break away and lapse into techno-speak (or techno-babble).

Pellegrino chronicled his thoughts on the *Titanic*, along with ruminations on what it was like for the humans who perished.

Many of those who came running out headed aft, but some must have gone after the only boat then remaining: . . . filled with women, and soon to be swamped, with none of the women inside ever to be heard from again.

Pellegrino's letters often turned philosophical, and he pondered the meaning of this *Titanic* expedition and even its title.

Ghosts of the Abyss. . . . No, I don't really believe that our spirits somehow walk the Earth after we are gone. But archeologists and paleontologists are still the biggest storytellers in the world.

Then, in the next sentence, Pellegrino draws a contrast between how different members of his family have experienced childhood wonder—some embraced it, some forgot it. This distinction, n a sense, gets at the heart of exploration.

And thank you, Kyle and Ashley and Kelly, for noticing that [your uncles] said they used to like dinosaurs when they were kids but did not like them anymore . . . and that when they grew up they stopped thinking about them and liking them.

"But daddy, you never grew up." No, and I hope you too will hold onto that childlike sense of wonder that so many adolescents allow to drain away, never to recover it again. . . .

I've carried the ghosts of the dinosaurs with me for a long time. The ghosts exist inside our heads; we breathe life into them with our imaginations. . . . After a while, one gets used to them. After a while, one does not want to be without them.

One of Pellegrino's notes is a handwritten scribble with little context, written in all caps:

Charlie: DO NOT DRINK THE WATER OUT OF THE SHOWER (OR THE TOILET, DIRTY DOG).

Pellegrino jotted down his objectives for the expedition, such as to "compare status of rusticles from 1996 to 2001." He made guesses about where he'd find rusticles in the *Titanic*: the promenade deck, the stern, the port anchor, the handrail.

He gave detailed accounts of the day-to-day:

August 19, 2001

We had our first lifeboat drill yesterday. There are approximately 120 of us aboard (100 crew). . . . There is lifeboat space for all. Funny that this should be new . . . on expeditions to the Titanic.

Mary worked in New York City near the World Trade Center, and she was often in the Twin Towers. So, several times in Pellegrino's letters in a bottle, he made reference to the Twin Towers.

August 21, 2001

We are 2 and a half miles (10 World Trade Center Twin Tower lengths) above the Titanic.

Pellegrino, of course, had a physical copy of his *Ghosts of the Titanic* book on hand—he could update it in real time—anc he wasn't the only one reading it.

> At the 8:30 a.m. meeting, [Bill] Paxton stated that he began reading *Ghosts of the Titanic* last night, and that it really disturbed him and kept him awake when he was supposed to be catching up on sleep for Dive 1.

Pellegrino had hoped to get email restored, but this was not tc be. He sent more letters.

> August 21, 2001
>
> It turns out, my Mary and my rodents [his kids], that we cannot yet get linked for email. . . . I've resorted to putting messages in bottles overboard.
>
> Dear Mary,
>
> I miss you, and the "little rodents," and the mooks more than can be described by words.
> Am A-okay out here, but we've run out of Skittles and Mars Bars. Running low on Aero Bars and Coca-Cola. Help!

Then this particular message in a bottle took a sudden pivot. He asked Mary, in his own roundabout way, to marry him. He sent a marriage proposal in a bottle.

> The Russian kitchen crew is very good; but I miss your cooking, and all those nice little things you do for me. It's very peaceful out here, but it's peaceful, too, at home with you—and since you've come into my life, I miss the peace I have with you more than I love and miss the peace of the sea.
> Wanna talk about making an honest man outta me?

When Cameron heard about Pellegrino's marriage proposal, he laughed and called it a "chicken-man proposal." Cameron's theory: It's a chicken move. No one's going to receive that bottle, so there's no chance she says yes!

Pellegrino missed Mary and his "little rodents." (This is a long-time joke because the twins were born in the Chinese Year of the Rat.) But of course, he also focused on his work, which included analyzing the rusticles. He lovingly described the science in letters to his kids and the woman he hoped would someday be his wife.

August 26, 2001

Mary and little rodents,

Exqueeze me, because I'm going to get all techie about rusticles again. Dissecting yet another rusticle from the #8 rail, have found one with growth bands growing in whorls.

While on the expedition, Pellegrino never lost his childlike sense of wonder.

August 29, 2001

Dear Mary,

I sometimes have to pinch myself . . . into believing that I am here on the *Keldysh* with what is probably the finest scientific and historical team ever assembled on salt water. . . .

[Unlike prior expeditions], this time I have someone (and some special little someones) to miss.

But missing and loving and knowing that you are missed and loved back is a very good place to be.

We're also coming up with plenty of new questions—a lot of "I don't know" in the rusticles alone. We're never afraid of not having the answers; it's running out of questions that we should fear most. Being confused ("What the hell is that?") is the best place for a scientist to be.

> Love you, miss you.
> —Your Charlie

As the expedition progressed, Pellegrino's letters in the bottles contained a mix of scientific observations and a longing to see his children and his girlfriend.

> Today I've been mostly reviewing 1912 transcripts, and looking at the huge samples of invertebrate fauna from the mud several miles from Titanic. . . .
>
> As I say in my sea-mails, I miss you guys and I love you so much that it hurts, being way out here . . . especially when so many who survived lost loved ones.

Pellegrino had pictures of his kids with him on the *Keldysh*. That helped tide him over.

> August 29, 2001
>
> Dear Ashley, Kyle, Kelly,
>
> I've got your pictures spread all over my cabin, and they will in fact be going 2½ miles down to the bottom with me. . . .
>
> My two biggest wishes for you guys are that (A) you grow up to own your own lives and (B) Just as you told Daddy last month, that he's different from your uncles because he still loves the dinosaurs and the moon and Mars. . . .
>
> Oh, may you never stop asking new questions, never outgrow that childhood sense of wonder.
>
> > Love and kisses and hugs,
> > —Daddy

Sometimes instead of jotting notes to put in bottles, Pellegrino would write actual emails that he knew couldn't be sent—or at least not until the internet was restored. He tried to send another email to Arthur C. Clarke:

August 31, 2001

Dear Arthur:

Internet contact is going to be a bit spotty. . . . I am happy to report that this Cameron expedition is run so well that it makes every other voyage . . . seem amateurish by comparison. . . . All in all, it's been the dream expedition of a lifetime. . . .

Don't be surprised if you get a message in a bottle. I've been sending a half dozen per day from the Titanic site via Squid Mail.

See you later, Charlie P

It was almost time for the dive, but he still had more life advice for his kids.

September 3, 2001

Dear Mary—Ashley, Kyle, Kelly,

. . . My little "rodents": A reporter once asked me what it takes to do this kind of job, and I said, "You have to be one-third explorer, one-third fish, and one-third crazy." Well . . . not that crazy. Some of us are just lucky enough never to put away the wonders of childhood.

That childhood sense of wonder about dinosaurs, or where the sky ends—or time itself. I'm sure you'll get teachers who tell you to stop asking about those things because they don't know the answers. The secret is that no one knows how deep into the

Earth's skin the water seeps, or where the universe ends. Truly no one.

You ask those questions, and you're in unexplored territory. Your Daddy was lucky enough to have parents and teachers . . . who encouraged him to never stop asking questions, never to give up that sense of wonder, the thrill of mystery. And you've got a Daddy who hopes that wherever you go, you will never forget the miracle that is a simple leaf in the palm of your hand.

Fortunately these long expeditions only occur every 5 years or so. I'll stay safe out here for you, and I'll be home to you in early October—home with you all for a long time.

Love, and kisses and hugs,
Your Charlie, Your Daddy

In just a few days, it would be time for Pellegrino's dive inside the *Mir I*, the three-person submersible that would tour the *Titanic*. Pellegrino sent Mary a joking letter from Jim Cameron, stating the real reason he was about to plunge to the *Titanic*.

September 9, 2001

Dear Mary: I'm sending Charlie down to the stern tomorrow because he's finally reached the stage where he can be more annoying up here than down there.

—Jim Cameron

Mary: I love you / Grrrrr . . .

On Pellegrino's dive to the *Titanic*, he would bring letters he'd written by hand to other members of his family—his mother (who had passed) and his father. He wrote notes to them on flattered Styrofoam cups, and he strapped the cups to the outside of the *Mir I*.

September 10, 2001

To DAD:

Thanks for getting me this far.

Love, Charlie

To his mother:

For Jane Pellegrino

May 26, 1935—Feb 25, 1993
Thank you, Mom, for believing, and nudging me closer to believing, when experts said you shouldn't believe, couldn't believe, must not believe. Wherever you are, a part of you will be with me in the rusticle garden—along with that silly little story, which you seemed to overuse.

Love, the little engine who thought he could

Thirteen books later—I owe you, too, Dad, for believing in that reading-disabled boy who just needed the right parents and teachers, and got what he needed.

And Pellegrino, of course, wrote a Styrofoam cup to his beloved Mary, who he knew to be safe and sound in New York City, in the financial district, near the World Trade Center.

September 10, 2001

To my Mary:

With love, from 10 Twin Tower lengths down—at the World's Ultimate Haunted Mansion.

Love,
Your Charlie

Pellegrino had his dive to the *Titanic*. He wrote again later that day.

> September 10 (late night), 2001
>
> Dear Mary, Ashley, Kyle, Kelly:
>
> . . . After an initial period of being stricken speechless—when we reached the bow section and I found myself "feeling human again," I began actually to scribble corrections into a dog-eared copy of *Ghosts of the Titanic,* with the actual Titanic right outside my viewport—correcting what I'd gotten wrong about the stern in my drawings, which were based previously only on video and photographs.
>
> Hope to see you soon for big group hug.
>
> Love, Your Charlie,
> Your Daddy

After the dive, in the early hours of September 11, Pellegrino was in a state of sensory overload. He couldn't sleep, so he wrote a three-page letter chronicling all his emotions.

> Early morning of September 11, 2001.
>
> . . . I think what I found there, way down there 10 Twin Towers lengths at the stern, was the color that has no words. The color no one can describe.
>
> When I was sixteen and the first men were about to walk on the moon, I wondered how they would describe it, if they saw, out there amongst the rocks, a color no one had seen before, and for which there were no words. . . .
>
> It snuck up on me and bit. And it bit hard. It bit so hard that all I wanted to do was get away from the stern. Can you believe that? No scientific observations. Can you believe that science wasn't even in it? Not one damned bit? I kept closing my eyes and sud-

denly I felt so exhausted I could easily have dozed off and slept the rest of the dive. I was so bitten that I would have been happy if our pilot, Victor, took us anywhere else but there—even straightaway back to the surface.

Pellegrino did not sleep long after that dive. He woke up three hours later, on the morning of September 11. While Cameron's ship did not have email, it did have a satellite phone, and it could receive faxes.

The bridge of the *Keldysh* received a fax. No one knew what to do with it, when to show it. Logged at 12:10 p.m. for the time zone of the *Titanic,* transmitted to the bridge by Mary at 10:40 a.m. eastern daylight time.

> To: Charlie Pellegrino
> Terrorist attack on World Trade Center.
> Both buildings are gone.
> Pentagon attacked.
> I can't find Mom.

Like the rest of the nation and the world, Pellegrino struggled to process what he'd just learned. He thought about how Mary traveled through the World Trade Center every day on her way to work. He thought about how, incredibly, so many of his recent letters had been peppered with references to the Twin Towers. He lived in Long Island, so he thought about all his family and friends. He knew nothing for many hours. He went into his office and stared at a Skor chocolate bar that had been given to him by Mary. He kept staring at that Skor bar. And somehow he just *knew*: Mary was okay.

Hours later he confirmed what his gut told him: Mary was alive and safe. She had the flu, and that had kept her from taking her normal commute through the World Trade Center. He could exhale.

But he soon learned that his cousin Donna, whom he grew up

with, was "missing." Gone, right where the starboard wing of Flight 11 struck. He learned that a dear firefighter friend was kil ed. He learned that so many of his extended family and friends vere missing.

Pellegrino immediately wrote Mary and the kids:

Dear Mary, Kyle, Kelly:

Dove to the Titanic yesterday and was ready to tell you all about it in today's log—but that's not even in this.

I'm so agnostic that I'm next of kin to atheist, but I've been praying that you all are alright, that you, Mary, never got that transfer [to the World Trade Center] that you were worried about, or that the trains were not all screwed up and you got your connection on time and were across the river at 8 am, or that the flu kept you in bed another day. . . .

I'm reasonably certain that all of our family are still together. I'm just as certain that some of our friends are in trouble. And Mary, it had better be a trick of the imagination from staying up most of the night . . . but I seem to feel your presence here, as with your father. You're the truest love of my entire life and we've got so much work to do. Don't be going ghost on us, okay? . . .

Sorry guys, I'm really very tired right now and I don't know where to go with any of this train of thought. . . .

Love you all,
Your Charlie,
Your Daddy

p.s. Mary—Strange feeling, like you're here beside me telling me that I worry too much and that you weren't near it.

Several days later the internet was restored. Mary and her mother were fine (though Mary had been caught in a surge of dust clouds).

Pellegrino sent an email to Arthur C. Clarke and a small group of friends to give an update of the *Titanic* expedition, especially in the wake of tragedy.

> The whole subject, the gray lady, seemed suddenly so irrelevant and insignificant—despite the fact that my experience down there had involved all of the emotions in such intensity that I came to regard it as the single most all-encompassing emotional event of my life—and hours later it was replaced by an even more all-encompassing event.

Pellegrino then addressed what everyone really wanted to know. Would they continue with the exploration?

> Oh, my friends, to not go on and finish what we started, even if no one in the world will any longer care about the Titanic, we remain right now "in attack mode to complete the mission," no matter how sorry that may sound to the world outside. It is really, in our minds, our act of solidarity and defiance against terrorism. We defy the bastards—as we failed, collectively, to defy our ignorance and our complacency . . . as we failed this decade past to recognize the bumps of all those little icebergs along the way. . . .
>
> Ignorance. Education. Ignorance. We've all been educated this week. Education. There is no substitute.
>
> Every expedition to the Titanic has left a calling card, of sorts—usually little brass plaques saying, though not in quite these words, "Hi I'm Bob Ballard, or George Tulloch, or some dot com millionaire on an expensive camping trip and I was here on such and such date."
>
> Jim [Cameron] brought a simple statement carved into bronze but he did not really know if he wanted to put it down there, and he brought it out the other day, and he cradled it and he wept, and it is here with me right now at this table, all too

prophetic. It reads: "THE 1500 SOULS LOST HERE STILL SPEAK, REMINDING US ALWAYS THAT THE UNTHINK-ABLE CAN HAPPEN, BUT FOR OUR VIGILANCE, HUMILITY AND COMPASSION."

Even with the restored internet, Pellegrino kept writing handwritten letters.

September 17, 2001

At first, six days ago, the mood here was much like it must have been in New York on April 15, 1912. People were trying to get through and find out what happened to friends in New York.

And an email to Mary, still grasping onto humor as healing:

September 19, 2001

Dear Mary,

. . . I do miss you and I love you—even more than Skittles and Aero bars and Coca-Cola. And I love you more than bananas, too; and I love bananas because they have no bones. I love you more than the core of the Indian Point III nuclear power plant, and the smell of ozone in the New York City subway. I love you more than stepping on some glass, or burping raunchy gas in the submarines. And I love catching me the flu, making monkey stew, cooking me a rat, and bats. And I love you too.

Love,

Your Charlie

In the days after 9/11, on the *Keldysh*, Pellegrino stared out a porthole, looking at the open sky, weeping. He tried to process the fact that even now, in the twenty-first century, in this age of scientific marvel. humans could still destroy other humans. And he tried to reconcile his despair with his spirit of childhood wonder.

In the midst of this heartache, Pellegrino found comfort and even hope from one reliable source: his family of explorers on the *Keldysh*. The ship was packed with both American and Russian scientists. On the morning of September 11, the national borders disappeared. "Up until 9/11, a bit of a membrane of the Cold War was still there," says Pellegrino. "Now none of that mattered."

On that terrible day, via satellite uplink, Pellegrino received a message from the International Space Station (ISS). In another island of isolated humanity, inhabited by Russians and Americans, the astronauts and cosmonauts looked out the window from the space station and could see smoke coming from Manhattan. They sent the *Keldysh* a message of shared grief and solidarity.

The email from the ISS, in a strange coincidence, was nearly word for word something that Pellegrino had written many years earlier, in one of his sci-fi novels. And the message from the ISS was eventually carved into a plaque that now resides at the 9/11 Memorial. The ISS's message:

Tears do not flow the same way in space.

Finally, weeks later, Pellegrino made it back home to Long Island. He made it home to the little rodents. He made it home to Mary. And they all had that big group hug.

Several months later, off the coast of Ireland, a man named Michael Walsh took a walk on the beach. He noticed a bottle in the sand and opened it. The bottle contained a marriage proposal to a woman named Mary, along with instructions on how to forward it along. Walsh sent the message.

Mary finally received her proposal in a bottle. By then, of course, she and Pellegrino had reunited in person, and he had popped the question in a more traditional style. Mary said yes. They're still married.

The letter from the bottle now hangs, framed, in their living room.

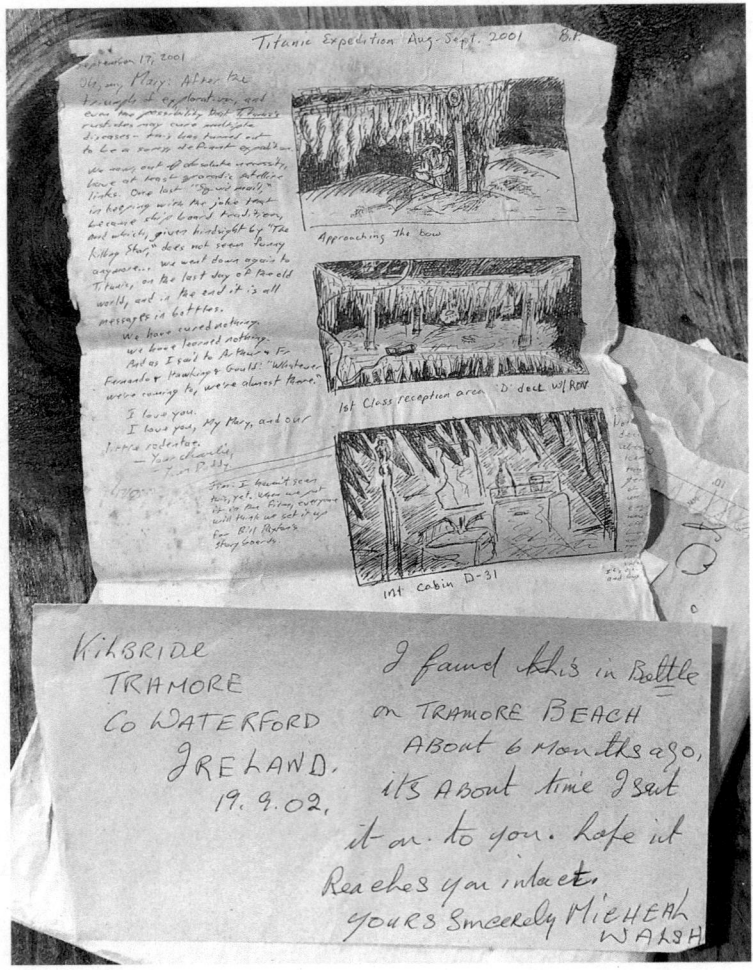

HALF DEAD OR HALF ALIVE?

Tiffany Duong

SURVIVAL IS POSSIBLE, and miracles exist—particularly in nature. This is what Tiffany Duong found off the coast of Tela, Honduras, when she learned of an almost magical stretch of coral reef.

The coral defied all logic. Much of the world's coral is bleached, damaged, and dying—thanks largely to pollution and climate change—but this coral, somehow, had survived. It was even pristine. Colorful. Gloriously alive. "It was a coral ecosystem thriving despite being in hot, silty, polluted waters," says Duong.

Because it rebelled against the grim forces that would normally spell death, Duong called it the "Rebel Reef." When she first laid eyes on the reef, it was so visually overwhelming—swirling bright technicolor, teeming with life—that she had to look away. And the crown jewel of the Rebel Reef was a coral colony that stood twenty-five feet tall and eighty feet across. It almost looked like a beautiful little house, so Duong named it "Casita."

In 2023, Duong donned her scuba gear to conduct research at Casita along with two of her friends and colleagues, Juli Berwald and Heather Kuhlken. They were just as dazzled. They hoped to discover what made Casita tick. How could it be so resilient? What could it teach us about how to protect the rest of the planet?

Scientists now know that coral plays a crucial, outsized role in our marine ecosystems. It's the ocean's backbone. Coral accounts for less than 1 percent of the ocean's area, but it supports a quarter of all marine life. "If we think about protecting coral reefs," says Juli Berwald, "we protect over 860,000 species." Some studies show that coral supports $9.9 trillion of economic impact; one billion people rely on coral for protein.

For Duong, the Rebel Reef represents the "wonder and awe that could help us fight for this planet." And for Heather Kuhlken the reefs are something even more. She gives eco-focused classes and adventures for kids and teenagers, and sometimes she'll take kids to see coral reefs in Key Largo. Her goal is to inspire them, but thanks to rampant pollution and climate change, Florida's reefs are so bleached and scarred that they can be depressing.

On bad days, the kids just see dead fish. Kuhlken once took them out after a 101-degree heat wave, and the kids felt anxious and nauseous at the sights underwater. Even Kuhlken found the scene wrenching. "It was horrific," she says. "I did everything I could not to throw up underwater." The kids saw corpses of sea urchins. Sludge. An aquatic graveyard. Instead of being inspired by the environment, they stared at a dystopian future.

Kuhlken sensed they had an acute case of eco-anxiety, and she gave them something of a pep talk. "What you just saw was so traumatic," she told them, acknowledging the reality. But then she cheered them up: She told them about the Rebel Reef, from which she'd just returned. She showed them photos from her phone. "Here's what the reefs look like in Tela," she said, her voice thick with emotion. She clung to Casita as a symbol of hope.

Then, just weeks after Kuhlken, Duong, and Berwald visited the miracle of Casita—and after Kuhlken used it to inspire her students—they received a text from Antal Borcsok, who runs Tela's Marine Protected Area.

Borcsok's text: "The reef is dying."

. . .

THE THREE WOMEN were shocked. This made no sense. They had just visited Casita, and it was thriving. Duong likens this to visiting a healthy parent or grandparent, having a lovely time, and then returning home to discover they have terminal cancer.

They knew they had to return to Casita. As soon as they could, they cleared their schedules and hopped on flights, strapped into their diving gear, and joined Antal Borcsok to once again explore the Rebel Reef.

As they swam underwater, all three remembered the magical colors they had seen just months ago. An ocean bursting with life. And then they saw the current state—and they each felt a stab of grief. What had been alive and vibrant was now dead and brown. "We swam through fields of dead skeletons," Duong remembers. They suspected this was caused by stony coral tissue-loss disease,

which has ravaged coral throughout the Caribbean. And then they watched, spellbound, as Borcsok—who had first discovered Casita—swam to the base of the coral. He gently lay a hand on the devastated bottom part of the coral, bowed his head, and thanked the coral for her strength and perseverance.

As Kuhlken took in the sights of the carnage, snapping bleak photo after photo, she was overwhelmed with sadness. She took photos of dead coral: brain coral, mountainous star coral, lettuce coral. One species after another, now all brown. Photos of hope that was shattered. She had been clinging to this very reef as hope for the planet—even telling stories of it to teenagers—and now she had nothing. Kuhlken had never felt such despondence, or perhaps even nihilism, about the planet's fate. As she swam through the brown death she thought, for the first time ever, about quitting her profession. What was the point of environmentalism? Maybe now she'd just spend all her time playing video games.

The defeated scientist swam, silently, to join her friends Berwald and Duong on the boat. And when she caught up to them, she was stunned by what she found. Berwald and Duong, too, were on the verge of tears. But these were happy tears. They were almost tears of joy.

"There's hope, still," Duong said, overwhelmed with relief.

Kuhlken asked what she meant.

While the bottom of Casita was scarred and violated, somehow, the top part—everything taller than two feet—appeared to be alive and colorful and pristine as ever before. This would not have been possible if the culprit was stony coral tissue-loss disease, which would have infected the entire reef or none at all. Something else had caused the damage, and the top had somehow survived. The top part of the reef still had life.

Duong saw the same coral devastation as Kuhlken, but she focused on this aspect. She focused on the upper part of Casita and the Rebel Reef—the sprawling chunk of colors and magic—that had somehow survived the carnage and sat miraculously untouched.

"I couldn't be sad anymore," Duong says now. "She [Casita] survived. And the fact that she did gave me so much hope."

When Duong had swum back from the Rebel Reef, she'd been exuberant. *Casita is still alive. She's still there!* Duong had journeyed to what she calls the "emotional edge," and in a way, Duong and Kuhlken were on opposing sides of that same edge.

Since then, Kuhlken has had more time to reflect. She was initially in a state of shock, but then she collaborated with her colleagues, and they developed theories on how the fifty-fifty carnage could have happened. They asked more questions and conducted more research, and in the coming weeks, all three regained their sense of hope.

They already knew that it was almost certainly not the disease that had jeopardized all the Caribbean's coral elsewhere. Then there was the evidence from Antal Borcsok. When he first noticed that the reef around Casita was dying, his text described a "clear to milky white" substance on the reef. That told them that the substance had to be denser than sea water, which itself was a clue.

"We suspect it was a spill," says Kuhlken. A man-made chemical spill is an eco-tragedy, yes, but it's not a sweeping existential threat to the ecosystem. It's an outlier. Since then, the trio has done more sleuthing—using ship-tracking software—to identify the potential culprit, and they're hopeful they will soon have an answer. As Kuhlken puts it, "We're hoping to find a lab that's going to help us Erin Brockovich this."

For all three women, the Rebel Reef remains a symbol of hope—and in some ways it's more poignant than before. The partial loss makes them treasure what remains. Yes, climate change is ravaging the planet; and yes, humanity has endless work to do; and yes, the problem is real and the clock is ticking. But the planet is not doomed, we are not doomed, and Casita is not dead. The earth is resilient. Humans are resourceful. We have agency. Progress is possible. There's hope.

And sometimes that hope lurks in places we don't think to check. "We're terrestrial beings," says Berwald. "We don't look beneath the waves as often as we should."

KIDNAPPED

Will Roseman

IN 1982, WILL ROSEMAN'S journey to Zaire was off to a shaky start. Just after leaving the Kinshasa airport he was robbed. It felt like a war zone; he saw cars on fire on the side of the road and skirmishes in broad daylight. The air had the stench of burning rubber and was filled with smoke from burning charcoal.

Roseman didn't exactly have a detailed plan for his expedition, and perhaps it wasn't even an "expedition," in the modern sense. Roseman was simply curious about the Baluba people and their art, so he planned to visit the Mbuji-Mayi region to spend time with them. That was the extent of his plan.

He was able to get to Lubumbashi, then Kamina, and then Mwene-Ditu, about eighty miles from his elusive goal of Mbuji-Mayi. There he was instructed by some people masquerading as refrigerator repairmen (who turned out to be CIA agents) to go no farther, given the rampant violence. Roseman was advised that members of U.S. Agency for International Development would be driving through in five days, and they could escort him to Mbuji-Mayi.

But Roseman was impatient, so he left on his own.

On the first day of his eighty-mile walk, he encountered a group of Lingala-speaking soldiers, their eyes stern and their rifles menacing. One of them also spoke broken English.

"Where's your permit?" the soldier asked him.

"What permit?"

"Your permit."

The soldier told Roseman that since he did not have a permit, he was under arrest. The only way to avoid arrest, the soldier said, was to fork over money for a permit.

"How much?" Roseman asked.

$5,000.

Roseman knew he was being hustled. But he also knew he didn't have anything close to $5,000. He had maybe $50 dollars to his name, having previously been robbed, and he was surrounded by soldiers with rifles.

So the Lingala-speaking soldiers put Roseman under arrest. He suspected they might not be part of the official Zaire military, but rather some sort of informal group of mercenaries that traveled from village to village, looting what they could.

Held captive, Roseman walked with the mercenaries on the road to Mbuji-Mayi. They walked for days. Roseman soon realized that the soldiers were broke. They didn't have handcuffs to secure him, instead loosely tying his hands with rope. Their jeep sputtered and died—a symbol of their desperate straits—and they simply left it on the side of the road. At one point, they steamed the stamps off an envelope with the hope of later selling them. It dawned on Roseman that they were so impoverished that their guns likely did not have bullets, but he wasn't willing to test this theory.

Days bled into nights. The soldiers were hungry, and Roseman was hungry. The forced march was fueled by antelope, which were stolen from villages, and cassava, a starchy root vegetable that offered little protein. The soldiers doled out tiny portions to Roseman. The one thing the soldiers had in abundance, Roseman found, was palm wine. They guzzled palm wine every night, they became inebriated, they passed out, and then they slept until noon the next day.

After ten days of captivity, the soldier who spoke broken English gave Roseman some paper and a pencil.

"Write," the soldier said.

"Write what?"

The soldier explained that Roseman needed to write a letter stating where he was, and that he needed money sent to him immediately. They wanted a ransom letter. And the price for Roseman's freedom?

The soldiers demanded five million U.S. dollars.

Although maybe that wasn't the case . . . Roseman was confused. Given the language barrier and the chaos of misinterpretation, Roseman wasn't entirely sure if the soldiers demanded $5 million, or $5,000, or $500. For all he knew, perhaps the shakedown was for only $5. The one thing he knew for certain was that his life depended upon someone sending him a ransom that ranged between $5 and $5 million.

Roseman thought about who he should write to. He considered his parents, but the last thing he wanted was for them to receive this letter after he was dead. So he wrote to his then-fiancée, Lorie.

The letter was a lifeline, a fragile thread back to civilization written under duress. He kept it simple. He wasn't even sure if the soldiers could afford the postage to get the letter to New York. But he didn't have much choice, so, at gunpoint, Roseman scribbled his letter:

Send $5,000 to the Grand Kasaï hotel.

—Will

Shortly after writing that letter, Roseman realized the soldiers would kill him if the money did not come soon. The signs, though subtle, were unmistakable. He sensed that they were looking at him differently, and even treating him more kindly—it almost felt like pity. At dinner, in an unprecedented act of generosity, a soldier gave Roseman his own share of cassava. This felt like a last supper.

Roseman knew he needed to escape.

The escape plan hinged on two crucial factors: The soldiers never tied his hands securely, and every night they got blackout drunk. In some ways, the escape would be cartoonishly easy, as the soldiers had the air of Keystone Cops in a war zone. Their incompetence could be his salvation.

Roseman waited until the soldiers were passed out, drunk on their palm wine, as usual. Then he slipped his hands from the binding and simply walked out of camp, gingerly stepping over one of the sleeping soldiers. The silence was broken only by the snores of his captors. He didn't know where he was going. He just walked straight into the bush, hoping to find a friendly village. He was weak and hungry and thirsty, and he had already lost thirty pounds.

Knowing he was being pursued by his captors, Roseman kept walking through the bush, moving forward for two straight days. Finally, he found a Baluba community, where he met a villager who had been raised by missionaries. His name was America, and Roseman couldn't imagine a more fitting moniker. He introduced Roseman to Methodist missionaries working in the area, and they helped arrange a way out of Zaire.

But getting out of Zaire was not a given. Roseman feared there were still soldiers hunting him down. To leave the country, Roseman needed to take a short flight from Lubumbashi to Kinshasa (the capital of Zaire), and from there, catch a flight to almost anywhere else. That was the plan. But it was possible—even probable—that the soldiers would have a presence at the airport.

The missionaries helped him get on an Air Zaïre flight to Kinshasa. The plane was small, rickety, and would have flunked most safety tests. There was no fabric on his seat; Roseman sat on naked springs. There was no door separating the cockpit from the cabin. A goat ran up and down the aisle. One woman sat in the back of the plane cooking her food over an open flame.

When this plane landed in Kinshasa, Roseman looked out the window . . . and he could see Lingala-speaking soldiers mustering on the tarmac. Then, adding to his fears, no one was allowed to leave the plane. That seemed ominous. Roseman knew they weren't being kept on that flight for any kind of safety protocol—could it be that the soldiers had found him? Ten minutes ticked by. Then fifteen minutes. He saw the soldiers had rifles, and these rifles would have bullets. He had just one simple thought: *I'm fucked*.

Finally, Roseman and the other passengers were let off the plane and corralled into a staging area. And on the other side of the tarmac, so tantalizingly close, Roseman could see the larger TAP Air Portugal plane—the one on which the missionaries had arranged his passage. It was three hundred feet away. Meanwhile, Lingala-speaking soldiers lurked nearby.

At that moment, standing on the tarmac, Roseman remembered a story he had heard years earlier from a World War II veteran. The veteran had said that your first chance to escape is always your best chance to escape.

So Roseman ran for it.

He ran toward either freedom or bullets. He figured it was fifty-fifty at best.

The flight crew from Air Zaïre, startled, tried to restrain him and told him that no one was allowed to leave. Roseman shoved them aside. He ran across the tarmac and toward the TAP Air Portugal plane. As Roseman ran, he could hear the soldiers shouting what sounded like "No, no, no!"

The soldiers yelled for him to stop. Roseman didn't stop—a response that was half survival instinct and half desperation. Then he heard them cock their rifles. He ran faster.

Just as Roseman neared the TAP Air Portugal airstairs, the plane's door swung open. The pilot stepped out and quickly descended the staircase. Roseman ran toward the plane, and the pilot ran toward Roseman. Then the pilot said to him, "Don't stop!" and kept running past him, toward the approaching soldiers.

Roseman bounded up the stairs to the TAP Air Portugal plane. From the staircase he could see the pilot arguing with the soldiers, and then the pilot gave them a wad of cash. The pilot then walked backward toward the plane, still staring at the soldiers.

The pilot boarded the plane. He looked at Roseman.

"Are you okay?"

"Yeah."

The pilot gave Roseman a seat in first class. As the plane took off, the flight attendant turned to Roseman and handed him some towels. "Please, sir, go into the bathroom and clean yourself."

Roseman realized he was given a first-class seat, at least in part, because he hadn't bathed in three weeks, and his stench filled the plane. After cleaning himself up, he returned to his seat and looked out the window, and then, finally, a torrent of pent-up emotion flowed free. Not from fear or sadness but out of cathartic emotional release. He wept tears of relief.

Roseman had no money, no phone, no passport, but TAP Air Portugal had ushered him aboard that flight, no questions asked. When the plane landed in Lisbon, they put him up in a hotel room and then sent him to New York for free. For decades Roseman would be a loyal TAP Air Portugal customer. Roseman never forgot the generosity of the missionaries or the people of Zaire.

This is not a story Roseman tells often. He didn't even include it in his application to The Explorers Club, where he has served as executive director for years. With his trademark humility, Roseman says that this particular journey had no rigorous *purpose* of discovery, so it was more of a wayward adventure than true exploration. "This was an introduction to exploration, and the importance of being prepared," Roseman says now. "I was a knucklehead."

But the story is useful as a cautionary tale, and it helps to delineate the distinction between adventure and exploration. It also helped nudge Roseman to think about the role of risk in exploration, and how one should responsibly calculate and manage risk—both to oneself and to others involved. This is true for the smallest and grandest expeditions. Roseman once asked Buzz Aldrin, for example, if he was ever afraid on the moon.

"There wasn't a moment where I was afraid or concerned," Aldrin told him. Aldrin explained that the absence of fear wasn't due to some kind of preternatural heroism but because he was so well trained by NASA that if x happened, he knew immediately to do y. Roseman posed the question to Jim Lovell, and Lovell told him the same thing.

Perhaps Aldrin hadn't thought of himself as being on the edge after all. Don Walsh said something similar about descending to the Mariana Trench—that, because he was so well trained, it was just "another day at the office." The edge is a relative concept. "Though I couldn't imagine being more on the edge than the moon, they never saw it that way," says Roseman.

If it's true that "the edge" connotes an element of risk, the way Roseman sees it, the seasoned explorer tries to do what they can to *not* be on the edge, but sometimes the mission goes sideways and they have no choice but to adapt. And they're willing to accept that risk—including the risk of their own life—because they can't ignore their burning curiosity.

"They say curiosity killed the cat," says Roseman. "It's killed more explorers than it has any number of cats."

THE RIVER OF DOUBT

Teddy Roosevelt

TEDDY ROOSEVELT APPLIED to be a member of The Explorers Club in 1915. Under the "qualifications" section of the application, Roosevelt wrote, "Various positions including . . . President of the United States."

But that was not the first qualification he cited. He first mentioned the Roosevelt-Rondon expedition to Brazil.

Roosevelt undertook the expedition in 1913, after his failed bid for the White House. Originally, he had two purposes for this trip: (1) to give a series of lectures throughout South America; (2) to join a cruise down well-known Amazon rivers, with the intent to complete a scientific survey along with other naturalists. That was the plan. But then Brazil's minister of foreign affairs asked him, almost as a challenge, "Colonel Roosevelt, why don't you go down an unknown river?"

Roosevelt found the idea irresistible. With scant planning, the Rough Rider switched gears and decided to journey down the uncharted Rio da Dúvida, or River of Doubt. (Of course, the River of Doubt was only "uncharted" to Roosevelt and those from the United States, not the Indigenous people who knew it well.)

Roosevelt's goal was to map the river. This was in spite (or maybe because) of the daunting challenges of hidden rapids, swarms of mosquitos, constant dampness that would rot supplies, and no clear way to retreat to safety. As Frank Chapman, a co-founder of The Explorers Club, noted with concern at the time, "It may be said with confidence . . . that in all of South America there is not a more difficult or dangerous journey."

Roosevelt's twenty-two-man crew included Cândido Rondon an acclaimed Brazilian explorer; two naturalists from the American Museum of Natural History; and his son Kermit. The trek started with a grueling weeks-long hike through the Brazilian jungle, which sapped the men of supplies and energy. Roosevelt's glasses fogged over in the humid rainforest, but he refused to complain and was even cheerful, marveling at the lush nature. "The lofty and matted forest rose like a green wall on either hand" when they reached the river, he later observed. "The trees were stately and beautiful. The looped and twisted vines hung from them like great ropes."

At first the river was calm. Then the rapids began to pound their canoes. The river twisted and turned and seemed to force itself in every possible direction . . . none of which was known. They truly had no idea where they were going. "We did not know whether we had one hundred or eight hundred kilometers to go," wrote Roosevelt.

They encountered waterfalls, a seemingly endless stream of rapids, and then minor setbacks compounded into disaster: Water leaked into one of the dugout canoes, the canoe sunk, and suddenly the men were forced to ditch most of their supplies. Kermit almost drowned in the rapids. One member of the crew actually did drown.

They became sick with malaria and dysentery. And then, while trying to rescue a canoe from the raging river, Roosevelt sliced his shin against a rock. "Blood spun out of the wound like an unraveling spool of thread, mixing with the muddy water and disappearing downstream," writes Candice Millard, author of *The River of Doubt: Theodore Roosevelt's Darkest Journey.*

The illness, injury, and exhaustion all set in. Because of his wound, Roosevelt could barely walk. And finally, when the ragged party reached a steep waterfall that looked impossible to traverse with canoes—and equally impossible for Roosevelt to manage on foot— the Rough Rider made a decision: He would rather die than compromise the expedition. He would do this in the name of exploration. "If I had to die anywhere," Roosevelt reasoned, "Why not die in helping to open up to the knowledge of the world a great unknown land, and so aid humanity in general and the people of Brazil in particular?"

Roosevelt considered an overlooked item that he had smuggled in his personal gear. Near his spare eyeglasses (he traveled with eight pairs), Roosevelt had stashed a lethal dose of morphine. And now he was prepared to use it.

Nearly delirious with pain, Roosevelt summoned the crew. "Boys, I realize that some of us are not going to finish this journey," he said. "I want you and Kermit to go on. You can get out. I will stop here."

That night, on the cusp of death, Roosevelt kept repeating lines from Samuel Taylor Coleridge's "Kubla Khan." Again and again he muttered, "In Xanadu did Kubla Kahn a stately pleasure-dome decree. In Xanadu did Kubla Kahn a stately pleasure-dome decree." At the start of the expedition, less than two months earlier, Roosevelt—the great bear of a man—had weighed 220 pounds. Now he weighed 170 "The expedition must not stop," Roosevelt insisted. "Go, and leave me here."

Two things saved his life. First, Kermit would hear nothing of abandoning his father, and he devised a clever way of using ropes to lower the canoes down the waterfall. Second, the expedition, led by the resourceful Rondon, eventually received crucial help through local seringueiros—Brazilian rubber tappers. When one of the seringueiros saw the sorry state of Roosevelt, he asked, baffled, "But is he really a president?"

The seringueiros gave the expedition new canoes, personally guided them through a tricky section of the jungle, and they gave pointers on the safest trails to lead them back to "civilization."

The Brazilian seringueiros had given them both direction and hope, but Roosevelt continued to grow weaker. His leg was infected, and the pain shot through his body. It required emergency surgery. "The operating-room floor was nothing more than the muddy soil of the riverbank," writes Millard. "Using only the simplest of surgical tools and no anesthetic, [the doctor] sliced deep into his patient's leg, releasing a mottled mixture of blood and foul-smelling pus that had collected in the abscess."

On brand, Roosevelt gritted his teeth and didn't say a word. Eventually, of course, the former president convalesced and recovered He took pride in having mapped 1,500 kilometers of this previously unknown (to them) river. As soon as he had access to a telegram, he sent a dispatch, dripping with comical understatement:

> We have had a hard and somewhat dangerous but very successful trip.

Roosevelt returned to New York, proudly bringing lantern slides that showed where he had been.

The next time he set foot in the Club, he likely asked for a glass of milk (his go-to drink at the bar) and shared tales of his journey on the River of Doubt. Or, as the Brazilians later renamed it, the Rio Roosevelt.

One could argue that the expedition was reckless and poorly planned. But, even acknowledging those caveats, Roosevelt had a keen sense of what separates exploration from tourism. "The ordinary traveler, who never goes off the beaten route and who on this beaten route is carried by others, without himself doing anything or risking anything, does not need to show much more initiative and intelligence than an express package," he explained.

Exploration is different. And when he returned from Brazil, he realized, "There yet remains plenty of exploring work to be done in South America." Roosevelt's words, if we broaden the scope, could serve as a theme for the Club: There yet remains plenty of exploring work to be done.

4

The Edge of
Culture

O ften, explorers set out to learn about a culture that is
different from their own. So much of modern exploration is focused on exploring cultures—sometimes pre-
serving, sometimes chronicling, and always learning.
The key phrase is "other cultures," as explorers now recognize that there is not one primary culture (i.e., Western) that's the center of the world, but instead a mosaic of
cultures that deserve to be better understood. This can
mean journeying through the South Pacific islands to research the secret history of tattooing, uncovering the
deeper truths of psychedelics in Nepal, or living with
local Bedouin tribes to understand (and prevent) deadly
floods in Petra.

Or sometimes explorers question the norms and as-
sumptions about the culture in which they were born. This
can mean retracing Thoreau's steps to better understand
how our culture has impacted climate change or, in 1917,

spending time in Jerusalem to meet a young officer the world had not yet heard of: Lawrence of Arabia.

These stories involve a desire to better understand how others in the world operate . . . and this, inevitably, brings a deeper understanding of ourselves.

WITH LAWRENCE OF ARABIA

Lowell Thomas

LOWELL THOMAS'S NAME is all over The Explorers Club. This is quite literal. The headquarters of the Club, a six-story mansion on East Seventieth Street in New York, is called the Lowell Thomas Building. At its annual dinner, the Club hands out Lowell Thomas Awards.

This is because Thomas, the legendary broadcaster, author, journalist, and traveler, was a Club mainstay for decades. His many stories from the field helped spread the study of and passion for exploration. Millions of people have learned about other cultures through the words of Lowell Thomas.

Consider what he wrote and then shared at the Club's long table, where explorers have gathered for decades to tell their stories:

> When we took off from the aerodrome at Heliopolis one afternoon in the autumn of 1917, I little knew what a dramatic, historic spectacle I was to witness. We had heard several reports in Cairo about the Palestine campaign, but they were all vague, technical, military, laconic. There was a rumor that Allenby was advancing, that a mysterious chap named Lawrence and his Arabs were bewildering and hamstringing the Turkish armies. . . .
>
> With a few loops above the Pyramids, a flip of our tail in the face of the Sphinx, off we zoomed across the Suez Canal and over the sand dunes of Sinai's mystical desert. To our left shimmered and gleamed the blue waters of the Mediterranean. Far to the south, almost lost in the heat haze, loomed portentously the dim

outline of the grim mountain where Moses, amid flashes of lightning and awful thunderclaps, received the tablets of stone that established the imperishable foundation of a code of criminal, civil, and religious laws which now govern the relations of human beings over some four-fifths of the earth's surface. . . .

About the time of the Duke's arrival, I was strolling through one of the winding streets of Jerusalem. As I passed a group of Arabs, one in particular arrested my attention. Though arrayed in a most striking Arab costume, he was beardless and a blond. Now the Arabs don't consider a man full grown unless he has a beard. They swear by their beards. And I knew there was no such creature as a blond Arab. So I made up my mind to find out all I could about that phenomenon. . . .

I went to the office of the Governor of Jerusalem in an old palace outside the Damascus gate. The British member of the office of tourism I met was Colonel Ronald Storrs. To him I expressed my reportorial curiosity about the blond Arab. Colonel Storrs stood up, opened a door and through it I looked into another room and saw the beardless chap in full Sheridan panoply, sitting at a table and reading a work on archaeology. . . .

"Let me introduce you to Colonel T. E. Lawrence," said Storrs and added, "the uncrowned king of Arabia." . . .

And thus it was that I was able to bring back the first account of the Revolt in the Desert, the first story to reach the ears of the world of the almost incredible adventures of Lawrence of Arabia.

TRACING THE INK

Amanda Fornal

IN 2006, AS AMANDA FORNAL journeyed through the South Pacific to research the history of tattooing, she sent daily emails to her mother as proof of life.

> Hi Mom—
>
> I am here safe. I interviewed a guy with a traditional tattoo. Very cool. The internet is super slow here and I will probably not have good access until September 7 when I go to Apia.
>
> The time and date here are different. . . . I crossed the international date line and I am now living September 2 all over again! I hope you are having a great day!
>
> Amanda

Fornal was in the midst of journeying through Tonga, Samoa, Rapa Nui, and seventeen other islands in the South Pacific. Two years prior, while traveling solo through India, she happened to photograph a woman in Gujarat and noticed some face and neck tattoos. These were not henna but actual tattoos. She kept coming back to that photograph. Why did she get that tattoo? What did it mean? And what insights does it reveal about Gujarat culture?

She did research back home in Connecticut but found nothing. "Our [Western] culture of tattooing originated in the South Pacific," says Fornal. "But there's not a lot of data out there, and especially not in 2004."

She carefully planned every leg of her journey, she devoured research books, and she read as much as she could. Then traveling with little more than a camera, a journal, and her curiosity, she booked a ticket to Fiji. She had made connections in advance when she could— for instance, getting permission from the government of Vanuatu to serve as one of two official cultural researchers. At times she lived in huts with no electricity and no running water, and at every stop she scribbled notes from the field. A sample:

> Another grass runway. Mota Lava is a small island in the northern province. . . .
>
> The small thatch-roofed hut had a bush toilette that consisted of a small bamboo hut with a hole and a box over it; lovely smell: Try old diapers on a hot summer day, especially fun at 4:00 a.m. when enormous spiders line up to have a shot at biting your butt. . . .
>
> Mota Lava's appeal was its remoteness, small size and its lack of documented information. . . . We discussed my project with Chief Brian (the names still seem to surprise me), and he welcomed me to both his village and the island and granted me permission to film and work with the people of his community.

Then Fornal gets to business, focusing on what brought her here:

> Our first interview was surreal. Joanne, a villager, stood in front of me in her tattered T-shirt as a semi-circle of villagers surrounded me and watched my every move. Franklin acted as translator as we discussed her tattoos. He was joined by a chorus of villagers, all keen to help out with the questions, be it by word or with smiles.

During Fornal's expedition, she found that every tattoo told a story, and they were often stories of pride that tapped into family and home and community. Tattoos connected people. Tattoos were a literal mark of culture, and those marks were undocumented and would soon vanish. So Fornal did what she could to capture these stories. As she learned from the tattooed woman in Mota Lava:

The traditional tattoos she had on her face, a sun-like symbol on her cheek and a sideways W next to her eye, were markers of her home. Her island. She was from Ra and would not be mistaken for any other island. Her tattoo acted as passport.

Tattoos were applied to women by women in the women's nakemal, or women's house. Tattoos on these northern Vanuatu islands were not only for chiefs' families but for everyone, quite liberal. During the tattoo application the women would sing songs and spend time celebrating together. The men were excluded from these ceremonies.

Fornal interviewed woman after woman on the island of Mota Lava, as she did throughout the South Pacific. Studying tattoos gave her insights about the wider local traditions, such as this observation from the same letter:

Three elderly women gathered in a triangle, the eldest in front. Their mouths opened and in unison they sang a soothing melody meant to relax the one being tattooed. Not used anymore, it was amazing they remembered it. This may be the only time this song has ever been recorded.

And along the way, as often happens in exploration, Fornal found that her overall perspective shifted:

On our way back to the bungalows we came across a group of men slaughtering a pig for a party. Most people in the U.S. don't see the source of their ham, bacon and pork chops going through the production process. It's quite possible that the more people see the less they will eat. It certainly has worked for me.

Franklin then led me on a journey to yet another village. A newly slaughtered cow was hanging from a tree as the village worked en masse to prepare the meat. Everything was done as a community, whether it was: building a house, gardening, fishing or preparing the slaughter. The cooperation was unlike anything I've ever seen at home, where I hardly even know my neighbors let alone work on community projects with them.

Fornal's own relationship with tattoos? She has none. (This often shocks people.) But that's the power of curiosity: Sometimes it crops up in unexplainable ways and gives you no choice but to chase it across the planet, regardless of your level of preparation. "I had no guidance, no mentor, and was rolling with it," she says.

Fornal donated her complete set of Vanuatu tattoo photographs to the Vanuatu Cultural Center for archival and research purposes. Through her work, Fornal sought not just to explore, but to document these stories before they faded from memory. To her, the edge means pushing limits and embracing the challenge of "keeping cultures alive while still moving forward with change and progress." And there's no guarantee that cultures will survive. Sometimes the culture is stamped as a tattoo, and sometimes someone needs to preserve it.

IN SEARCH OF THOREAU

Meg Haywood Sullivan

MEG HAYWOOD SULLIVAN saw the book in a second-hand store. It was old, dusty, and dog-eared, with a green fabric cover. She liked used books, preferring them to new ones. "I love to think about the eyes that have read them," she says, "and the hands that have touched them."

She found the book on Cape Cod, and in fact the book was called *Cape Cod*—Henry David Thoreau's ruminations on the region's nature and beauty. She read it. Then reread it. Her mind couldn't shake Thoreau's detailed, thoughtful observations of the Cape's plants and creatures. The spell of the book lingered for more than a year.

Then Sullivan had an idea. Maybe she could retrace Thoreau's steps around the Cape and see and chronicle how it (and the surrounding local culture) has changed. This would align with her larger work at the intersection of art and science, where she focuses on environmentalism and climate change. She creates art to tell stories and open minds.

The plan began to crystalize. She would hike through Cape Cod on a path that was as faithful to Thoreau's as possible. No technical gear, no Gore-Tex, no hotels. (Although she was forced to make some compromises. Thoreau slept under the stars on the beach; this was no longer legal, so she did the next best thing and camped in a friendly surf photographer's front yard.)

Before she started, Sullivan had a theory: The impact of tourism and climate change would have dramatically transformed the appearance, vibrancy, and biodiversity of Cape Cod, painting a sharp contrast to the idyllic days of Thoreau.

She was delighted to discover she was wrong.

• • •

FOLLOWING THE ARC of Thoreau's journey was trickier than it sounded at first blush, as there was no obvious path, like there is for a trek up Mount Everest. "He didn't have much of a plan," says Sullivan. "He was wandering, observing, and looking at the plants, animals, and people."

So that's what she did. Along with environmental filmmaker Nicole Gormley, a friend and fellow eco-focused artist, Sullivan loosely traced Thoreau's forty-four-mile hike and made detailed notes of the ecosystem. While she hiked, as was her habit, she wrote poetry and sketched artwork. This is her way of speaking with her subconscious and seeing truth. "These writings made sense of new experiences, forged connections, navigated failures," she says. It's a good reminder that, though a frequent goal of exploration is scientific discovery, science is not the only kind of wisdom. Excerpts from her poems:

THOREAU //

Rhythmic cadence of the sea-washed breakers my
    only companion
save a pair of plovers ambivalent to the clumsy hiker
    before them
prevailing wind upon my back tide comes. tide goes
Mist-veiled mirage of the Great Unknown.
Mist-cloaked dunes cascading to the sea
sewn together by grasses dancing.
Windswept dreams of a wayward wanderer
seeking everything—and nothing—all at once.

But the field is still the field, and that can bring complications for almost any expedition—even pleasant strolls to appreciate nature.

Sullivan had previously contracted Lyme disease, and the medication's side effects included photosensitivity, which meant she was supposed to stay out of the sun. Because she couldn't do that on her trek, she got sun poisoning, which made her entire body break out in a rash. She had a rare reaction that caused her to lose all her fingernails. (She still wrote and drew in her journal.)

CAPE COD

Death and life duke it out for the best hand
the kiss—or clash—of two elements at war
or in lust with each other depending.
Of sea and sun and mung and coyote track,
warm breath of a grey seal in the mist
bewitching.
Like two halves of a shell pried open,
The New Englander, moth
to a flame.

Sullivan was dazzled by the tiny miracles she saw every day. The Cape—at least the off-the-tourist-path Cape she was exploring—teemed with dolphins and seals and birds. Instead of the land being heavily impacted, as she had predicted, she was startled to find tranquil, lovely scenes that looked nearly identical to Thoreau's descriptions.

MAP QUEST //

Lineated scribbles of folded leaves
fluttering, ever gently, in a dry dust breeze
the road to nowhere is a road to somewhere
carved between lines of topography
a sliver of silence seducing a
page turner to the next unknown

Sullivan hiked through the overlooked section of Cape Cod, far from the tourists, and she was astonished to see its unvarnished beauty. Thoreau would have recognized it and loved it. One of the only differences, really, was that Thoreau describes a community of "pickers" who salvaged parts from shipwrecked boats; obviously, this has vanished. She was surprised to find very little trash. Among the only litter she found was a box of knotted ropes from lobster pots; she kept this as a keepsake.

WE WERE ONCE WILD //

We were once wild
and painted the sky black with our wings
soaring high above plains
of gold
flecked by the backs of brawny buffalo
no more.
The stories were once real.
We were once wild
the creatures you tried to ignore
and squashed beneath thumbs
our jeweled wings, millions of years of fine-tuned elegance
a masterpiece in creation, evolution of the fittest.
and finest,
dazzling swarms and hives and marches.
Wake up, humanity, Wake up.
It is time. It's your time
so flood the streets and the polls
have no fear except fear of sofa-bound apathy
The house is on fire. Our house. And your house.
Our dens and caves and nests and homes, little ones tucked
        under wing
the fate of life as we know it rests upon your shoulders
wake up.

Sullivan wondered, why was her theory so wrong? How did nature look so much *better* than she expected? Then she knew the answer. This stretch of the Cape was protected by conservation regulation and law. "And those protections worked."

That happy conclusion, to Sullivan, is worth sharing and even celebrating. Part of her work looks at the impact of positive versus pessimistic messaging on climate change. She has found that messages of hope can resonate, cut through the clutter, and get people to act. "It's not about looking through rose-colored glasses," she says, "but celebrating the progress being done."

Ultimately, for Sullivan, this is just another tool in the toolkit for getting humanity to pay attention to climate change. Or, as she—and many modern explorers—put it: getting people to wake up.

SEEKING TRUTH IN
BEDOUIN BOURBON

Tom Paradise

TOM PARADISE DIDN'T just study the local Bedouin tribes. He lived with them. He shared a tent. He got so close that he would routinely wake up to the sight of random children playing just above his head.

The kids were his roommates. This was in the early 1990s in Petra, Jordan. The large tent was made of goat and camel hair. Paradise learned their customs. He ate their cheese that somehow didn't need to be refrigerated, he participated in Bedouin wedding ceremonies, and he joined them in shooting ancient carbine rifles into the night sky. He lived with them every summer for years.

Why Petra? "Sandstone is easy to study," says Paradise. "It's so shitty." He clarifies that it's "soft and friable" and that sandstone, unlike a harder stone such as granite, is a sedimentary rock that's more easily affected by weather and chemical alterations. The bad news is that it's harder to preserve; the good news is that these many layers make it easier for geologists to uncover clues that unveil different moments in history.

And there's a lot of sandstone in Petra. Paradise, a multidisciplinary scholar who combines geology, petrology (the science of rocks), archeology, and history, has now been studying the sandstone of Petra for more than thirty years. The studies have solved mysteries, saved lives, and helped preserve millennia-old structures.

For this he can partially thank something called "Bedouin Bourbon."

One night, he drank Bedouin Bourbon—strong black tea loaded with sugar—with an old Bedouin. Like many of the B'doul elders, the old man liked to talk, and he shared a story from the Bedouin oral history about an ancient flood, which filled the streets of Petra and claimed countless lives and shut the city down.

Paradise later thought about this conversation. He jotted down notes in his field journal, recording the old man's wisdom.

> B'doui like Hamoudi talk about old stories from elders in the tribe about ancient floods along Main Street. This is hinting at such catastrophic floods indicated by deposits and geomorphology.

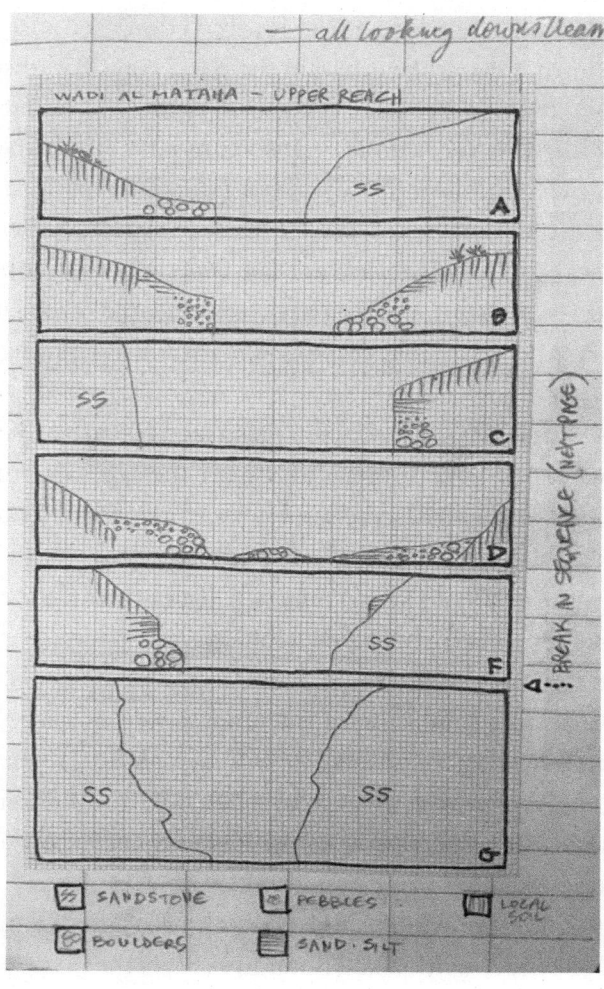

And he began to make connections—a link between this oral history of floods and what he could glean from the science of sediment analysis. He knew of other catastrophic floods in the region, such as one in 1965 that killed twenty-five tourists. Patterns soon emerged, and he sketched them in his journal.

Thanks in part to the old man's oral history, Paradise published a series of academic papers that gave a definitive account of the region's flooding. He explained the history and exposed the risks, which let communities take preventive actions—they built new dams, and the location of these dams was informed by Paradise's research on where the floods had been most deadly. "I don't see another major flood ever hitting Petra like it had in the past," says Paradise.

His work didn't stop there. Petra, of course, is home to iconic structures like the Treasury, a mausoleum that was carved into a sandstone cliff, popularized in *Indiana Jones and the Last Crusade*. These historic buildings are at risk of degradation. When Stephen Spielberg was filming, in fact, Paradise was there to give him pointers on how to do so in a way that respected the structure. (Years later, Denis Villeneuve used Paradise's maps for the filming of *Dune: Part Two*.)

Paradise knew the sandstone of these iconic structures was eroding. But why? He later showed that even though sandstone was a "wimpy" (his words) rock, the structures could generally handle the rain, survive the baking sun, and endure the punishment of centuries, but there's one element that could easily bring their destruction: humans. More specifically, tourists. "Humans have to touch everything, even if the sign says do not touch," says Paradise.

When analyzing tombs, he kept finding a curious white substance on the walls. At first, he thought it was some kind of salt emerging from the rocks. Then he ran an analysis, and the mysterious substance turned out to be stearic acid—which is, as Paradise observes, "a common ingredient from suntan oil."

He connected more dots. Sandstone, at heart, is nothing but sand with a bit of binder in it. When humidity enters the picture, moisture is absorbed between the grains and the stone splinters. And when tourists (and their suntan oil) entered structures like the tombs, the humidity rose. In fact, the numbers leapt off the chart. "Tour groups of thirty or more made the humidity jump twenty to forty percent," says Paradise. "That's enough to mess stuff up."

Paradise's proof was so compelling that the Jordanian government, upon considering his work, immediately closed the Treasury to tourists. (For a while, the tour guides hated him.) That response from the government, however well intended, was not exactly what Paradise had had in mind. "Manage it, don't shut it down," he says. He later proposed a radical technology that would allow for tourists but keep the humidity in check: a fan.

Problem solved. The revenue from tourists, who are crucial for Petra, again flowed into the local economy, and these iconic structures are more likely to survive for millennia to come. So now, when you visit the Treasury, you will see a fan, and for this you can thank Tom Paradise and an old Bedouin who liked to tell stories.

SWAMI AND THE PSYCHEDELICS

Robert "Rio" Hahn

MOST MEMBERS OF The Explorers Club wear many different hats—they're also marketing executives, anesthesiologists, U.S. presidents. Captain Robert "Rio" Hahn is no different. Sometimes he leads expeditions as a sea captain, sometimes he's a photographer, and sometimes he studies the impact of psychedelic drugs.

Hahn has studied psychedelics since the 1970s, when he became close friends with Albert Hofmann, the discoverer of LSD. He has a background in biochemistry, so he understood the science. In the 1970s he traveled to Nepal to research the impact of datura, a psychedelic plant that is sacred to Shiva and many yogis. The practice of chewing datura is ancient and was even chronicled by Marco Polo.

In Hahn's dispatch from Nepal, he notes:

> Revered and feared throughout the world, Datura is considered one of the most mysterious and frighteningly powerful sacred plants. Traditional cultures have treated Datura with cautious respect, and Datura has often been associated with the practice of sorcery and witchcraft. Datura is reputed to have been a major component of the salve European witches used to anoint their broomsticks, an effective means for women to self-administer the drug.... The popular image of the flying witch is no doubt one of mystical flight, an out-of-the-body sensation in which the journey is not through space but across the hallucinatory landscape of the witches' own mind.

The drug is potent. As Hahn explains:

> Datura is highly psychoactive and has been described as an intox-
> icant or a hallucinogen, but calling it a deliriant is probably most
> accurate. Ingestion of Datura causes symptoms of spectral illu-
> sions, delirium, dilated pupils, thirst, dryness of the mouth and
> muscular incoordination.

Just as ayahuasca is now praised by many for its powers of unlock-
ing a higher form of truth, datura has been used for millennia in
China and India. Given the frightening potential side effects, Hahn
had one simple question: Why?

In his quest to understand datura, Hahn met an eighty-five-year-
old yogi and Sanskrit scholar named Swami Dharmjyoti. Swami (as
he liked to be called) invited Hahn to religious rituals and ceremonies
that involved datura; Hahn was the only westerner present. He later
chronicled and filmed these rituals on flag expeditions for The Explorers Club.

Swami began to trust Hahn. They spoke deep into the night about
philosophy and eastern religion. Swami told Hahn that he did more
than simply use datura occasionally; he used it almost every waking
hour.

From Hahn's dispatch:

> By his own report, supported in part by my direct observation,
> Swami regularly takes at least eight daily doses of Datura in the
> form of the betel chew. Typically, he ingests the betel chew in the
> morning at 7:00 am, 8:00 am, and 9:00 am, then again in the after-
> noon at 2:00 pm and 3:00 pm (or 3:00 pm and 4:00 pm), and then
> at night. . . .
>
> One would expect such a dosage level to render Swami con-
> fused, disoriented, unable to think clearly, and incapable of re-
> membering almost anything. In Swami's case, just the opposite

appears to be true. Swami reports that without his daily regime of Datura, he is unable to remember the vast number of books he has read and Sanskrit writings he has studied.

Hahn learned that Swami had been consuming datura since a young age and had built up an extraordinary tolerance. Hahn dug into the research and could find no precedent for this in all of history. His curiosity was at a fever pitch. Ultimately, Hahn decided that for him to truly explore the impact of this sacred plant, he needed to properly try it himself. And who better to mentor him than Swami?

The ancient yogi, at first, was resistant to the idea. As Hahn writes:

> His concern appeared overstated to me, but he insisted saying he didn't want the death of a Westerner on his hands as it would cause problems for him with the local authorities!

Once before, almost on a whim, Hahn had had the tiniest taste of datura. It didn't go well. "Just give me a little bit, just a taste," Hahn had asked Swami, who relented. As they were getting out of a taxi, Swami gave Hahn a small dose—nowhere close to his normal amount—and Hahn fell to the ground. He didn't even remember falling; he had blacked out.

But Hahn was undeterred, and now he wanted to properly prepare for the drug—to ingest it in the right context and give it the respect it deserved. So, in Swami's apartment in Kathmandu, on a simple wooden bed, Hahn lay down and could feel the fresh air wafting in through a window. He could hear the chants, bells, and prayers coming from outside. Swami burned incense.

As Hahn writes:

> The effects of my Datura experience lasted for approximately the next 36 hours, slowly decreasing in intensity. During this time I experienced an "elevated state" of mind and exhibited, according to external observation, a euphoric disposition.

Hahn's vision became more intense. His hearing became more intense. His overall awareness became more intense. Hahn was reminded of Plato's allegory of the cave, the classic thought experiment where people live in a cave and see shadows of objects on the wall, and they mistakenly think these shadows are the real objects, being unable to perceive the truth. By analogy, he thought, perhaps what we experience as normal consciousness is just the shadow of objects in the cave, and a heightened experience on datura can reveal the underlying reality.

There was no "bad trip." Hahn gained a deeper appreciation of why Swami and the ancient yogis have used datura for centuries. He published his findings in academic journals, and this is part of a growing body of research that has removed much of the stigma of psychedelic drugs.

Hahn stresses the importance of caution, safety, and deep knowledge and preparation when experimenting with a substance like datura. He's skeptical of tourists dabbling in ayahuasca as a fad, saying, "I wouldn't go into it willy-nilly."

But study after study has suggested that—when taken safely and responsibly and in certain contexts—psychedelics can have benefits such as alleviating depression, reducing anxiety, treating PTSD, and enhancing creativity and personal well-being. Conducting that research meant, in a sense, going to the edge of reality. "I explore these deep psychedelic states of consciousness," says Hahn. "That's my nature as an explorer."

THE SEARCH FOR THE SKULL

Justin Fornal

IN 1800, NAT TURNER was born into slavery. In 1831 he led a slave rebellion that some consider to be the first battle of the Civil War. It was the deadliest slave revolt in American history.

The rebellion killed approximately sixty white people, including some women and children. So Turner was hunted down, captured, and then hanged by white Virginians. His legacy is complicated. Some find the collateral damage done to innocents unforgivable; others consider him a champion of racial justice.

The exact details of Turner's death, too, are shrouded in mystery. We know for certain that he was killed. After that, the history tilts toward myth and legend. According to some, his head was chopped off. According to others, he was skinned, with his body parts used as leathery human trophies. And for nearly two centuries, one mystery remained: What happened to Nat Turner's skull? Where was it now?

That question haunted Justin Fornal, an explorer and "cultural detective" who specializes in solving historical mysteries. In 2016, he worked as a producer on a film about Nat Turner. But he wanted to do more than just make a movie—he wanted to solve the mystery.

Fornal began sleuthing, and he tracked down letter after letter that claimed knowledge of the location of Turner's skull. He discovered a letter, for example, that showed how Turner's skull was passed from the coroner to future generations:

TO WHOM IT MAY CONCERN:

This skull, to the best of my knowledge and belief, is the skull of Nat Turner, the negro executed (I am told) in the tide water area of the state of Virginia. It came into the possession of my father, Dr. Albert Gallitin Franklin, a practicing physician in Richmond, Virginia, circa 1900.

It was given to him for his office by a young woman (name long forgotten) who inherited it from her father, a physician who was in attendance at the execution.

After my father's death in 1927, my mother who lived with me for many years, and who died at the age of 88 in 1964, kept it in her trunk for many years in memory of my father, and gave it to my children before she passed on.

He also found a letter sent to Patricia Cornwell, the true-crime novelist.

Dear Ms. Cornwell:

I need your help or advice. . . .

I have the skull of Nat Turner. It has been in my family for about a century as you can see from the enclosed copy of a letter to me from my father.

Now in my twilight years, I wish to find an appropriate resting place for Nat if possible. . . .

Ownership of the skull carries with it some sensitivity, and even if it is not Nat Turner, one might logically say "so what". I'm not proud of having the skull, but family loyalty and respect for the deceased, make me reluctant to simply dispose of it.

One Saturday night while in his office, sipping whiskey and re-searching Nat Turner, Fornal discovered something that surprised him. He learned of a fundraising event in the early 1990s, at which the skull itself was given to a man named Richard Gordon Hatcher.

Hatcher was the former mayor of Gary, Indiana. He had made history as the first African American mayor of a city of more than one hundred thousand people, and he served as mayor for twenty years.

The man was a legend. Now it seemed that he was trying to establish a Civil Rights Hall of Fame. Could Hatcher somehow have the skull?

Fornal called up Hatcher's office and spoke to the man himself. After some pleasantries, he asked him, point-blank, "Do you have the skull of Nat Turner?"

Hatcher said he did not.

But Fornal dug deeper, and he became convinced that Hatcher possessed the skull. The situation was now almost awkward. Hatcher certainly had the best intentions, but he was keeping the skull in his own private collection, and it was important to Nat Turner's descendants—and the NAACP—that the skull be returned to the family or a museum. That seemed only right.

How could Fornal make inroads? As it happened, he now had personal relationships with a respected Black performer named Tony Wilson, who also goes by the "Young James Brown" (he had toured with the real James Brown), Nat Turner's family, and the NAACP. Young James Brown made some calls to Black mayors of other cities, who then called Hatcher on Fornal's behalf, vouching for him.

After this relationship building, Fornal once again got Mayor Hatcher on the phone. "Mr. Hatcher, I just want to say something to you," Fornal said. "I do believe you have the skull of Nat Turner. And I've read your biography. And you've achieved so much in the realm of civil rights. It would be heartbreaking if something was to happen to you, and nobody knew what happened to the skull of Nat Turner."

Fornal respectfully said to Hatcher that Nat Turner needed to be returned to his family, and that a failure to do so would be dehumanizing. He said to Hatcher, "His spirit needs to come home. You're holding him in purgatory."

That seemed to do the trick. Hatcher asked to speak to Nat Turner's descendants, so Fornal arranged a call between Hatcher and Turner's fifth-great-granddaughters. Hatcher told the women that he had a profound respect for their ancestor and viewed him as an inspirational historical figure. Then he began to get emotional.

"I have his skull," Hatcher said on the call, and began to cry. "I have his skull."

Hatcher said he could no longer keep this to himself and needed to lift the weight off his shoulders. "I'm putting the skull in the mail tomorrow," he said. "What's your address?"

Fornal, who had been silently listening in on the call, was skittish about the skull being dropped in the mail. He suggested that they all meet in person on Hatcher's turf—Gary, Indiana—for a properly ceremonial skull transfer.

They met at a casino that Hatcher owned. The scene likely struck everyone as surreal: Mayor Hatcher, Justin Fornal, Young James Brown, and the descendants of Nat Turner met in a casino hotel room for this transfer. Cameras for National Geographic (which had commissioned the story) stood at the ready. Mayor Hatcher then produced a white cardboard box—the kind of box that might hold a pair of sneakers. The box was filled with Styrofoam packing noodles. Rattling around in the noodles was the skull of Nat Turner.

The skull was presented to the descendants, and then Fornal—with blessings from National Geographic, the NAACP, and Nat Turner's family—personally transported it to the Smithsonian.

On his way to D.C., Fornal did not let the skull out of his sight. He kept it next to him when he slept. At the request of the African American diaspora spiritual community, he conducted a ceremony to "cleanse the energy" of the skull—an apology, of sorts, for it being stuck in a closet for decades.

The story was published in National Geographic (without any of these behind-the-scenes details of how the skull was recovered), and it was widely read. In fact, the story was read by a descendant of Gerónimo, the legendary Apache warrior who symbolized Native American resistance.

The Gerónimo family got in touch with Fornal, who by now had some renown for tracking down lost relics. Gerónimo's skull, too, had been missing for more than a century. And the Gerónimo family had reason to believe that it was being kept by Skull and Bones, a secret society at Yale University. Fornal consulted with tribal elders and a former U.S. attorney who had tried to solve the case.

After months of research, Fornal wrote a detailed letter to a former member of Skull and Bones. This member's grandfather, according to Fornal's evidence, had removed the skull from Gerónimo's grave. Fornal worked with members of The Explorers Club to get a working address for the man and wrote him a letter, clearly detailing what he knew and asking for a response—just as he had with Mayor Hatcher.

Justin Fornal sent this letter to former President George W. Bush:

> Dear Mr. Bush,
>
> My name is Justin Fornal. I am a writer, explorer and student of American history. I write to you with hope in my heart as we stand together at a cross road of our nation's legacy. My passion in life is orchestrating positive resolutions to history's loose ends, and I believe together you and I can bring fresh closure to an old story.

Fornal then described his work returning Nat Turner's skull to his descendants:

> Mayor Richard Gordon Hatcher, who had the skull hidden in a closet, has contacted me on multiple occasions since the relic's return and thanked me for lifting the burden from his soul and his family's legacy. The skull is currently in possession of forensics expert Douglas Owsley at the Smithsonian Institute as we await DNA results. Once the research is complete, the relic will be buried in Southampton, Virginia, giving the family and members of the national African American community a sense of closure to a dark chapter in our nation's history.
>
> Following the printing of my article, I was contacted by descendants of the great Apache medicine man and warrior Goyaaté

(Geronimo). They asked if I would be willing to help with the re-patriation of his skull, which they believe was removed from its resting place at Fort Sill in 1918. As it is believed that your grand-father Prescott Bush was among the group of young Bonesmen who removed the relic, there is no better living individual than yourself to aid its safe return. . . .

In a private audience of Mescalero elders, I made a vow to do everything in my power to return the alleged skull to the Apache people. I did not and will not accept any money for this activity. It is my belief that payment cannot exchange hands when dealing with spiritual matters. . . .

I am a member of several private fraternal orders and have al-ways had a great respect for brotherhood, time honored tradi-tions, and the power of mystique. I am proud to call myself a 'fellow in residence' at the Explorers Club, a society for field sci-entists established in 1904. Our members have been the first to the peak of Mount Everest, the Mariana Trench, and the moon. In my opinion, the Club has made many positive changes over the years, such as permitting the membership of women in 1981. The Club has evolved from a fraternity of adventurers and big game hunters to a scientific institution at the forefront of global protec-tion and awareness. I can speak for many members when I say that we are a better club than we were 100 years ago.

This is the perfect moment in history to return the 'most spec-tacular crook' to its people. This simple gesture would display that the Skull and Bones society and the Russell Trust Associa-tion of today are as benevolent as they are powerful.

Fornal then offered to sign a nondisclosure agreement and sug-gested possible logistics for the returning of the skull.

Mr. Bush; it is a pleasure to meet you under these optimistic cir-cumstances. I am excited to hear your thoughts and ideas on this matter. This is one of America's greatest stories, and you, sir, are in the unique position to be the hero.

Very truly yours,
Justin Fornal

The letter came back marked Return to Sender. Fornal is still on the case.

To be continued . . .

5

The Edge of
Humanity

While The Explorers Club is not technically a humanitarian organization, it's also true that many members are driven by a desire for social impact. These include explorers like Jane Hamilton-Merritt, who, in the shadow of the Vietnam War, risked her life to live with Hmong refugees and tell their untold story.

Or the explorer who followed the footsteps of Charles Darwin in Patagonia to better understand what the father of evolution got wrong about humanity. Other explorers use photographs to give a voice (and face) to the world's unseen refugees, and still others dive into the front of an active war, eager to give food and medicine.

Exploration for humanity, however, isn't always about solving macro societal problems.

Sometimes the edge of humanity is on a smaller scale. Micro instead of macro. J. R. Harris explored the edge of humanity by doing something unusual—and unexpected— for his brother. Another formed a surprising bond with a girl in South Sudan. And Dr. Richard Harris, an anesthesiologist and cave diver, was forced to make agonizing choices when a soccer team was stuck in a flooded cave system in Thailand.

So, what does "the edge of humanity" mean in this context? At its heart, exploration can involve more than the cold, hard, objective answers to scientific questions. Sometimes we travel, search, chronicle, give, and serve out of profound respect for our shared humanity.

TRAGIC MOUNTAINS
AND SECRET WARS

Jane Hamilton-Merritt

MOST AMERICANS HADN'T heard of the Hmong. Especially in the 1960s and '70s, most were unaware that this Indigenous people from Southeast Asia—an ethnic minority throughout the region—were involved in a secret and tragic arc of the Vietnam War.

Jane Hamilton-Merritt knew about the Hmong. She was familiar with their language, ate their food, and was deeply immersed in their culture. After the communist victory in Vietnam and Laos in the mid-1970s, she embedded herself in Hmong refugee camps so she could help share their stories.

By then she had been in the region for years. A young photojournalist, Hamilton-Merritt happened to have a PhD in Southeast Asian Studies. "So when my generation went to war," she says, "I thought I should cover it." She covered the fighting in Vietnam and won awards for her frontline coverage. She also tried to cover the "secret war" in Laos, which was embargoed to journalists.

Hamilton-Merritt had discovered that Laos was a critical but secret theater of the Vietnam War. The communist North Vietnamese Army needed control of northern Laos, then the Hmong homelands, so they could move men and materials through Laos to South Vietnam via the Ho Chi Minh Trail. In 1962, President Kennedy had reached a deal to keep Laos "neutral" and out of the regional fight for control—no foreign forces were to operate there. When his administration realized that U.S. adversaries did not withdraw their forces, Kennedy's CIA covertly recruited, trained, and armed Hmong to be the "American boots" on the ground in northern Laos. The Hmong, under Hmong General Vang Pao, would become a guerrilla-blocking force against the North Vietnamese Army invaders. And significantly, Hmong would later serve as spotter pilots for U.S. strike aircraft and Ho Chi Minh Trail watchers and were tasked to rescue American pilots downed in Hmong territory.

All of this was done at great sacrifice by the Hmong. While Americans didn't know about this secret war and the U.S. alliance with the Hmong, those whom the Hmong were fighting knew and ultimately vowed revenge.

The fighting in Hmong territory was an off-limits area to American journalists. "That didn't particularly stop me," says Hamilton-Merritt. To discover what was really going on, she would head to Laos and visit the bars where the Air America pilots drank beer. She chatted them up and began to piece together the puzzle. She personally studied the flight patterns of U.S. aircraft. "I could see F-4 Phantom fighter jets carrying bombs underneath their wings rise out of the rice patties [of northern Thailand] heading toward northern Laos," she says. "They weren't going to North Vietnam, because they returned too quickly with no bombs attached." (It shouldn't be a surprise that Hamilton-Merritt was nominated for a Pulitzer.)

A tragic epitaph to this secret is that in the wake of the communist victory in Laos, the Hmong tried to flee to Thailand to escape violent retribution for their long alliance with the United States. At the time, there were no bridges across the Mekong River. To reach Thailand and hope for safety in a refugee camp, the Hmong had to cross the river using makshift boats, bamboo rafts, tire inner tubes, or anything that might float. As Hamilton-Merritt says, "Many Hmong died trying to cross the Mekong River."

Hamilton-Merritt made it her mission to speak with survivors who made it to (relative) safety in the refugee camps in northern Thailand. "I believe that journalism is the first draft of history," she says. "I had the obligation to record interviews, to document with photos, and to preserve the history of what I was witnessing."

She didn't do this from the cozy comfort of a hotel. Hamilton-Merritt lived in the Hmong refugee camps for months at a time. She slept in huts. Her "bed" was usually a wooden board. Breakfast was rice, lunch was rice, dinner was rice. As she remembers now, the rice was often filled with "stones and rat shit."

The Hmong welcomed her into their community, shared their stories and did their best to keep her safe. When she slept in a hut with several young men, for example, two of them volunteered as de facto guards, sleeping on either side of her with knives.

One thing that helped keep her safe was the fact that she befriended the Thai commander who ran the refugee camp. In her initial visits to the camp, the commander was friendly to her. This didn't last. He eventually grew suspicious of her motives and interrogated her. His soldiers held her at gunpoint. The commander asked Hamilton-Merritt how she had arrived at the camp. (In truth, she had snuck in.) Hamilton-Merritt knew she might be harmed or worse, but she tried to act like nothing was wrong, saying to the commander with a smile, "How are you? It's so nice to see you!"

With a gun in her face, Hamilton-Merritt kept gushing pleasantries to literally disarm the commander, such as "It's so nice to see that the rose is blooming in your garden!" She told the commander she was about to travel to Bangkok, and that she would be visiting with some influential people whose names he would recognize—higher-ups in the Thai military and members of the Thai parliament. There was some truth to this, as Hamilton-Merritt was then writing for the *Bangkok Post* and had connections. At gunpoint, she told him with a smile, "I'll report that I had a lovely time here!"

The Thai commander, whether charmed or convinced or confused, let her go, and she continued her reporting. She scribbled all her notes in journals that she keeps to this day. She snapped photographs. She now estimates that she has "tens of thousands of photos" and "stacks and stacks of notebooks."

Her reporting showed that sometimes the Hmong refugees made it safely from Laos to Thailand, but many times they did not. This is a difficult but important story to hear. Consider these gutting journal entries from 1979.

. . .

July 27, 1979

The river and freedom are in sight. A group of 189 Hmong—30 men and 159 women and children—have endured a two-month trek through the mountainous high jungles of Laos, running from the Pathet Lao and North Vietnamese soldiers.

Tonight, they sit by the edge of the Mekong River waiting for darkness to provide cover for a crossing into Thailand—the final obstacle to freedom. Adults have not eaten for many days to preserve food for the children. Small amounts of the remaining rice are forced into mouths of children—many only skeletons. Afraid to light fires for fear of detection by enemy soldiers, they wait in the monsoon darkness. Children are given more opium to keep them quiet: Any noise may alert soldiers known to patrol the banks of the Mekong searching for Hmong trying to escape.

Hmong who have escaped Laos tell of Pathet Lao and North Vietnamese soldiers killing children for nothing, women for their silver necklaces, men because they are soldiers. They say that enemy soldiers take their rice, chickens, and buffalo; that poisonous gases are dropped from planes on their villages and that their people die. They are convinced that the communist soldiers intend to kill all the Hmong. Yet the Hmong continue to fight the Communists in Laos although they have few weapons left and no meaningful support from outside.

July 28, 1979

At the darkest time of night, they cross the Mekong, only to discover as the dawn mists lift that they have miscalculated and have crossed at a very wide part of the river. They land on a long river island and still far from the Thai banks. Hurriedly the Hmong gather vines to weave into ropes to attach to mounds of sand and patches of river reeds to make a link to shore and safety. There is so little time, for the river is rising noticeably and storm clouds hang over the mountains to the north. They could all drown if the river suddenly rose. Now that they believe themselves off Laotian territory and safe, they build fires to boil water in United States Army canteens. Women take off their blouses and, with sticks for frames, make shelters for the sick, babies, and old women.

Many Thai soldiers appear on the Thai bank along with a machine gun mounted on a jeep. Soon a Thai patrol in two boats lands on the island to inform the Hmong leader that they must go back to Laos—they cannot cross into Thailand. The Hmong tell the Thai soldiers that they will build bamboo rafts and leave during the night. Since the Thai side of the island is lower than the Laotian side, the Hmong huddle on the lower side hoping that enemy soldiers from Laos will not see them.

Men and women cut bamboo from small clusters on the island while others continue to make survival ropes. In the afternoon, Thai soldiers in boats cut the vines, the Hmong lifelines to freedom. Night falls and the Hmong take up guard. They have no food and the river is rising.

August 1, 1979

Morning brings signs of another torrid day. . . .

As I stood watching the Hmong marooned on the island, I remembered the stories of so many who, like those on the island, had fled Laos under the most terrifying circumstances. Drumming in my mind were the words of one young man: "I feel sad for my wife. Her clothes are shreds and she's sick with malaria, yet she cares for my brother's five children. The youngest is four and he's so weak he cannot stand alone; she must carry him. My brother and his wife are dead. His wife disappeared while searching for food. I often think of my American friends. They gave me their addresses but I've lost them. It seems so long ago that the Americans left—maybe four years, and now the fighting is even more difficult, with so few weapons and no one to help us. We Hmong are all so tired. So many Hmong are dead. We Hmong people are so pitiful."

The Hmong who fought under General Vang Pao for the Americans in Laos against the Communists since the early 1960's find it difficult to accept that no one cares about them, hardly anyone writes about their tragedy, no American friends seek to help.

August 2, 1979

A group of 30 to 40 Pathet Lao soldiers land on the island. Shooting breaks out and the Hmong are massacred. It is not known whether there were any survivors. These 189 brave Hmong men, women and children did not know that the island on which they had landed was Laotian territory.

After so long a struggle, freedom never came.

As Vang Yee, the Hmong chief, holding the rank of colonel, said to me: "We Hmong fight, work like buffalo, run, starve, and die—and no one knows."

· · ·

HAMILTON-MERRITT'S MISSION TO come back and tell the Hmong story—no matter how painful—did not end in Southeast Asia or in the 1970s. She'd made a commitment to Vang Yee, the Hmong chief from the refugee camp, that she would continue to raise awareness of the Hmong. And she would honor that pledge for the rest of her life.

First, she synthesized her reporting (including these journal entries) into the book *Tragic Mountains: The Hmong, the Americans, and the Secret Wars for Laos, 1942–1992.* Then she did what she could for the Hmong who were resettled in the United States, unknown and unwanted despite having fought for American interests.

"In the 1980s, it was clear that the Hmong could not go back to Laos. They would be tortured and killed," says Hamilton-Merritt. This is why many were resettled to the United States, where the refugee agencies—largely ignorant of Hmong culture—plunked them in cold cities like Detroit and Minneapolis. Most couldn't speak English. Many suffered from PTSD. They were often the victims of assault. And they were severed from their homeland and their culture.

Hamilton-Merritt remembered her promise to Vang Yee, so she created an exhibit that made good use of her photos of traditional Hmong life, as well as photos of the ensuing tragedy. She included physical samples she had saved of their beautiful textiles. She had no idea if this exhibit would find an audience, but after some glowing press coverage, the exhibit soon went on tour. Then it traveled to all the major cities where the Hmong had resettled. And what mattered to Hamilton-Merritt was that the Hmong themselves seemed to respond to the exhibit.

"The Hmong were so proud of what they saw," says Hamilton-Merritt. "And the tragedy was there, too." For decades Hamilton-Merritt gave speeches about the Hmong at universities, gave career support and guidance to young Hmong, and did what she could to help preserve their culture. She knows that nothing can undo or atone for the unfathomable loss. But she also felt that "I had to preserve it. I had to do something about the fact that nobody seemed to know."

FINDING CHARLES DARWIN

Marcio Pimenta

IN 1831, AS A YOUNG MAN, Charles Darwin spent two years traveling through Patagonia. He was struck by the region's staggering biodiversity, its geology, and the variety of the species. Patagonia influenced Darwin intellectually, personally, and professionally. He later called the expedition "by far the most important event in my life" and claimed that it had "determined my whole career."

Darwin wrote extensive notes and letters while in Patagonia, making detailed observations:

> I paid particular attention to the mammalia and birds. Of the latter I procured, within the distance of a morning's walk, no less than eighty species, of which many were exceedingly beautiful—I think even more so than those of Brazil. The other orders were not neglected. Reptiles were numerous, and nine different kinds of snakes were taken.

These notes and letters were part of Darwin's larger expedition on HMS *Beagle*, a five-year journey exploring South America He later published his thoughts in the now classic *The Voyage of the Beagle*.

Darwin's insights from his trip to Patagonia led to *On the Origin of Species*, the book that ultimately changed our entire understanding of the natural world. Marcio Pimenta, a Brazilian photographer, considers Darwin's landmark study "the most important single scientific work ever published." Pimenta happens to love Patagonia, and he journeys there frequently, so he was surprised that little is known of the personal details.

So he decided to follow in Darwin's footsteps.

Pimenta embarked on a forty-day journey to retrace Darwin's path in Patagonia, hoping to better understand the scientist's perspective. Darwin was a complicated man. In addition to being a brilliant naturalist, he harbored many of the ugly prejudices of the nineteenth century, and that prejudice extends to the people of Patagonia. In one of his letters, Darwin described the Indigenous people he encountered as "miserable degraded savages." He wrote:

> I could not have believed how wide was the difference between savage and civilized man: it is greater than between a wild and domesticated animal.

And also:

> Viewing such men, one can hardly make oneself believe that they are fellow-creatures, and inhabitants of the same world.

Pimenta struggled to reconcile the intellectual curiosity of Darwin with his ignorance about humanity. He thought about the dilemma often as he traveled the 6,800 miles—a mix of hiking and traveling by jeep. (Darwin rode a horse.)

Along the way he reread Darwin's field notes from Patagonia, marveling at his eye for detail:

> When at the Rio Negro, in Northern Patagonia, I repeatedly heard the Gauchos talking of a very rare bird which they called Avestruz Petise. They described it as being less than the common ostrich (which is there abundant), but with a very close general resemblance. They said its colour was dark and mottled, and that its legs were shorter, and feathered lower down than those of the

common ostrich. It is more easily caught by the bolas than the other species.

Patagonia is not easy terrain. The wind can travel at one hundred miles per hour—comparable to a Category 2 hurricane—and literally knock you off a ridge. Insects are everywhere. Pimenta took some comfort knowing that Darwin had dealt with much of the same. From Darwin's letters:

> We have been surrounded by insects. One evening, when we were about ten miles from the Bay of San Bias, vast numbers of butterflies, in bands or flocks of countless myriads, extended as far as the eye could range. Even by the aid of a glass it was not possible to see a space free from butterflies.

Pimenta, who is married, struggled with loneliness as he continued the forty-day journey. He sometimes wondered if what he was doing made any sense. He wondered if anyone would care. But then he would again gulp in the bounty of Patagonia's ecosystem—both the sweeping panoramic views and the tiny miracles of its creatures—and his resolve would be restored. He loved the beetles and birds and lizards. So did Darwin. From Darwin's letters:

> On the arid plains a few black beetles (Heteromera) might be seen slowly crawling about, and occasionally a lizard darting from side to side. Of birds we have three carrion hawks, and in the valleys a few finches and insect feeders. . . . In the stomachs of these birds I found grasshoppers, cicadæ, small lizards, and even scorpions. At one time of the year they go in flocks, at another in pairs: their cry is very loud and singular, and resembles the neighing of the guanaco.

Again and again, Pimenta found new appreciation for Darwin's exacting attention to detail. Darwin constantly made surprising connecions between the species. He observed the animals at the edge—or at least the edge for him—and this contributed directly to his understanding of the world. It was in Patagonia that Darwin found fossils, and that further fueled his thoughts on evolution:

> I have been wonderfully lucky with fossil bones—some of the animals must have been of great dimensions: I am almost sure that many of them are quite new.

When Pimenta glimpsed the ocean, he imagined the *Beagle* docked at sea. He visualized Darwin strolling the beach, scribbling notes in his journal. And he reminded himself that while in Patagonia Darwin was still a young man, nowhere near a finished product. "Before Darwin explored the world, Darwin was exploring himself," says Pimenta. "This was the first time Darwin left Europe to travel the world. It was all new for Darwin."

Darwin's chief insight was that species evolve. And this, ultimately, is how Pimenta reconciled Darwin's prejudice with his brilliance: Darwin himself evolved.

The naturalist wrote his initial letters about the Patagonian people in 1834, when he was twenty-five years old. He grew up. He matured. And he spent much of his later life fighting racism. "Darwin came to believe that we are all one," says Pimenta. "We all evolved from the same place."

As Pimenta fought the wind and fatigue and loneliness, in these rough conditions he keenly felt that there were no geopolitical borders or nationalities—just creatures and humans and nature. Darwin would come to see the same thing.

"We are all one. We are passengers of the world. When I die, a new generation will take my place," says Pimenta. "So why are we occupying our time on the planet with stupid fights? Let's just enjoy it."

THE POWER OF FACES

Theresa Menders

and Daniel Farber Huang

VISUALIZE A REFUGEE CAMP. What do you see? Most people see an image of dirty water, tattered clothes, and overall misery. Theresa Menders and Daniel Farber Huang, a wife-and-husband exploration duo, would prefer us to visualize something else entirely: the refugees' human faces.

The idea started when Huang, a longtime photographer, was chronicling a refugee camp in Chios, Greece, in 2017. He made eye contact with as many people as he could. He tried to smile. He cites the importance of "our willingness to smile," as "the only thing we can do is acknowledge that we see people." He says that as he was smiling and waving, he might have looked "like a dope," but at least the refugees realized he was not armed police.

Then he noticed something that surprised him: When refugees saw his camera, they asked him to take their picture. At first that struck him as odd. Most refugees had some version of a smartphone, and even the most basic phones had a camera, so what good would his photos do them?

Back at home, Huang and Menders spoke about this at length. "What we realized is that they've lost everything," says Menders. They were forced to flee their homes. Their possessions were all gone. "Why were they asking for photos? It's almost a way to show people that they exist."

Menders and Huang thought more about the problem. It occurred to them that when people see refugee camps in the news, they tend to see the wretched conditions that most of us just visualized. But what if we could see the faces of the refugees in a different context, something with less squalor, more humanity?

So in 2017, Menders and Huang returned to the refugee camp in Chios and set up a makeshift photo studio. The goal was not to capture the brutal conditions—that's important work, but there's plenty of others doing it. Instead, they hung a bright orange sheet from a fence and used that as a backdrop. They took thousands of portraits. The photos were happy and upbeat, full of smiles, almost like family holiday cards or high school graduation shots.

Huang scribbled notes in his field journal when they finished, chronicling the experience.

> Back to Chios. We printed 1,500 photos for refugees and some for volunteers as well. We spent 2 days in Souda camp, 1 day inside at the CESRT Creative Center on Sunday, and 2 days at the Vial refugee camp.
>
> The weather had blistering hot sun, maybe 90-100 degrees regularly, and just harsh all around. . . . We spent more time taking beauty shots of people, both refugees and volunteers. . . .
>
> We were [near] the portable toilets. Blistering sun, weird smells and God knows what was on the ground in the dirt.

Huang tuned out the sun and the dirt and the smells. He focused on something more important. "I was always drawn to their eyes," he says. "If you're able to look into a stranger's eyes, hopefully that will help you fear that stranger less." Menders and Huang set up portable printers at the refugee camp and gave each person a physical photo as a keepsake.

> From a technical standpoint we were able to run an efficient process in very harsh conditions. The [printers] we were given worked exceptionally well in the direct sunlight for hours, but the blowing sand sometimes marred the prints. We should bring pressurized air to keep them clean.

> The paper frames . . . made all the difference so people could really keep their prints for the long term. This showed the refugees that we were trying to give them something meaningful.

He spent as much time as he could with each. "They want to be seen," he says. "Being seen is validating for people."

> When we set up in the mornings and gave the first few people their prints, it was nice to see how quickly word spread and people got interested. The kids were crazed to get as many prints as possible. . . . It was nice to see how excited many were to have their portrait taken. Some women changed their outfits multiple times and I spent extra time with them to make multiple poses.

The project eventually morphed into a larger project called The Power of Faces and spawned TED talks and gallery exhibitions. "The edge we inhabit is the places where humanity is at risk of losing its way," says Huang. "The edge is where we use our voices to speak up for people who have had their voices taken away."

SHELLING IN UKRAINE

Peter Flo Grinde-Hollevik

DATA CAN ONLY tell you so much. At least, that was the perspective of Peter Flo Grinde-Hollevik, an undergraduate student at the University of California, Berkeley, who studied environmental economics and data science. He constantly worked with data. But in 2022, he felt like he was missing a crucial part of the equation. Where was the human connection? He felt tugged to somehow go beyond the objectivity of numbers to find something more emotional, more visceral, more human, more real.

So he left the comfy halls of Berkeley to spend a month in sub-Saharan Africa—a region that was being impacted by climate change—working in the fields of Rwanda and Uganda. "I was able to go to the primary source of our data and understand the connection between what we're doing as researchers and what we should be doing with people," says Grinde-Hollevik.

While in Africa, another type of data kept ticking into his phone: the number of people killed in Ukraine. He felt guilty for being a mere bystander. He felt a desire to help. And he felt some desire to better understand what was really going on—to see the frontlines in Ukraine as more than just the data of the dead.

Grinde-Hollevik thought about how he could help. He wasn't a doctor, nurse, or soldier. But he knew of a group of people in Norway, where he's from, members of a community called Paracrew, who quit their jobs, packed their cars, and drove to Ukraine as soon as the war broke out, on a mission to deliver humanitarian aid. Paracrew was founded by a mother and daughter, and they delivered aid to places too dangerous for the Red Cross.

The first thing Grinde-Hollevik did was solicit donations from his friends and contacts at Berkeley, as he knew that what the relief workers really needed was money. With cash, they could buy whatever they needed on the ground. (This aligns with a broader shift in humanitarian aid. Many groups now give cash instead of jackets or beans or goats, as cash gives more agency to the recipients.) Funding secured, Grinde-Hollevik took a flight from Rwanda to Amsterdam, then a twenty-eight-hour bus ride to the border of Poland and Ukraine.

Throughout his time in Ukraine, whenever he had internet access, he sent letters (via email) to his donors, typing into his phone and shaking with adrenaline—giving them dispatches from the edge of war.

> On Thursday I expect to arrive at the border near Lyiv, Ukraine. We'll spend Friday planning and packing the trucks, and will leave toward the Eastern Front on Saturday morning.
>
> Without giving too much detail, I've been informed that the first supply mission will head toward the Kharkiv region. In addition to a normal supply run, we'll also assist transporting medical personnel to an undisclosed location that needs it the most.
>
> I'll keep you posted as my time down there progresses.

Grinde-Hollevik woke up at 3 a.m. for his first supply run. He joined a team of two other aid workers, and they drove sixteen hours from the Polish border toward the eastern front. On the first night, Grinde-Hollevik slept wearing silicon earplugs. He couldn't hear anything. He woke up to learn that in the middle of the night, Russian S-400 missiles had just missed his shelter. The aid workers packed their truck with basics like clean drinking water, food, and any items requested by civilians near the front—everything from medicine to saws to adult diapers.

On another supply run they delivered a truck full of dog food.

Most Ukrainians were forced to abandon their homes and leave their dogs behind, meaning that hundreds of stray dogs remained. These dogs were hungry. "I'm running in the forest in a semi-military uniform, with dog food," says Grinde-Hollevik. "And I'm delivering it to dogs. Never did I think I'd be doing this."

> Just arrived back at the Polish border after some intense days in Ukraine.
>
> A lot of impressions hard to describe over an email, but I'll do my best. . . .
>
> Our first delivery was a large batch of needed foodstuffs, clean water, and hygiene products to a Ukrainian volunteer named Antôn. He's distributing this further to local organizations that need it the most. . . . Their former apartment block was completely leveled during the liberation of Kharkiv last summer.
>
> After this we headed toward the Eastern Front. We . . . arrived at a military hospital. . . . Our mission was to pick up an American doctor and transport him and surplus equipment to the pediatric hospital in Kharkiv. . . .
>
> [I'm] impressed by the unwavering positive attitude the Ukrainian people have. War consumes a society, and it is clearly the case here.
>
> From "Support our Troops" campaigns at the local gas stations to endless amounts of vehicles heading toward the front, I have nothing but the best to say about these people.

At the war-zone hospital mentioned in the above email, Grinde-Hollevik spent time in the surgery ward. He saw soldiers—maybe teachers or accountants just months earlier—about to get limbs amputated. He saw people, clinging to life, with burn injuries on every inch of skin. One victim was mummified from head to toe, unable to use his arms, and his friend held a cigarette up to his mouth.

Another dispatch:

> The Antonivka Bridge is an incredibly important strategic point for both the Russian and Ukrainian forces. . . . "Strategic point" is another word for "shelled the fuck out of." Pardon my French but it's hard to describe it in any other way. . . .
>
> Getting to Antonivka is no joke. In Kherson we put on body armour and met up with our contact. . . . A stretch of around a mile leaves us very exposed to Russian firing. Luckily, no one is enforcing speed limits. The road itself is an amalgamation of old military equipment, abandoned bunkers, glass, and shrapnel. We learnt this the hard way as we punctured our tire.
>
> On arrival, we were met with big smiles from locals of all ages. 12 or so people helped us unload the truck and asked us in for a coffee. With heavy rain coming down, we sat there drinking as the roof was slowly coming to a collapse. At least they have the tools to fix this now.
>
> This fix is probably the least of their problems. In a street of 10 or so houses, I could only see a couple of houses standing. A Russian grenade had landed in their backyard. I can only imagine how the life of constant shelling must be. Or the life under Russian occupation.

Grinde-Hollevik was surprised to find Odessa, which was under constant bombardment, alive with cafes and bars and people playing music in the streets. He even called his father to tell him this was the most beautiful European city he had ever seen. The city felt safe enough for him to lace up his sneakers and go for a run, and along the way he passed a cathedral that he considered so beautiful—and he's not a religious person—that he reverently put a hand on its front door.

Two days later, after he had left Odessa, he learned of an intense missile attack on the city. That cathedral had been bombed to pieces. He has many memories like this.

Months later, back in the academic bubble of Berkeley, Grinde-Hollevik would take a class on Tolstoy. He was asked to read aloud a passage from *Sevastopol Sketches,* which is an account of the Crimean War. Grinde-Hollevik's body shook with emotion when he read aloud to his classmates. He struggled to process the insight. The gruesome war imagery described by Tolstoy matched—almost too perfectly—the horrors he saw in the surgery ward. "A hundred sixty years later," says Grinde-Hollevik, "and we're still shooting metal objects with explosives at each other."

Multiple times while being interviewed, Grinde-Hollevik stressed that he was not any kind of hero, and that all the credit should go to the Ukrainian people and the regular volunteers at Paracrew, who have been doing this work for weeks and months and now years.

Now, back in his world of studies and academia, Grinde-Hollevik doesn't have any easy answers. But he has learned something. "Whenever I see a data point, I know there are thousands of people having limbs amputated or needing prosthetic legs," says Grinde-Hollevik, who also remembers the generosity, grit, and even cheeky humor of the Ukrainians—like the soldier who kept insisting he would personally build a submarine (out of spare parts) to beat the Russians. "Those data points are more than just data points. They're human life."

A GIRL AND A WELL

Shawn Small

TWELVE-YEAR-OLD JINA LIVED in South Sudan. It was 2010, and her job was to provide water for her family. The nearest water hole was two miles away. So she spent six hours per day, every day, walking back and forth to the water hole, carrying an eight-gallon tank above her head.

She lived in a ten-by-twelve-foot cement-block house, which had just one room. She shared the space with her five siblings and her blind grandmother, and she took care of all of them. Jina's father was away in the army; her mother had died of waterborne illness when Jina was six years old.

There are many deaths like that of Jina's mother in South Sudan. In 2006, 90 percent of the nation's nine million people had no access to clean water, and 80 percent of all hospital calls were from waterborne illnesses. This was why the nonprofit organization Water is Basic came to Sudan in 2010 to install water wells, and this was why Shawn Small, a documentary filmmaker, traveled to the town of Lupapa (a few miles outside of Yei) to capture Jina's story.

South Sudan, at the time, was arguably the most dangerous place on the planet. For more than fifty years the nation had been ravaged by a civil war that sparked constant bouts of tribal violence. The regions fought over how to share the revenue from oil. (Most of the profits left the country.) Millions were displaced from their homes.

But you could argue the lack of clean water was the nation's biggest problem. This is why every morning, before dawn, Small woke up to quietly observe Jina's routine. (She and the parish bishop had agreed to this beforehand.) Small knew Jina wasn't just some outlier—

there are roughly one billion girls on the planet who are responsible for carrying their families' water. Many had to travel six miles each way—multiple times a day—meaning that Jina was "lucky" with her two-mile trek to the water hole.

Jina spoke four languages. Even though she was too busy carrying water to go to school, she informally served as a math tutor for several students. Small watched, amazed, as Jina tutored several junior high students. She did all the family's chores. She cooked.

At one point Small picked up the jerrycan of water that Jina carried every day. It held more than forty pounds of water, and many months later, when he premiered the documentary *Ru* at multiple venues, he would fill up the jug and ask people in the crowd to walk twenty feet with it. Most everyone struggled. And Jina carried that jug on her head—often without using hands—every day for twenty-four-thousand steps (Small tracked it). So do one billion young women around the globe. "The women carry this water until their bodies break," says Small. "By the time they're twenty or twenty-one, their backs are destroyed."

Jina never complained when she carried the water. She never complained that her kitchen was outside the cement home, meaning that she cooked over a simple fire. She never complained as she cleaned the straw beds where her grandmother and siblings slept. And the dirt floor, somehow, was always clean.

"We all fell in love with her," Small says of Jina. "She was so intelligent." Sometimes Jina sang a little song while she carried the water, and Small marveled at her optimism.

And Small was there, with Jina, on the day that the well went into service. (Importantly, the wells were a project ultimately operated and managed by the village collective, giving them long-term agency.) Jina used to walk a total of twelve miles (two miles each way, three times a day) to the water hole; now it was just ten minutes from her home.

Within a week she enrolled in school.

Small, of course, headed back home when the project was complete. He often thought of Jina, and he even worried that his team might have inadvertently put her in danger. What if other villagers thought she was getting money from the filmmakers? Would they rob her? This is a classic problem for impact-driven documentary filmmakers: the concern that observing someone's life might harm someone's life.

"It felt like we were leaving her to the wolves," says Small. "It was scary to me. Everyone is watching what's going on." It turned out that Jina was indeed getting hassled—lightly—"but it was nothing she couldn't handle."

And then Jina's life began to change.

Small and Jina stayed in touch—at first sending handwritten notes, then emails, then WhatsApp messages back and forth across the Atlantic.

From Jina to Small, whom she began calling "father":

> To my lovely father Shawn Small,
>
> I have been crying for help from God and he answer me by sending you as his faithfully and lovely servant God bless you and I want you to greet your wife as my mother, your children as my brothers and sisters tell them that I really love them so and very much and I promise that one day you take me and stay with you in America. Since I am in this school I pass very well in first grades.
>
> And I would like you to buy for me a clothes bags, clothes, stories books.
>
> May God bless you, thanks, yours faithfully, daughter Jina

They stayed in touch over many years. Jina enrolled in a private school, paid for by Small and a group including the Water is Basic organization. She began to ace her classes, first in the lower grades and then in high school. He received this email from a school administrator in South Sudan:

Good afternoon Mr. Shawn Small. I hope this email finds you well. Exam results were released last week on Sunday average performance where in all the four programs, we registered 100% pass in nursing, midwifery and laboratory. . . .

[Jina's] results were as follows,

1. medicine 65%

2. surgery 45%

3. pediatrics 71%

4. obstetric and gynecology 68%

5. public health 72%

6. practical paper 67%

7. health system research 78%

Jina is now to proceed with 8 months internship, meanwhile she will be able to do her supplementary paper in the June exam.

Jina finished at the top of her class and was accepted into a medical school in Uganda. Again she earned good grades. Then she was accepted to an internship at the hospital. Her texts to Small included funny details about some of the weirder medical issues she saw in the ward. "I don't want to see post-op pictures!" Small would say to her, joking. This is not to say that Jina's life is a fairytale, or that the wave of a nonprofit wand can solve all the world's problems. Small acknowledges that Jina has had "a few hard years."

Small did return to South Sudan a few years after they installed the well. The town of Lupapa had tripled in size. The community started a brick factory, because now they have water to make bricks. Hospital calls have plummeted. There's no question this is an improvement, but Small resists the narrative of "sad village becomes happy, thanks to westerners." For starters, who's sad and who's happy? Small objects to simplistic views of the South Sudanese plight. "I hate these 'boo hoo' films of 'look at how poor these people are,'" says Small. "I hate it. I hate it. Because it's not what I've seen in humanity."

Small observed that even though the South Sudanese had been

through fifty years of civil war, they were often "filled with joy." They sang songs. They laughed. For perspective, he notes that $70 million would have brought clean water to nine million people in South Sudan, and that in 2023, people in the United States spent $700 million on Halloween costumes for pets. This is why Small doesn't feel *sorry* for the Sudanese. "I feel sorry for us."

Back on that visit in 2010, before Small left Jina and South Sudan, he thought some more about the song she sang when she carried the jug of water above her head. The song was beautiful. He asked her if she could sing it for him and the camera.

Jina told him that before her mom died, they'd always collected water together, and her mother sang this song.

"What does it mean?" Small asked her.

"Oh, it's my prayer of thanksgiving."

Small asked her what that meant.

"It's real simple," she said. She explained that it's a song to the Creator, and that she was thankful for what has been created.

"I thank you for the air I breathe," Jina sang. "I thank you for my family that surrounds me. I thank you for the beautiful weather today. And that you provided water for me today."

Jina kept rattling off more things she was thankful for.

Before long, Small and his team were in tears, moved by the deep gratitude of this girl who seemed to have nothing. Which is why Small now wonders, who helped whom?

LLOYD MOUNTAIN

J. R. Harris

EXPEDITIONS AREN'T CHEAP. The reality is that most modern-day explorers aren't *always* in the field, and they juggle their trips to the edge with the usual grown-up responsibilities, such as having a family, maintaining a career, and making a paycheck.

J. Robert "J. R." Harris knows this balancing act well. He has felt the pull of exploration since he was a teenager in the 1960s, when he went off on his own to wander through Alaska or the Yukon. But he also had bills to pay. In the early 1970s, Harris worked in marketing at NBC, General Foods, Pepsi, and other companies, where he was always one of the few African American employees in his department. "I was the only one out there," he says now with a chuckle.

Harris was good at his job, and his employers noticed. His reputation grew. So he hung his own shingle and launched a marketing consulting firm in 1975, but he faced some headwinds for obvious reasons. Cold-calling is never easy, and it was harder still as one of the very few Black-owned firms in 1970s corporate America. But Harris kept at it. He had a wife and two little kids, and he needed to do right by them.

Still, even as he hustled to establish his new business, he felt the urge to explore. It was just how he was wired. He longed to bring a sleeping bag into the wilderness and roam by himself for weeks. Colleagues told him he was crazy—that given the pragmatic challenges of growing a business, he needed to wait at least five years to go off the grid. Or maybe he had to face the fact that those days were gone forever.

But Harris didn't want to wait. He wanted to do it now. So he recruited his secret weapon, someone who could let him both grow his career and nurture his thirst for exploration: his little brother Lloyd.

"Little" is a relative term. Lloyd stood an imposing six feet, four inches, but J. R. always felt protective of his younger sibling. "Don't mess with my kid brother," he'd tell anyone who needed to listen. J. R. was the first person in his family to graduate high school and go to college; Lloyd was the second. Chuckling, J. R. remembers that when Lloyd received a full scholarship to go to Harvard, he told their mother, "But I don't want to go to Harvard. I want to go to Brown."

Their mother smiled at Lloyd and said, "You're going to take your little brown ass to Harvard and stay there for four years."

Lloyd went to Harvard. And just after Lloyd graduated from Harvard, J. R. happened to be starting up his marketing consultancy.

"Listen, why don't you come with me?" J. R. told his brother.

Lloyd said he didn't really have the experience.

"You know what you know, and I'll teach you the rest," J. R. told him. "We'll do it together."

Both in hindsight and at the time, J. R.'s idea was wildly ambitious. No one in their family had ever started a business of any kind, much less a marketing consultancy. As J. R. remembers, there were only a handful of Black marketing consultancies in the entire United States.

Lloyd heard J. R.'s pitch and thought it over. Then the Harvard graduate said, "Yeah, but I want to be a flight attendant."

But big brother was persuasive and Lloyd soon began working for JRH Marketing Services. That was in 1975, and the brothers looked at each other and said, "Wouldn't it be cool if we could stay in business for fifty years?"

It was the only job either of them would ever have.

J. R. taught Lloyd the ropes, and—as he expected—Lloyd was a natural. Lloyd became so good at marketing, in fact, that he quickly became partner and could man the fort while J. R. went exploring. J. R. didn't need to wait five years after all. He could feed his curiosity by wandering deep into nature, eventually backpacking thousands of miles across the globe. He would be gone for weeks at a time, with no way for anyone to reach him. But he could do it with peace of mind, knowing that Lloyd had everything covered. The company flourished, and J. R. was eventually inducted into the Market Research Council Hall of Fame.

So, did Lloyd join J. R. on his explorations? Not exactly. "What he wanted to do was go to the south of France, sit on the beach, and say, 'Bring me another martini,'" J. R. says with a laugh. "He didn't like carrying heavy packs or sleeping on the ground."

Lloyd and J. R. worked together for thirty-seven years, until Lloyd developed a rare and devastating disease called PML, or progressive multifocal leukoencephalopathy. For two years, J. R. visited his brother every day while he was sick. He even refused to do any traveling or exploration—to the end he'd be there for his little brother. Lloyd passed away in 2016 at the age of fifty-three.

Before his brother passed, it was important to J. R. that Lloyd knew how much he was valued—not just at the end of his life but throughout those thirty-seven years of working together. This is one of the quieter aspects of exploration that rarely gets discussed: Usually it can't happen without the support, patience, and generosity of others in your life. That bedrock of support could be a spouse, a parent, a child, a coworker, a friend, or a six-foot-four kid brother.

Decades earlier, J. R. had wondered, how could he show Lloyd what he meant to him? How could he show Lloyd how much he cared? How could he convey how crucial Lloyd was to his own life and exploration?

In 1986, he had his answer.

J. R. traveled to northern Alaska to explore the John River on foot and by canoe. The 125-mile river flows through a remote stretch of mountains called the Brooks Range, and more importantly to J. R., the Brooks Range had a tradition: If you made the first ascent of an unnamed peak, you got to name the mountain.

When J. R. first arrived at the gateway to the Brooks Range, in a small Alaskan town called Bettles (population of fifty-three at the time), he visited the ranger's office. The office had a huge topographical map on the wall.

"Which of these mountains are unnamed?" J. R. asked the ranger.

The ranger told him that out of a hundred mountains, less than a dozen had names.

Perfect. So J. R. walked ten days across a tundra, and from there he arranged for a bush pilot to fly him and a canoe to the base of an imposing unnamed peak. He stashed his canoe and headed up the face of the mountain; of course, there was no trailhead—J. R. was almost certainly the first human to climb this peak.

He reached the summit of the mountain on August 28, 1986, just a few days after Lloyd's birthday. He took out a piece of paper. And then J. R. wrote his five-word letter from the edge:

Lloyd, this is for you.

He dated the letter, sealed it in a ziplock bag, and tucked the bag under a pile of rocks near the summit, where it likely remains to this day.

Before he inserted the letter, J. R. jotted down the new name of this peak: Lloyd Mountain. And in 2025, exactly fifty years after Lloyd came onboard, the company they started was still in business.

THAI CAVES AND
AGONIZING CHOICES

Dr. Richard Harris

RICHARD HARRIS GOT the text in the middle of a surgery. Dr. Harris, an anesthesiologist, was working on a thyroidectomy. This is not a simple operation. Normally he doesn't check his phone in the OR, but this text stopped him in his tracks:

> There's stuff to talk about. They're not being dived out by Thai navy. Could you sedate someone and dive them out??

The date was July 5, 2018. The text was sent by Rick Stanton, the legendary British cave diver. Stanton specializes in cave rescues, and now he was working on a rescue that had captivated the world: a boys soccer team that had been trapped in the Tham Luang cave of Thailand.

Like the rest of the planet, Harris had been closely following the story. He knew that the team had been found by divers three days ago, and he also knew that there were no good solutions. The boys were stuck. Thanks to the divers, the twelve boys (aged eleven to sixteen) and their coach now had food and water and blankets, but there was no way to safely extract them through the 2.4 miles of underwater caves, which had flooded thanks to the annual monsoon.

It's not a stretch to say the entire world was involved. The rescue mission included ten thousand volunteers, more than a hundred countries, Navy SEALs, the Thailand military, and ninety of the world's premiere divers. But almost no one had the very specific expertise of Dr. Richard Harris, which was why he received that text.

Harris was both an anesthesiologist and a cave diver. He'd had extensive cave-rescue training. And he happened to be near Thailand, as he lived in Australia. For days he'd been texting and calling the diving teams and volunteering his services.

Now they were needed.

This was the problem that vexed the Thai government and the divers: It would be impossible to train these boys how to cave-dive the 2.4 miles of tricky and deadly terrain. They only had a matter of days to escape before the next monsoon arrived, and this wasn't enough time for training the boys. Rescuers were told the boys couldn't even swim. That was a nonstarter. If the boys tried to dive, they would die.

Every other proposed solution, from drilling a rescue shaft to finding an alternate entrance to deploying Elon Musk's submarine, had come up empty. So this was the last option considered: Give the boys anesthesia to render them unconscious, and then the experienced divers could carry them out as cargo.

Harris hated the idea. He thought it was doomed to fail. "There's no possible way that these kids are coming out alive," he told Stanton after getting the text. "I'm not doing that. But I'll come if you want me to."

While the idea of "just sedating the boys" sounded simple on the surface, Harris knew it was far more complicated. It was almost certain to kill them. "You don't have to be a cave diver or an anesthesiologist to know that after a three-hour journey, they're not going to be alive at the other end of that," Harris says now. "It's a no-brainer."

His logic was informed by both academic knowledge and his experience in the field. Harris had himself, as an experiment, once explored the idea of sedation underwater. He put on a full face mask and went underwater. He pretended to be unconscious. "I found that very slowly but surely, water would ingress," says Harris. If this happened, they would die. Or perhaps the tongue would fall back and obstruct the airwave, which was a problem anesthesiologists faced even in the perfect conditions of the operating room. Three hours underwater? Harris knew they'd be dead.

But he was eager to help in any way he could. As he continued to research the problem, a couple of things changed. One, he learned that the masks available to the boys, which had a positive pressure function, should provide a better seal than the one that had leaked. Perhaps that would boost the odds.

The second variable? They were out of options. "The fact was they had racked their brains with how to get the kids out," says Harris. And diving while conscious was even worse than being cargo while unconscious. For any beginning cave diver, says Harris, "you realize that panic is a moment away when you're in an unfamiliar environment. To be suddenly immersed in this and expect to live for three hours . . . the chance of this killing them is 100 percent." He pauses. "Unfortunately, it's very hard to explain that to non-cave-divers."

The moment Harris finished that thyroidectomy operation, he called Rick Stanton and heard something chilling. Something that hammered home the stakes.

"If you want to come," Stanton told him, "prepare yourself for the reality that you're going to dive in through the cave and see these children. And they're beautiful kids. And then you're going to turn your back on them. And they're almost certainly all going to die."

•　•　•

BEFORE HE KNEW IT, Harris was strapped into his diving gear and squirming through the complicated system of the Tham Luang caves. The rain had eased, so he didn't face the raging torrent he had feared, but the caves were difficult to navigate even for world-class divers. Some spots, called "flatteners," were so tight that he could barely fit through, even wearing his air cylinders on his sides. He could feel the walls of the cave on both his chest and back. "It's a three-dimensional challenge that normally can be quite fun," Harris says. "There was nothing fun about this."

After the challenging three-hour dive, Harris emerged into the chamber where the boys were huddled. By now they were accompanied by four Navy SEALs. Harris was surprised to find them upbeat and even happy. Morale was high, despite how thin and sickly the kids looked. One weighed sixty-four pounds.

In the cave, Harris consulted with a Thai Navy SEAL who was also a doctor. Dr. Pak Loharnshoon spoke reasonable English. Pak helped Harris examine the boys, checking their skin and guts and lungs. Then Harris asked Dr. Pak to explain his plan by reading a letter to the boys:

> Tomorrow we will return to take 4 of you out
>
> 4 will be dressed in wetsuits and receive a tablet to make you feel relaxed
>
> One by one you will come down to the water to sit with Dr Harry
>
> You will get one injection in each leg which will make you fall asleep
>
> Once you are asleep, we will finish dressing you in diving equipment
>
> A British diver will take you out of the cave
>
> When you wake up, you will be in the hospital

Pak took the liberty of changing the word hospital to "outside," fearing the boys would be scared. But the boys weren't scared. As Pak read the letter, Harris closely watched the faces of the kids. They were unbelievably calm. They were trusting. Some even gave a thumbs up. As Harris says now, "You'd think it was the best idea they'd ever heard."

Harris and Pak knew they needed to get the kids on board with the plan. "One thing I knew I couldn't do was drag any of these kids kicking and screaming to the water's edge and assault them with a syringe of ketamine," says Harris. "I wasn't prepared to do that."

Harris took video footage of the boys. He did this for the parents. He knew that most if not all of them were unlikely to survive, so the parents should have something, anything, as a final message from their children.

Yes, Harris knew that the plan would likely send the boys to their death. But he knew they had no choice. They needed to be completely anesthetized, so they could not flail or kick or panic. "At the very worst, the boys would die when they were asleep," he says. "And then they'd be returned to their parents."

If they don't go with the plan?

"They would die over the next two to three weeks of starvation or infection or exposure, and their skeletal remains would return to their parents in four to six months." Harris pauses. "Those were the two options I was given."

∙　∙　∙

EARLY THE NEXT MORNING, Harris learned two things. The first was that the Thai government had indeed green-lit the grim plan. The second was that if the plan failed, Harris might personally be used as a scapegoat and perhaps locked in a Thai prison. Harris didn't have the time or the bandwidth to worry about that threat. As a rescue cave diver and an anesthesiologist, he was uniquely qualified to do this job—so he would do the job.

He had to give an anesthesia class to the other divers, who would need to top up the anesthetic drugs during the journey out. There simply wasn't enough time for him to personally escort all twelve boys from the cave. He explained the basics. Then he had the divers practice injecting empty water bottles with syringes. As he remembers, "It was basically six years of postgraduate training in twenty-five minutes."

The clock was ticking. They only had four of the highly pressurized facemasks that gave a better seal, so at most they could save four boys per day, and that was if all went miraculously well. They would need to get four boys the first day, four boys the second, four boys *and* the coach the third. There was no margin for error. To make matters worse, the monsoon rains were predicted to return in the next three to five days, and that would spell the end of the rescue mission. It had to be now.

The first four boys, at Harris's instruction (translated through Dr. Pak), had fasted overnight. Harris gave them some antianxiety tablets, and then he got to work. He spoke to the first boy. He was going to give the boy sedation, and he knew the boy would likely never wake up; his was likely the last face the boy would ever see. The boy's final memory. The boy's final moment.

Knowing all of that, Harris did the only thing he could: He remained upbeat and settled into the usual banter he would give to any anesthesiology patient, even though the boy couldn't speak English and Harris couldn't speak Thai. Pak translated. Harris talked breezily about soccer ("What position do you play?") as he prepared the needle.

Harris held up the syringe. Then he injected one of the boy's thighs, then the other thigh.

The boy remained calm. No screaming, no crying, no fighting. "They just accepted it," says Harris. Sometimes they even pressed their palms together in the universal symbol of gratitude. "It was heartbreaking," says Harris. "They're thanking me for euthanizing them."

After the boy appeared to be unconscious, Harris and the boy's British escort prepared him for the dive. Putting the mask and gear on the unconscious child was harder than he expected. It felt like dressing a rag doll. The boy flopped on his lap and almost fell off, but Harris stuck with it and sealed the mask, with so much force he almost squashed the boy's nose. He strapped a cylinder of 80 percent oxygen to the boy's chest.

Everything depended on the seal of the mask. If water seeped in, the boy would die. If the mask was somehow dislodged, he would die. If the child woke up, panicked, and peeled off his mask, he would die. To ensure it was sealed, Harris had to do something that should not be done—something that just felt wrong. He dunked the boy's face underwater and held it for five seconds. He needed to do this to inspect for leaks.

Five seconds, no leaks. Good.

Then he dunked the boy's head for thirty seconds. Thirty seconds feels like a long time when you're holding an unconscious boy's head beneath the water. Harris hated this, but it had to be done.

Thirty seconds, no leaks. Then, finally, he worked up the courage to put the child's face underwater . . . and leave him there for several minutes. As Harris says now, "It felt like I was drowning kittens."

He only felt worse after that. Next, he had to tie the boy's hands behind his back, then tie his ankles together. He needed to be restrained. Tying their limbs ensured the boys were as streamlined as possible, to minimize the chance they would hit rocks or the walls of the cave and so that, if they somehow woke up, they'd be unable to rip off their masks.

So Harris, after securing the boy as best as he could, gave him to the first British diver. The diver left with the child. Harris worked on the second boy, then the third, then the fourth. He knew he was doing the right thing, and he knew they were likely to die. Both these things were true.

Finally, after the fourth boy had departed, Harris himself donned his diving gear. It was a three-hour swim to the base cave, where he would learn the fate of the children. He tried not to agonize over something he could no longer control. He tried not to think about their deaths. He even tried to appreciate the natural beauty of the Thai cave itself, remembering why he began diving in the first place.

When Harris finally reached the edge of safety, he immediately saw the air force officers who had greeted all the divers, and who would know if the boys had lived or died.

The air force officer approached Harris and said, "Four out of four, doc."

Harris tried to process what he had just heard: Four out of four of the boys had died. He had prepared for this, he had expected it he had warned of it. But hearing it was gutting.

The air force officer, upon seeing Harris' reaction, immediately clarified: "All four are alive!"

. . .

THANKS TO THE COURAGE, resourcefulness, collaboration, and humanity of Harris and the divers, and thanks to the unprecedented global rescue mission, four out of four boys lived on that first day. And on the second day, four out of four boys lived. On the third day, four out of four boys and the coach lived.

On that final day, as Harris remembers it, after they realized that they had somehow cheated certain death, "everyone was standing around with smiles. No one had found the words to describe what happened." Someone produced a bottle of Jack Daniels. There were no glasses, but someone found a pack of tiny paper cups that nurses use to dispense pills. They poured whiskey in those cups with giant grins on their faces. "We were all so exhausted," says Harris. "Goofy and happy."

At the time he thought, "We're really going to party tonight." Then he had one beer and passed out.

6

The Edge of
Boundaries

George Kourounis lit himself on fire and lowered himself into the boiling lava of the "Doorway to Hell," something no human had ever done. Mariah Wilson studied elephants in the Congo to navigate the strange world of "poop trees." Lonnie Schorer crossed the boundary of the Iron Curtain during the peak of the Cold War . . . on a secret mission for her country.

These stories have different settings, mission objectives, and even stakes—some are life-and-death, some whimsical. But they're all, at heart, about exploring the edge of boundaries, which can be internal or external. Nations have boundaries. Earth's outer crust is a boundary. Rules and laws can act as boundaries, which is why Carl Sagan wrote a letter to crack the boundary of a cruel, senseless, and long outdated glass ceiling.

Boundaries, at times, can hurt those on both sides. Explorers can cross these boundaries to make surprising connections.

THE DOORWAY TO HELL

George Kourounis

GEORGE KOUROUNIS WANTED to go to hell. Or, more precisely, he wanted to touch the "Doorway to Hell," the nickname for Darvaza, a flaming gas crater in Turkmenistan, which has been burning for more than forty years. It looked like suicide. No one had ever dared to go inside the crater.

Kourounis didn't have a death wish. "But I love these extremes of nature," he says. "I love it so much." By 2010, he had a reputation as a daredevil who hurled himself into disasters like earthquakes and hurricanes—often so he could share a story in the name of education. "I feel like I have an obligation to share what I do to get kids interested in science and nature," says Kourounis. "To show the craziest shit imaginable. That's what kids love."

He showed the craziest shit imaginable on his TV show *Angry Planet,* and in 2012 he pitched the Doorway to Hell idea to National Geographic, also for a TV show. Even the show's name was ominous: *Die Trying.*

And there was another reason Kourounis was willing to die trying—on top of the stunt value and the spectacle and even the educational content: Kourounis had a hunch that the methane burning in the crater could be important. It had implications for space exploration. Darvaza happened to be a hot, methane-rich environment, and he knew that planets outside our solar system had hot, methane-rich environments. Was this environment habitable? "If I could find examples of bacteria living at the bottom of the crater," says Kourounis, "that could give us hints and clues of where we could look for signs of alien life."

So, with the support of National Geographic, the U.S. Embassy, and a crew that tirelessly worked to avoid getting him killed, Kourounis set out for hell.

. . .

BUT BEFORE THE FIRE came the paperwork. And the paperwork was daunting. One unsexy but critical step in exploration that's usually omitted from the story is that even getting *permission* can be challenging, especially in Turkmenistan. His team spent more than a year wrangling with authorities. "Turkmenistan is an extremely oppressive dictatorship, with some of the worst human rights violations on the planet," says Kourounis. "One former leader erected a giant statue of gold of himself that always faced the sun." (This same leader changed the names of the days of the week to those of his family members.)

Meanwhile, Kourounis trained for descending into the flames as safely as possible, "safely" being a relative term. "We have this joke: hashtag safety third," he says with a laugh. "First is look good, second is get the shot, third is safety."

Kourounis planned to descend into the burning crater using an elaborate system of ropes that would stretch across the opening, so he practiced this over a river gorge in Ontario. His team hauled him up and down. While dangling on the ropes he wore a self-contained breathing apparatus and fire-resistant suit, just as he would in Darvaza. It was hot and hard to breathe, but it had to be done. They cleverly designed the rope system so that even if Kourounis fell unconscious, his team could still lift him up to safety. Assuming he wasn't charred to a crisp.

But practicing over a river is one thing, and descending into the flaming jaws of hell is something else. Kourounis realized he needed to set himself on fire. That was the only way he wouldn't panic during the real thing. "It's okay to be afraid, but panic will get you killed," says Kourounis. "And one of the things that causes panic is fire."

So Kourounis hired stunt coordinators who normally worked on Hollywood films, and he asked them to blast him with flames. Even though he wore a fire-resistant suit, the risks were real, and so was the fear.

The stunt coordinators shot Kourounis with fire as he walked toward them and into the inferno, feeling the flames envelop his body. The heat ate through the fire-resistant gel that coated his face. His back began to burn. Only millimeters of protection kept him from death, and those millimeters began to corrode and vanish. His eyebrow caught on fire. Soon that would be his eyeball.

The fire burned through the first layer of his suit. Soon his skin would be at risk, but he kept walking into the flames. "I had no choice. Keep walking forward," he says. "The number-one rule is to keep walking forward." The moment he felt the fire penetrate his suit, he dropped to the ground, and his team—prepared for this—snuffed the flames with a fire extinguisher.

He was hot and exhausted and a little bit burnt, but he was ready. Time for the inferno.

. . .

THE MISSION WAS almost scuttled at the last minute. It's always the little things that go wrong. Kourounis would be wearing air tanks on his back as he descended into the crater, but you're not allowed to fly in a plane with pressurized tanks, so the team planned to fill them in Turkmenistan. But they discovered to their horror that the fittings on the North American tanks didn't match the local settings, which jeopardized the entire operation. Luckily, someone from the U.S. Embassy figured out a way to MacGyver a conversion. As Kourounis says, "You take air for granted until you don't have access to it."

Finally, years after Kourounis had first had the idea, they made the four-hour drive to a remote stretch of land speckled with sand dunes. There was nothing to see for miles, and then, with no warning, appeared an almost perfectly circular hole with a diameter of 220 feet. It looked like a volcano but it was not—it was a burning pit of methane gas.

Kourounis walked up to confront this burning crater he had obsessed over for years—his white whale. He had studied every single photograph and video anyone had ever taken of Darvaza. No one knew it like he did; he was the world's foremost expert. He had done everything he could do to prepare. And as he finally stepped up to the edge, armed with the reassurance of his training, his brain was seized by one clear thought.

I can't do this.

None of the photos did the crater justice, nor did the videos. Even though Kourounis first viewed the crater in the relative calm of daylight, the flames and the heat eclipsed his wildest fantasies and fears. It was a pit full of fire. He had known that in advance, but he wasn't prepared for the wind that blew across the crater and smacked him in the face. It felt like he had cranked up the oven to five hundred degrees and opened the door and stuck his head inside. Then there was the sound. The crater hissed like a jet engine.

Kourounis took a deep breath.

Okay. He realized this would be a hell of a lot harder than he had imagined, but he thought about an aphorism: How do you eat an elephant? One bite at a time.

So Kourounis and the team set up camp. He spent several days studying the crater. "If you're intimidated or afraid of something," he says, "the best way to get over it is to learn about it." The team of engineers took measurements. They fine-tuned their calculations. They set up and tested the rope system.

They thought about precisely how and where Kourounis could descend into the crater. They realized—happily—that the safest place to descend was actually at the very center of the crater, as that had the least amount of heat. It didn't hurt that going down the very center of the pit of flames made for a good photograph and good TV.

On the eve of the big day, as a trial, Kourounis clipped himself onto the ropes. He did some last-minute check-ins with his crew. One thing he insisted on was that anyone on his team, at any moment, for any reason—even the most junior member—had the authority to abort the mission, even if he personally objected. There were two reasons for this. The first is obvious: that it was possible that Kourounis could be knocked unconscious or unable to give clear directions, so he empowered his crew to prioritize safety. (The "hashtag safety third" joke, ultimately, truly was a joke.)

The second reason is more subtle: Kourounis was all too aware of summit fever. "You're so close. And it's right there, it's right fucking there," says Kourounis. "You want to keep going but it will cost you your life." Kourounis didn't want to succumb to summit fever, which was why he let anyone outrank him when it came to safety.

Now that he was clipped onto the ropes, he did a "flyover test" by traversing from one side of the crater to the other, hovering over the flames. This helped him ease into it.

The next day, he was ready to descend into hell. Kourounis consulted with his checklist. He wiggled into the flame-resistant suit. He strapped on his air tanks. He affixed not one but two GoPro cameras—one facing out to see what he could see and one inside the mask, pointed at his face. The interior camera blotted out his left eye, meaning he was half blind. (No one said TV was easy.)

They attempted their descent at night, when the flames illuminated the entire sky like a searchlight. Moths, insects, and flocks of birds converged on these eerie flames. It was haunting and terrifying and beautiful.

Kourounis grabbed the rope, put all of his weight on it, and took a few deep breaths. A system of pulleys lowered him. There wasn't much to do at this point. He felt like a piece of laundry drying in the sun.

Before he knew it, he looked up at his teammates on the edge of the crater, and they were small and getting smaller. Then his feet touched the ground. And it hit him that he was standing on a place that no human had ever stood before.

But there was little time for reflection. Kourounis had work to do and the clock was ticking; the tanks only provided seventeen minutes of air, and in that time he dug for as many methane-rich rocks as possible. (He also, naturally, made time for a quick photo with The Explorers Club's flag number 150.)

All around him flames shot upward from holes in the ground. He checked the field thermometer he had plunged into the ground—over seven hundred degrees Fahrenheit. Kourounis walked as close as possible to the primary flame. He gathered more samples. Soon an alarm went off, signaling that his oxygen was low. He knew it was time, as he puts it, to "GTFO."

Kourounis signaled his team. They pulled him up. High fives all around. Then he immediately handed the precious goods—soil and rock samples—to a scientist on his team, who began the analysis on the spot. Later DNA analysis would show that, yes, amazingly, there were thermophillic microorganisms thriving in this hot cauldron. "We believe that some of them are using that methane gas to metabolize as food, and not using photosynthesis," says Kourounis. So, if life could exist in this inferno, it could exist in the same climate on distant planets.

This was an important scientific discovery. And he knew that kids would be inspired by this crazy shit, and perhaps one would be so inspired they'd grow up to be a scientist. But he also, at heart, knew he had pulled off something outrageous and special. "Twelve people stood on the surface of the moon," says Kourounis. "Only one person has been to hell and back."

THE NORTH KOREA TRAVEL GUIDE

Arnie Weissmann

ARNIE WEISSMANN WANTED more than just a tour. He loved to travel, but he wanted to do it on his own terms, without guidance, free to wander and explore other cultures. In the 1980s he quit his job and began an open-ended trip around the world, bouncing from country to country in Africa and Asia.

To sort out his logistics, Weissmann occasionally asked travel agents for some basic information. (This was decades before the public internet.) They kept trying to sell him tours. But Weissmann didn't want to go on a tour—he just wanted basic facts so he could do his own thing. Eventually, he found a well-traveled agent who helped him get started, and the two of them created a subscription service for travel agents containing information about every country in the world. That service, Weissmann Travel Reports, still exists today as Travel42.

Weissmann could visit or find correspondents for most countries, but there was one tricky nation that he didn't know how to crack: North Korea. He wanted a real glimpse inside the country itself, but at the time, almost no American civilians were allowed access. Still, Weissmann was determined. He enjoyed going off the beaten path, and as he says now, "There was no place that was further off the beaten path." For perspective, more Americans summit Everest every year than visit North Korea.

In 1991, at a London trade show, Weissmann met the rare tour operator who said he could book a trip into North Korea. They chatted a bit, and then the agent shook his head.

"Look, you're a journalist," the agent said. "You'll never get a visa."

Weissmann thought that was the end. Then the agent added, "So, what do you want to be?"

"I'll be a teacher," Weissmann said.

"Every journalist says 'teacher,'" the agent said. "You'll be an accountant."

So Weissmann, who knew nothing about bookkeeping or debits or credits, told everyone he knew that he was an accountant, in case their intelligence agency had their eyes on him. Weissmann was one of only six Americans to receive a visa that year.

He and his then-wife flew to Beijing and then took a twenty-three-hour train ride to Pyongyang. And he wrote a detailed seventy-seven-page letter to a friend about the trip, which he sent the day after he left North Korea.

> Dear Ed,
>
> We arrived today in Pyongyang, North Korea (D.P.R.K.) without much fanfare. . . .
>
> We arrived on a train from Beijing. Everyone's first question was, "Who has invited you?" In fact, that's the 2nd question. The first is, "From what country do you come?" When we say "United States" they are literally shocked out of their smile. For all the literature we have come across, the bitterness of the Korean War has kept a very strong feeling about the U.S. alive.
>
> We were the only non-Koreans on the train. All the other passengers had a pin with the likeness of Kim Il Sung, the Great Leader, on their lapel. The door to the next car up was locked. Much to our dismay—we were cut off from the dining car, and had brought no food for the 23-hour trip.
>
> Still, the trip was not without its pleasures. We went to sleep to the flat plains east of Beijing and awoke in a beautiful, mountainous area. . . .
>
> After crossing into Korea, our cars were uncoupled. Korean immigration collected our passports, then returned.

At the border, the North Korean immigration officer collected the r passports and, seeing they were from the United States, did an almost comic double take. He left and returned with an armed soldier. The immigration officer said, "Arrest."

"What?" said Weissmann.

"Arrest," said the official.

"Why?"

The officer's English wasn't very good. "Okay to leave train," he stammered. "Have a rest."

Weissmann was permitted to leave the train station and have a rest, without arrest.

> The station building had a huge mural of the Great Leader and his son, the Dear Leader, Kim Jong Il, painted in brilliant reds, yellows and oranges, on a panorama with the setting sun behind them. It simply glowed, like a cross between Peter Max and Maxfield Parrish. Visible from the platform was a giant statue of the Great Leader—perhaps 3 stories high. . . .
>
> Rice was being harvested and bundled along the tracks. . . . This Sunday is a huge national holiday, honoring the harvest. All in all, the scenery was lovely. We were met at the station by a young man named Kim, who is to be our round-the-clock guide for the next week.

As much as Weissmann blanched at the idea of a tour guide, he knew this was the only way he could see any of Pyongyang. (Kim hadn't been born with the name Kim; his family had changed it to Kim, after the Great Leader.)

> In the lobby of the hotel was another large mural of the Great Leader and Dear Leader, walking along a bridge with a flock of pigeons at their feet. Kim came up to our room with us to discuss our itinerary. He is a very sincere young man of about 25. He believes very strongly in the good and unique position North Korea

holds. He asked us several times to try hard to understand the Korean way, and how good it is. He said that everyone is very happy here, thanks to the accomplishments of the Great Leader. The Great Leader, he said, is very talented, and it is important that someone can continue on after him, so it is very good that they have trained his son to do this. . . .

The hotel has a bookstore, and many of the books are homages to the Great Leader and Dear Leader. All the books—even guide books—tell of the accomplishments and the Korean philosophy of socialism. Our guide Kim explained that socialism in Eastern Europe had become corrupted, and that is why it had failed.

Weissmann didn't speak Korean, so he was heavily reliant upon Kim to show him around. He asked to see and meet as many people as possible and was amused at how Kim—who was almost certainly an agent of the North Korean government—filtered the translations. For example, Kim took Weissmann to a Buddhist temple to show that North Korea was tolerant of many religions. When Weissmann met the head monk, he asked the monk (through Kim) how he could reconcile being a religious leader in a country that's officially atheist and seemed to worship a secular leader.

There was considerable back and forth between Kim and the monk. After this long conversation, Kim simply said to Weissmann, "He sees no conflict."

There were two channels operating on the television—one was of a man making a speech, the other showed various aspects of the society's progress, interspersed with historical footage of the Great Leader. . . .

Our experience here has been very much colored by our guide, Kim; I was quite far off in guessing his age—he's 33, not 25. He joined the People's Army in 1973 (the exact date is tattooed on his forearm. The tattoo is the shape of a bullet. Just above that is the gold star, the symbol of the Worker's Party, which shares a shoulder with Communism's party.)

What Weissmann wanted most of all was to meet more of the North Korean people, but somehow, that never seemed to happen. Kim would grandly offer to take Weissmann to a popular restaurant that was packed with locals, but then he took him to a private room. Weissmann asked to see a movie theater; Kim wouldn't take him. Supposedly, the city had bowling alleys, but Kim wouldn't take him.

Finally, near the end of Weissmann's trip, Kim offered him something real.

"You've been asking to see how North Koreans live?" Kim asked.

"Yes."

"Let me take you to my apartment."

Once Kim brought him into his private apartment, Weissmann says, "he became a completely different person." Less gushing about the North Korean government. More authenticity, even vulnerability. Maybe Kim felt it was safer to speak here. Or maybe he just felt more comfortable. Whatever it was, Weissmann sensed he was now getting the real Kim.

Kim served Weissmann some cookies and apologized for "their poor quality," and then the two men sat on his couch. Kim opened a scrapbook and showed Weissmann pictures of his family and a poem he wrote the night his daughter was born. They broke bread, and they bonded.

"In just that one step through the door, his humanity was revealed," Weissmann says now. He realized that the North Koreans had a side that they couldn't show in public, "because I'm perceived to be the enemy of the state," but at heart, beneath that façade, was a shared humanity. It reinforced Weissmann's convictions to keep his opinions about a nation's government separate from its people. "I've been to 125 countries, and I've yet to be anywhere where I have not made a strong connection with someone," says Weissmann. "Regardless of differences in religion or culture, at the end of the day, everyone cares about their family. Everyone wants to eat."

Weissmann thinks about how astronauts often speak of the "overview effect," where when you look at Earth from space, you don't see borders or nations or politics—you just see the gorgeous blue marble that's shared by all. Weissmann tries to carry that mindset down here, on the planet's surface. "We're all cousins, descended from the same female ancestor," he says. "It's striking that we can't see it."

YOUR EDGE, THEIR HOME

Mariah Wilson

EVERY YEAR, HUNDREDS (perhaps thousands) of forest elephants get poached and slaughtered. Environmental filmmaker Mariah Wilson wanted to expose this. In 2016, she planned an expedition to the wilderness of the Congo Basin, seeking elephant clearings that were truly at the edge of civilization. These clearings are rarely visited by humans—except for the poachers looking to slay elephants, and the eco-guards hoping to protect them. Wilson was likely the first woman to visit some of these clearings. And almost as soon as her expedition began, she realized why the world didn't know more about these forest elephants: "They're really hard to film."

Wilson kept a detailed log of her expedition, using the same kind of trusty field journal as Ernest Shackleton and Edmund Hillary and Jane Goodall before her: the Notes app on her iPhone.

NKI NATIONAL PARK, CAMEROON, 2016:

A) I almost got shot by an eco-guard after going off to do secret poo away from camp. They thought I was a poacher.

The edge of civilization, naturally, does not come equipped with toilets, so, early in the expedition, as the rest of the team—the filmmaking crew and the eco-guards—sat around the campfire, Wilson—not wanting to announce her activities, for obvious reasons—discreetly peeled away into the darkness for what she calls her "secret poo." While she was taking care of her business, suddenly everything became quiet and she heard guns cocking.

The guards called out in French, "*C'est qui? C'est qui?*" (Who is it? Who is it?)

Wilson's first thought: The guards had spotted an elephant poacher. *Yes!* This was precisely what she was trying to film. This would make for a hell of a scene for the documentary. She was ecstatic. She hoped her camera guy was already filming.

Then she realized, *Oh my god. I'm the poacher. They think I'm the poacher.*

Wilson emerged with her hands up. "Don't shoot! It's me!"

B) Our tent was covered in buzzing, fucking flies (literally fucking) and it made me have a mini-nervous breakdown one night, because it sounded like I was in a horror film soundtrack.

C) We drank muddy jungle river water with iodine tablets and crossed our fingers.

This is iodine water experiment, day 1.

D) We broke our bodies to hike 12 miles into the densest jungle imaginable to see basically no animals at all because poachers are the worst.

E) Today, I said the words "I've never been covered in so much fly jizz" and "no sex flies allowed in our tent!" as the tiny maggots rained down upon me through the tent mesh.

F) Our badass eco-guard lady Sidonie was crouching in the bush with her gun in hand, ready to take on poachers. Her "office hours" are insane.

G) Tonight I bathed in the river with blinking fireflies all around. It was lovely and enchanting.

H) Ok dammit, the sex flies have now laid maggots into our equipment bags. Ew.

I) Just saw a large abandoned poachers camp right by an animal clearing. So sad.

The eco-guards destroyed it, at least.

J) Still zero animals have been filmed.

This is one of the trickiest parts of filming animals in the wild—actually finding the animals, especially forest elephants. Even though the elephants are gigantic and loud while rumbling through the forest, they somehow have the sneaky ability to stand right next to you in the trees without you realizing it. Wilson respected the fact that these elephants would make their own clearings, crashing down trees to create a comfortable habitat. As she sees it, "They're kind of like the architects of the forest environment in a really cool way."

K) Actually, ok fine, we did see a duck. And some hornbills.

L) I cannot wait to eat literally anything aside from bony fish and rice.

M) Time for a maggot cleaning sesh! Still no animals. Lots of prints in the mud.

N) The flies are back. God, how I hate them so.

O) A bullet ant bit me near my butt. Felt like a damn bee sting!! I'm covered in bites, scratches, blisters and bruises, but that one is by far the hurtiest (so far . . .)

P) Iodine water experiment, day 5: man down! Man down!

Q) Hiked to a new clearing. Saw a sitatunga. That was neat.

R) Iodine water experiment, day 6: man back up again, soldiering on.

S) Got so sick of bony fish rice that I added peanuts and sriracha to rice. Now it's surprisingly tasty.

T) Tonight, a firefly tried to mate with my headlamp as I bathed in the river . . . it was kinda magical.

U) We had a beautiful scorpion on our tent this morning! Then the eco-guards killed him with a machete. Also, I got stung by a bee yesterday. Wheee.

V) This forest doesn't want to let you go. It wants to eat you alive. Its prickly vines hold on to your hair and feet, its insects slowly eat you, and its thorny vines keep bits of your flesh and blood behind. These are my thoughts as we hike seven miles of unforgivable terrain today.

W) Ughhh. We HEARD the elephants tonight. Two of the eco-guards briefly saw them on patrol. I think they are torturing us by not allowing us to film them.

X) This was our last day to film. Zero elephants captured on camera! Devastating.

Good material with eco-guards, though.

Y) We saw a cephalophe on the drive out. It's like a tropical antelope. Also, that's a fun word to say. Cephalophe!

Z) The first food we were offered upon our return to quasi civilization at a Cameroonian border town? A cephalophe stew, of course. Sigh. That somehow seems an appropriate place to end.

Despite cheerfully enduring all the bee stings and silent poos, Wilson failed to spot any elephants or poachers in the entire expedition. That happens. But she didn't give up; instead, she made a second effort the next year.

BATÉKÉ PLATEAU, REPUBLIC OF CONGO—2017

Here we go again.

A) We came all this way to see . . . pigeons eating shit. I could have seen that in New York. This is all we filmed today on the clearings. Ugh.

B) To be fair, they are eating elephant shit. So that's a bit different. Also a hopeful sign for elephants being nearby. . . .

C) I was told today by our biologist Clement that I am the first woman ever at these particular clearings, and we are the first team to film in them!

D) Day 3. Still no elephants. We've brought the infrared camera this time, so will sleep out in the clearings (on a tall platform/mirador) so we can try to film at nighttime.

E) Turns out, it's hard to pick a wedgie in waders.

F) In this platform/mirador, we are sleeping like the sardines in the tin we are eating. It's like sleeping bag tetris to fit four humans up here.

G) Saw a poached elephant carcass today. A young male, whose tusks had been cut off. He was rotting back into the forest floor. The smell was overpowering, and the sight was hard on the soul.

H) Still no elephants filmed. It breaks my heart to see how timid they are to enter their own home.

I) TONIGHT! It HAPPENED!! Elephants!!! Mothertrucking elephants!! We woke up to the sound of them, and turned on the infrared camera. Seeing them splash around in the water is like magic. They were drinking and dunking amongst the blinking fireflies in the clearing that they created. We even saw a mother breastfeeding her baby. I'm so happy right now.

J) As we drove out of the forest today and back toward civilization, we saw poachers going the other way on motorbikes. Maddening.

Wilson, in the end, did find her elephants. They were worth the wait. And despite having done all her research before entering the Congo Basin, she felt a new appreciation for how elephants protect and nourish the larger ecosystem. "The forest elephants help to plant the forest," says Wilson. They stomp through the vegetation, they eat seeds, and then their gut helps germinate the seeds. This is why when Wilson gives presentations to elementary students, to drive home this point, she has a slide that simply says, "Poop trees."

The elephants create their own clearings, and these clearings benefit the forest. "Without the clearings and the pathways, other animals would struggle to get around as much," says Wilson. "Birds of prey wouldn't have this nice open area to hunt in." The elephants are even good at dispersing hardwood trees, which serve as carbon sinks that help fight climate change. Studies have shown that, without the elephants, more carbon would be in the atmosphere.

On her trips to the Congo Basin, Wilson discovered that the "edge"

for some is home for others. "I live in New York City. I'm a city creature for most of the time," she says. For most of the expedition she
was out of her comfort zone and dealing with bruises, iodine water,
and bee stings. "But his place where I struggle to find any kind of
comfort is a place where the elephants and creatures are comfortable.
This is their happy place. This is where they thrive."

Thriving, of course, is getting harder and harder for these elephants. "Those that are still around are nervous about coming out
into the clearings when they smell humans," says Wilson. "They seem
to understand that humans are trouble, for the most part. And they
aren't wrong."

THE VOLCANO LOVE FILTER

Ulla Lohmann

ULLA LOHMANN ALWAYS thought she had to choose: Follow her dreams of exploration or have a romantic partner.

For her, that choice was easy. It had been her whole life.

When Ulla was an eight-year-old girl, her father took her to Pompeii and showed her the ruins of the volcano. She was hooked. "From this point on," she says, "I read everything about volcanos I could, and I dreamed of going into a volcano and to the center of the earth," like in the Jules Verne book.

She studied volcanos, visited volcanos, fantasized about volcanos. She professionally photographed volcanos. She literally devoted her life to volcanos. She taught herself to be a rock climber, mainly so that she could descend into craters. "When I was fifteen," she says, "other girls were interested in boys. I was interested in earth science."

Ulla knew that spending so much time and energy on volcanos would naturally mean sacrifices to her personal life. Especially with dating. She'd be away on expeditions for weeks or months at a time, and in some years, she'd barely be at her home near Munich.

So Ulla developed a novel strategy to combine dating and exploration: She'd use volcanos as a test for her partners.

If a suitor wanted to get serious, he'd first need to pass her test in base camp. "It's actually quite a good test," Ulla says. "When you're both sharing a tent for weeks or hanging on a rope, you have to pull the same way if you want to go somewhere."

Ulla notes that for fellow members of The Explorers Club, it's totally normal to enjoy a muddy and freezing expedition for a month, with no showers or hot food. "We're happy being cold and miserable," she says. Most of humanity, however, is not wired that way. So Ulla liked to find this out about a potential partner sooner rather than later. "One time my underwear got moldy it was so wet from four weeks in base camp," she says. "Somebody who comes from the 'normal world' would have to live with this."

So, for years, Ulla asked romantic partners to join her at volcanos. Could they handle eating dried noodles for a month?

None of them could.

"I test every partner with the volcanos," she says. "All of them fail."

In 2011, she met a fellow rock climber named Basti Hofmann, who was also an alpinist and a geologist. They began dating. At the time, Ulla was still nursing her lifelong dream of descending to the bottom of a volcano; maybe Basti could hang? They had been dating for a while, she liked him, and now it was time for the test.

Ulla and Basti traveled to the island of Ambrym, in Vanuatu. The weather was rainy and gloomy, and base camp was rough. No toilets, no showers, no heat, and not much to eat besides noodles.

"No showers? Great," Basti said. "That's easier."

Basti didn't mind eating noodles for every meal. "It's okay,' he said. "I'll just put some artificial flavor on it. It's fine."

Ulla found herself getting antsy about the bad weather, which jeopardized her descent into the volcano. Basti was a reassuring presence. They killed time and joked around together. Ulla had already liked Basti before the trip began—they'd been dating for many months—but this was the first time her feelings had grown stronger on a test instead of waning.

Finally, toward the end of the trip, the weather cleared enough for Ulla and Basti to scale and descend the volcano. She tried to avoid her usual nagging thoughts, like *This is where he's going to screw it up*. It helped that Basti was a skilled climber, and the two of them nimbly scampered up the side of the volcano.

The view from the top looked otherworldly. From the peak they could see another volcano in the distance, emitting puffs of smoke, as well as sweeping views of the ocean. As Ulla remembers the view, "It looked like the origin of the earth." They walked along the rim of the volcano, looking for a good spot to descend with their ropes. The sunrise was spectacular. Ulla felt the wind on her face—crisp, cool, and almost like a dream.

Soon they secured their ropes and began their descent. Now they were wearing gas masks; this was an active volcano, after all. Basti skilfully darted lower, and Ulla had to grudgingly admit that she was impressed. In no time, they had descended two hundred meters to the first terrace.

To Ulla, all of this was surreal. In some ways it felt like paradise, but also, they were headed toward molten lava, which, as Ulla says, "feels like you're approaching hell." (She laughs, clarifying that, to her, this kind of hell is heaven.)

Ulla and Basti walked along the terrace, staring down at the lake of lava. This was the closest she had been, and it was everything she could have hoped for. Those stirrings from childhood had never quieted, and now that she stood inside the volcano, just above the lava, she felt almost overwhelmed.

"Basti, give me the backpack," she said. "I want to take some pictures."

But Basti didn't give her the backpack.

"Basti, the backpack!"

Clearly, Basti's mind was somewhere else. He didn't reach for the backpack. Instead, he grabbed her hand. Then he removed his gas mask and motioned for her to do the same. Basti just looked at her.

"How cool is this?" Ulla said, motioning to the lava and the sides of the volcano.

Basti held her eye contact. He didn't respond to her question. Instead, he had one of his own.

He asked her, "Do you want to marry me?"

Now, more than a decade later, Ulla doesn't remember the exact words of her response, but she thinks it was something like "Why not?"

Basti passed the test. Ulla and Basti married. They became romantic partners and expedition partners and partners in every conceivable sense. Ulla had never wanted to get married or have kids, because she'd assumed this would preclude her exploration; now she'd found someone who could truly speak her language.

"On expeditions, sometimes it's very lonely," Ulla says. "All of those long nights in base camp. Or all of the times waiting in weird airports." With Basti she shared an almost unspoken language of exploration, scaling up and down volcanos together.

They found a compromise for their honeymoon: Basti was an alpinist and wanted to go somewhere as high as possible, and Ulla (obviously) wanted to go to a volcano. So they traveled to Chile and went to the world's highest active volcano, Ojos del Salado. They spent four weeks acclimatizing to the 22,500-foot elevation. In the freezing cold they slept in separate sleeping bags, side by side, and every morning there was a layer of frost between them, so they cut a little hole in the frost, and they each said, "Hello, darling." Ulla literally couldn't imagine anything more romantic.

Ulla had never wanted to have kids before. How do you go exploring with a baby? Then she and Basti had a child, Manuk, named after

a volcano. When Manuk was five days old, he joined Ulla on an expedition. When he was ten days old, he joined her rock climbing. Manuk visited his first volcano when he was six months old. Ulla took him with her to a photo job in Indonesia; he was strapped to her back as she snapped pictures for the client. By the age of five, Manuk has been to fifty countries and had explored ten erupting volcanos.

Before all of that, on the morning of that engagement, Ulla snapped a photo of the scene and sent it to all their friends and family—her letter from the edge. She jokes that, of course, she had to say yes. It was that or the molten lava. She laughs again and says, "Hottest proposal ever."

CRACKING THE GLASS CEILING

Carl Sagan

WOMEN HAVE BEEN EXPLORING for centuries. Explorers like Amelia Earhart, Mary Jobe Akeley, Gertrude Bell, Bessie Coleman, Ethel Tweedie, and Ada Blackjack all journeyed to the edge . . . yet were denied membership to The Explorers Club. Astonishingly, as late as 1981, the Club still refused to admit women to its ranks. This was a full sixty-two years after women received the right to vote in the United States.

So Carl Sagan wrote a letter.

He wrote it to all his fellow Club members, urging them to remove this outdated boundary.

When our organization was formed in 1905 [1904], men were preventing women from voting and from pursuing many occupations for which they are clearly suited. In the popular mind, exploration was not what women did. Even so, women had played a significant but unheralded role in the history of exploration—in Africa in the Nineteenth Century, for example. Similarly, Lewis and Clark were covered with glory, but Sacajewea, who guided them every inch of the way, was strangely forgotten. All institutions reflect the prejudices and conventions of their times, and when it was founded The Explorers Club necessarily reflected the attitudes of 1905 [1904].

Traditions are important. They provide continuity with our past. But it is up to us to decide which traditions are essential to The Explorers Club and which are accidents of the epoch in which it was institutionalized. Times have changed since 1905. It is very clear that a foolish rigidity can destroy otherwise worthwhile institutions; they are then replaced by other organizations more in tune with the times. . . .

Today women are making extraordinary contributions in areas of fundamental interest to our organization. There are several women astronauts. The earliest footprints—3.6 million years old—made by a member of the human family have been found in a volcanic ash flow in Tanzania by Mary Leakey. Trailblazing studies of the behavior of primates in the wild have been performed by dozens of young women, each spending years with a different primate species. Jane Goodall's studies of the chimpanzee are the best known of the investigations which illuminate human origins. The undersea depth record is held by Sylvia Earle. The solar wind was first measured *in situ* by Marcia Neugebauer, using the Mariner 2 spacecraft. The first active volcanos beyond the Earth were discovered on the Jovian moon Io by Linda Morabito, using the Voyager 1 spacecraft. These examples of modern exploration and discovery could be multiplied a hundredfold. They are of true historical significance. If membership in The Explorers Club is restricted to men, the loss will be ours; we will only be depriving ourselves.

Soon after Sagan wrote this letter, the Club formally welcomed women to its ranks.

LIFE BEHIND THE IRON CURTAIN

Lonnie Schorer

IN THE SHADOW OF World War II, in the 1950s and '60s, Lonnie Schorer had a typical American upbringing. Her family was patriotic. Her mother had been a wartime aircraft spotter, and the men had all fought in the war. An uncle was one of the "Monuments Men" who concealed art masterpieces from the Nazis, later inspiring the book *Saving Italy* and the George Clooney film *The Monuments Men*.

So perhaps international service, intrigue, and diplomacy were in Lonnie's blood. In high school she served as an American Field Service exchange student in Istanbul. At Connecticut College, she was voted president of the International Relations Club. She was a representative to the Collegiate Council of the United Nations in New York, where she was one of five delegates invited to dine with Eleanor Roosevelt.

Her college major was originally French. Then, in 1962, John F. Kennedy gave his speech on the Cuban missile crisis. Lonnie's patriotism surged as she realized the growing conflict with the Soviet Union was more important—even urgent—than she imagined. She immediately switched her major to Russian, becoming one of only two students in the program.

Lonnie's career path wasn't entirely open to her, as 1960s America expected her to be a housewife, teacher, secretary, nurse, or perhaps a sociologist. Then one day, the college dean asked to see her. "There's someone who would like to speak with you," the dean said. "From Washington, D.C. If you're willing."

She was.

For many decades the details of that meeting remained a secret. Only recently, she shared what she agreed to do that day on the Connecticut College campus.

The government official was from the CIA.

During countless interviews in D.C., they grilled her, put her through a battery of psychological tests, and then asked her to serve her country.

. . .

AFTER GRADUATION, Lonnie moved to D.C. and roomed with four college friends. They knew her as an analyst who worked for the air force. On weekends they invited her to join them at their summer cottage rental in Ocean City, Maryland. She always told them, twisting the truth for reasons of national security, that she couldn't go because she couldn't afford it. Lonnie loved the beach and would have happily joined her friends, but her weekends were devoted to the CIA's skydiving club. While participating in "the Company's" club, she tested chutes for performance.

Over forty years later, seeing her D.C. roommates for the first time since graduation, she was allowed to reveal the truth. "I couldn't join you at the beach. Didn't you hear all those thuds coming from my bedroom?" she asked them with a laugh. "I was jumping off my bed to practice landing a parachute behind enemy lines."

Her work life complicated much of her everyday life, including dating. One of her neighbors growing up was a guy named Dave. His Dartmouth roommate went to a D.C. Christmas party thrown by Lonnie and her roommates, and after the party, the friend wrote to Dave saying, "Your old neighbor Lonnie has some really cute roommates."

Before long, Dave swung by the Eighteenth Street house to check out Lonnie's roommates. But only Lonnie was home, with her broken leg in a cast, hobbling around after a ski accident.

"He felt sorry for me and asked me out to dinner," Lonnie says now.

That dinner led to another, and soon Lonnie and Dave began eating. It became increasingly difficult to keep her place of employment a secret, but she couldn't let it slip. Dave said he also worked for the air force, and she was nervous he might invite her to lunch at the base. This was tricky because Lonnie was never *actually* at the air force base—she worked elsewhere, for the Company. So she told him she was overworked and never took time for lunch.

Eventually, the truth came out. But the entirety of the truth didn't just surprise Dave; it also floored Lonnie. It was true that he was her neighbor growing up. It was true that he had been the neighborhood newspaper boy and was a supportive boyfriend. And it was true that Dave served in the U.S. Air Force. But there was something he hadn't told her.

It seems, Lonnie and Dave both worked at the same place.

· · ·

THE CIA HAD RECRUITED Dave in the same manner as Lonnie. They became the real-life Mr. and Mrs. Smith. Suddenly, Lonnie found a true partner she could confide in, and Dave found the same. They got married and became partners in all phases of their life. Whenever she and Dave told their families they were headed off on a vacation, grandparents assumed they were sunbathing at the beach. In reality, they were traveling to "the farm" to learn and practice tradecraft.

They gained facility with weapons. They learned how to ram vehicles through barriers. They practiced high-speed car exercises, including spinning a car in the rain. "You should know how to do that," Lonnie says. "If you're by yourself, and you're coming to hostile enemy forces, and they're either going to detain you, kidnap, or shoot you, you drive up to them slowly, and then [she makes a car zooming no se] you throw the car in reverse, you step on the accelerator, spin the car, and get out of there."

They worked individually. They worked together. The CIA spotted the potential of this duo and assigned them as one of the nation's three first husband-and-wife overseas teams. "They tapped our abilities," Lonnie says. "Separately and together."

After they married, the CIA deployed them for a three-and-a-half-year mission in Bangkok. (What they did there, exactly, remains a mystery.) Later, Dave enrolled in language school to learn Russian, and Lonnie brushed up on hers. This was to prepare for their crucial new mission, an assignment their educations had prepared them for: They would go to the Soviet Union.

In the 1960s, Cold War tensions between the United States and the Soviet Union were precariously high. The United States had an official embassy in Moscow, but the consulate in Petrograd (renamed Leningrad in 1924, to be changed again in 1991 to Saint Petersburg) had closed in 1917 during the Russian Revolution, and it had been closed ever since.

As members of an advance party, it was part of Mr. and Mrs. Schorer's assignment to initiate some changes. Their mission was to establish an official U.S. consulate in Leningrad. Along with four other families, they were on the tip of the diplomatic spear. Part of their mission was to try to impact relations and the culture of the Cold War. "It was a kind of grassroots détente, an effort by the two governments to open more representation between the two countries," says Lonnie.

And they didn't travel alone. By now Lonnie and Dave had three children, ages three, two, and four months. The entire family would uproot and try to establish a sense of normalcy in this strange new world behind the Iron Curtain.

Before they left the United States, Lonnie and Dave stocked up on nonperishables and crammed them into boxes—jars of baby food, toothpaste, toilet paper, shaving cream, laundry detergent. The office had advised them to bring enough supplies for two years, as many of these simple household items were simply not available in the Soviet Union. Toilet paper in public restrooms consisted of cut-up squares of newspaper.

The family arrived to find the actual day-to-day conditions almost comically awful. To stock up on milk, they needed to drive ten hours round trip to the nearest grocery store in Finland. Without a freezer, they would keep milk on their outdoor balcony, where it would stay nearly frozen for the entire year.

There was no commissary, and sometimes no heat. No insulation. An old chandelier hung from the ceiling, and the walls were so thin that when the wind blew, the chandelier swung back and forth. The water that fed into the bathroom and kitchen sinks first piped through the radiators, meaning that it was always rusty. The water for the children's baths was crusty brown. In the apartment complex of six buildings, Lonnie and Dave owned the only car.

During this time, they were not allowed to receive mail, and their only contact with home was via an endless stream of letters to family and friends, chronicling life behind the Iron Curtain. These letters described their new home:

> It was quite an arrival with endless crates of canned goods and not a shelf in the place, no refrigerator, no hot water, no gas stove . . . 3 closets, but no poles or hooks for hanging anything, no showers, no cabinets, no towel racks, *stench from waste.*

Decades before email or texts, Lonnie sent countless postcards to her friends back in the United States. She made sure they were free of any operational details, because she knew the KGB read each one of them.

She carefully observed and chronicled the culture of Leningrad, even noting how the Soviet children were dazzled by her family's toys:

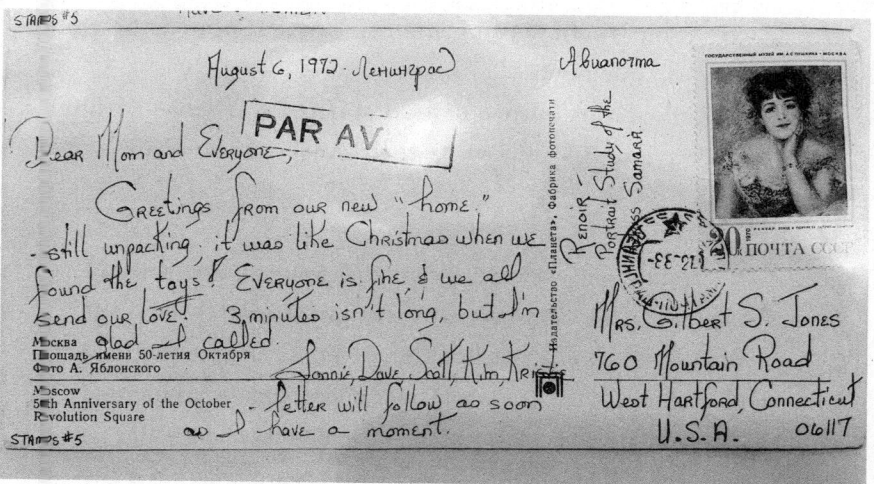

Three boys (11, 12, 14), Young Pioneers who came to the door collecting newspapers one day and ended up staying an hour and a half, returned each day to play with the toys. They long for an occasional wad of chewing gum (not a single chewing gum factory that we know of in the Soviet Union, but everyone knows about gum) and are usually still here during bathtime—astounded by the fact that we all bathe each day. They and others have told us that they bathe only on Sundays.—explains a lot.

Lonnie didn't just observe the culture of Leningrad; she actually influenced the underground economy. No one had storage materials such as paper bags, plastic bags, or screw-top jars. These were coveted. Lonnie had shipped over all the jars of baby food for her infant, and after she used each one, she rinsed it out and left it outside their apartment door. The jar would vanish before the next morning. She later learned there was a twenty-four-hour watch on their apartment door for the purpose of spotting baby jars and western magazines and newspapers. When her jars began appearing in the markets, she had a feeling of satisfaction in the knowledge that western capitalist products were penetrating Soviet society. They later learned that their reading material had supplied the underground with outside news.

Enduring all of this with a can-do spirit and a sense of humor, they were always uneasy, knowing their every movement was being scrutinized.

> An interesting episode which proves that watchful eyes perceive all happened not long ago when our Deputy Counsel General was suddenly called in to the local Soviet police department and handed a long list of U.S. Consulate traffic violations, committed by its 41 American employees, including families and US Marine Guards. The whole thing was humorously absurd, with never any mention of the Soviet cars which suddenly pull out in front of one forcing one to brake to an abrupt halt, or of the pedestrians who surge forward swallowing up one's car.

Soon, she realized, quite conclusively, that the KGB suspected she and Dave were more than normal diplomats. "They assume everyone in the state department is a spy," she says now.

And that could make life hell—even deadly—for her, her new friends, and her family.

. . .

THEY FELT THE PRESENCE of the KGB everywhere, including inside the walls of their home. Take Larissa. They had befriended Larissa, a young college student who lived in their apartment complex and liked to play with their children, because the toddlers had something wondrous that Larissa as an art major had never seen before—crayons!

One day, Larissa suddenly stopped coming by the apartment. "The KGB has gotten to her," Dave said to Lonnie in a whisper.

Each incident confirmed that their apartment was bugged. They knew it would be unwise to directly contact Larissa, who lived upstairs with her mother, so Lonnie baked a cake and asked Dave to take it upstairs. He knocked on the door, quickly thrusting the cake into Larissa's mother's hands, and said, "I'm sorry Larissa is sick."

The next day, Lonnie heard a knock on her door.

Larissa's mother.

Without a word, Larissa's mother handed Lonnie a cat.

"They wanted to say thank you," Lonnie says now. "They had nothing else to give us." This, to Lonnie, was tacit acknowledgment that after the KGB intervention, Larissa would no longer be able to be their friend, and they were offering their cat as an apology. Lonnie thanked Larissa's mother but insisted she couldn't possibly accept the cat.

Soon there were more mysterious disappearances. Another neighborhood woman, who worked as a bookbinder in a factory, loved Lonnie's children and frequently dropped by to play with them. Abruptly, she stopped visiting. One day she caught Lonnie's eye at the playground and shot her a look that clearly said, "Don't talk to me."

Lonnie and Dave soon realized that they couldn't speak to anybody without jeopardizing that person's safety. The KGB knew everything. Making a new Russian "friend" suggested one of two possible scenarios, both of them grim. In scenario one, the "friend" was truly a friend, and they would be in danger. In scenario two, the "friend" was a tendril of the KGB, and they'd have to report on everything you said and did. "We already knew not to say anything derogatory about anybody," says Lonnie. "You can't say, 'Oh, Joe drinks too much,' because that would be in Joe's file and used for blackmail."

Lonnie became accustomed to seeing her family occasionally appear in the newspapers. This started at the outdoor playground. The "playground" was a dusty plot of dirt. It had a broken seesaw, the empty metal framework of a slide, and chunks of glass littering the ground. On one of the officially declared cleanup days, Lonnie, Dave, and the children worked to clean the area, collecting trash and broken glass. They were the only family to do this, and it was covered in the local papers as a human-interest story.

But darker stories could also make the papers.

Early in the Leningrad assignment, at the ballet, she recognized the familiar notes of "Ode to Joy" from Ludwig van Beethoven's Ninth Symphony. A Soviet friend ("friend") corrected her, saying, "No, that's our composer Alexander Borodin's original work!"

"It's Beethoven!" Lonnie said, amused.

"No, it's Borodin!"

"Beethoven!"

Some weeks later, remembering the conversation, Lonnie bought a European album featuring "Ode to Joy"—with lyrics—while shopping at a department store in Helsinki.

Then one afternoon, when the kids were outside on the "playground" and she was having a rare quiet moment to herself, Lonnie heard the faint but unmistakable sounds of "Ode to Joy." The music was soft, but she was certain . . . and then she realized it was coming from inside the apartment, and she froze. Dave wasn't home. No one else was home.

Quietly, she crept through the apartment to follow the sound of the music to its source—but she saw nothing. Yet she could still hear the music, which now felt out of place and eerie.

She came to the living room wall, from which the music seemed to emanate. And she realized the inside wall between the living room and hallway was too wide for a normal wall and was likely harboring a room inside, a room where a Soviet tech was listening to the new record, thinking he was alone.

Lonnie and Dave already knew that nothing they said or did was secret or safe. They would later learn that when they checked their coats at the ballet or opera, the KGB inserted "spy dust" into the seams of their jackets, which was used to track them. Bugs had even been discovered inside shower heads. When returning from diplomatic receptions in the evening, they would find signs of intrusion:

cigarette butts in ashtrays (neither Lonnie nor Dave smoked) and all the children's Fisher Price toys and Lonnie's jewelry missing. But now the KGB was leaving proof that they controlled the family's space.

It was now clear that before her family moved in, the KGB had constructed a fake wall to hide a secret room. She became more sensitive to other sounds. Sometimes she could hear tech agents unspooling cable, which meant they were installing more listening devices. She knew the phone was bugged. Every day they lived there, their risk grew.

And finally that risk spilled into the open when, on a cold winter's day, Dave was apprehended and attacked. "David W. Schorer, the American vice consul in Leningrad, was roughed up by unidentified Russians in the streets of this Soviet city," began an AP story from January 20, 1974. "Details remained sketchy about the incident," the piece continued, noting, "The State Department declined to release any information."

To this day, whether for reasons that are personal, legal, or geopolitical, Lonnie demurs from sharing the full story of her and Dave's operation, but she says they left the Soviet Union thirty-six hours after Dave's apprehension. They packed quickly and abandoned almost everything they owned, bringing just one small suitcase stuffed with clothes for the children.

For Lonnie, the edge meant "not knowing what tomorrow, or even the next moment, would bring in terms of personal and family safety." And returning to the United States did not mean she was finished with risk-taking. Lonnie and Dave took some deep breaths, recovered, briefly reacclimatized to the United States, and then got ready to start all over again. They learned how to speak Turkish. Then they headed off for a three-year family assignment in Istanbul. Then another op in Rome. Then Oslo.

Most of Lonnie's stories are about missions, explorations, and operations that have never made the news. Her LinkedIn page says simply "Independent Architect and Author," and modestly notes that she is "skilled in Microsoft Excel." It doesn't mention the CIA. It doesn't note that she later became a pilot, searched for Amelia Earhart, is an emergency services first lieutenant in the Civil Air Patrol, and worked with Buzz Aldrin to promote private space exploration—decades before it became fashionable.

These all sound like disconnected ventures, but Lonnie doesn't see it that way. "My life is like a patchwork quilt," she says. "Each patch is different, but they're all connected."

And much of that quilt we can only wonder about—for example, vice consul Dave Schorer's assault by the Soviets that led to their sudden departure from behind the Iron Curtain. Their families learned of their departure from Walter Cronkite, on the evening news, and "that's the way it is."

Even now, half a century later, details remain murky to the public. But it's worth remembering that at the peak of the Cold War, every spark between the United States and the Soviet Union had the potential to trigger World War III. The world felt on the edge of nuclear war.

The CIA has declassified certain documents that are now open to the public, freely available on CIA.gov. One happens to be a 1974 letter from Brent Scowcroft—future national security advisor—to the national security advisor at the time: none other than Henry Kissinger. The letter was about what Scowcroft called "the Schorer incident in Leningrad" and outlined his suggestions for how to deal with media inquiries. The subtext was that if the story came out, tensions between the two nuclear superpowers could flare.

```
TO:        HENRY A. KISSINGER
FROM:      BRENT SCOWCROFT
SUBJECT:   PRESS GUIDANCE ON JANUARY 10 LENINGRAD INCIDENT

1. THE STATE PRESS OFFICE HAS RECEIVED A QUERY FROM SCRIPPS-HOWARD
WITH RESPECT TO THE SCHORER INCIDENT IN LENINGRAD. IT RESPONDED
THAT IT COULD NOT BE HELPFUL ON THIS AND HAD NO COMMENT. THE
```

"I would propose that we hold to the no comment line as long as it is feasible to do so," Scowcroft wrote to Kissinger. If the media asks if Schorer was injured? "I would best describe it as being roughed up" Scowcroft suggested. If the media asks if Schorer was in the CIA? "He is a State Department employee." And if the media asks to speak to Schorer, to get his version of the facts?

He proposed to Henry Kissinger that they say, "No, he is on leave."

7

The Edge of
the Universe

Astronauts blog from space; astrophysicists are trying to send holograms as a message to Alpha Centauri. And in a classical sense, perhaps history's finest letters from the edge are from Robert Falcon Scott, who scribbled his dying thoughts in letters to his loved ones. In doing so, he became a legend.

And finally, we close with a letter from one of the most dogged, faithful, and curious explorers of all time. Our final letter is from a Martian rover named Oppy.

Oppy, like most explorers, worked to understand our universe. And this is a mission that will never end.

BLOGGING FROM SPACE

Don Pettit

DON PETTIT IS a space station junkie. He first became an astronaut in 1996. He then blasted off to space again and again—operating robotic arms, mastering spacewalks, and conducting endless science experiments. In 2002 and 2003, he lived on the International Space Station for months at a stretch. He has now logged more than 370 days in space (and counting).

What does it feel like to spend so much time away from our blue marble? What are the days like? Pettit gives us the answers. "I like sharing the experiences for those who don't have an opportunity to go to the edge," he says. "I feel an obligation to share that experience in the best way I can."

In December 2011, Pettit traveled to the International Space Station for the third time. He would stay there for six months. While his chief responsibility was to conduct engineering experiments, he took the time to write a series of "Letters to Earth" that he shared on NASA's blog.

Some of these letters consider the evolution of exploration, contrasting the frontiers of space with the "conquering" explorers of yore:

> Gold, silk, and spices were tangible treasures from past exploration. The Conquistadors were particularly good at extracting gold from the local inhabitants. Sir Francis Drake, before he acquired the title of "Sir", brought back enough treasure from his circumnavigation of the globe to provide more than half of the income for the British crown for an entire year. The frontiers of space

likewise offer treasures won from exploration, treasure that will enrich our lives and enhance our standard of living. These treasures are golden but not gold. They contain secrets on the biochemistry of life and will allow us to increase our understanding of how life functions. No more silver and gold; from Space Station we have blood, spit, and urine, treasures that contain secrets more valuable than a chest filled with pillaged Aztec gold.

So how is Pettit studying these "secrets"? Decades earlier, Donna Oliver spent a winter in the Antarctic to study its impact on isolation. Astronauts do something similar at the Space Station.

As Pettit explains:

On the Space Station, we are human guinea pigs for a wide variety of medical experiments. The weightlessness of space offers a biochemical challenge to our bodies, which develop a host of fascinating maladies such as bone decalcification, cataracts, retina swelling, eye focus shifts, smooth muscle atrophy, fluid imbalance, gross weight loss, cardiovascular degeneration, and more. In spite of these maladies, humans can thrive in space proving that as a species, we are a hardy lot and can explore places where we were never meant to go.

We often think of space exploration in the loftiest of terms, but the reality is that there are some mundane problems that need to be overcome before we get to Mars and beyond. Exhibit A: drinking water.

Water is an essential ingredient not just for us, but for all life forms that we recognize. And water is always in short supply on a spacecraft. . . . If the toilet fails on a mission to Mars, the crew will run out of water and die.

So Pettit and the crew experimented with a system that transformed the urine from their own bodies into drinkable water. (Once again the lines between science and science fiction blur; this is essentially the same tech used in the space suits of *Dune*.) If humans wish to travel even farther from Earth, cracking the code for recycling urine is an essential part of space exploration. Pettit continues:

> Our recycling system on the Space Station is not a one-time demonstration, nor a test of astronauts' ability to handle the "yuck factor." It's a day-in, day-out operation, designed as an integral part of the overall spacecraft water balance. With this technology, we are truly on the frontier, and we have serial number 001 of a complex machine. . . . The first crews arriving at Mars will thank us for our urine-stained hands.

Pettit's letters share the day-to-day details of living in space, including details the rest of us take for granted. How, for example, does one shave in space? The answer involves miniature asteroid fields and black holes.

> I have never been able to shave with a safety razor without slicing my face, so I use a rotary electric razor instead. In weightlessness they work just as well, and the whiskers are captured inside the shaving head. But how does one clean out the whiskers in weightlessness? On Earth, you simply open the head and shake them out. Doing that up here would be a disaster.
>
> So once a week . . . I vacuum my razor. I hold the vacuum cleaner hose between my legs, and use both hands to carefully open the shaving head in front of the suction. A cloud of whiskers jumps out, appearing like a miniature asteroid field, then quickly disappears into a black hole, with no chance of escape.

In one of his final letters from space, Pettit gives a delightfully detailed breakdown of the hours of his day. He breaks his day into a pie-chart, then describes it slice by slice.

If my day on Space Station were a pie, it would be sliced into many wedge-shaped slivers.

It begins with a small slice for waking up, hygiene, and a bag of coffee (even in space, it is comforting to have a morning routine.) This is followed by a slice for reviewing and organizing the tasks that will make up my workday. . . . Then we have a morning conference with mission control.

Our workday then begins, consuming a 12-hour slice of time pie. At the end of the workday, we have another conference with mission control, followed by about an hour of work tying up loose ends. Then there is a slice for crew dinner. . . . This fulfills a very human social requirement, probably done since the discovery of fire, when the tribe would gather around the burning embers after the hunt (we now gather around our electric food warmer).

This leaves about a nine-hour slice of off-duty time [including sleep] until the whole routine begins anew. . . . At the end of the day, I am lucky to have an hour slice of truly personal time, often spent in the cupola gazing at the cosmos (writing these essays comes from this slice and competes with window time).

During the rare pockets of personal time, sometimes Pettit wrote poems:

STAIRWAY TO THE SKY

We climb the stairway,
that leads beyond the clouds.
The sky is not the limit,
at least anymore.
Atop the launch pad,
a passage into cramped quarters.
Is this the way to Heaven,

or possibly the other place?
Most definitely not business class.
We are perched atop a bottle of gasoline,
a personified Molotov.
Waiting;
more angst in front of news cameras than sitting here.
And finally,
fires hotter than hell.
That transforms us into a point of light in the sky,
thus a new star is born.
Blasted into space,
or blasted into bits,
In either case you are no longer on this planet.

After nearly six months at the International Space Station, on his final day, Pettit wrote his last letter. The letter reminds us that the concept of the edge (or, in Pettit's words, "frontier") is fluid and can mean different things to different people at different times. Sometimes the edge can become home, and this has happened since the beginning of humanity.

When a frontier feels like home, it is no longer a frontier; it has become "civilization." Those determined to wander must now pack their bags and move further into the cosmos.

Space Station is very much on the frontier. It is only my temporary home, and now it is time for me to venture back to my real home. For my generation, Earth is, and will remain, home. The technology for space travel is still in the process of development, and is not sufficiently mature to open this frontier to humanity. We are not prepared to call space our home—yet.

On Earth, the frontiers opened slowly. The technology of sailing was known and advanced for over a thousand years before the Earth was circumnavigated. Such bold acts require the technology, the will, and the audacity to explore. Sometimes you have one, but not the others.

I only hope that my small efforts here, perhaps adding one grain of sand to the beach of knowledge, will help enable a generation of people in the future to call space "home."

INTERGALACTIC HOLOGRAMS

C Bangs and Gregory Matloff

THE DATE DID NOT look promising. A mutual friend had tried to set them up, and they met at a cafe in the East Village. This was in 1982. Neither expected much; Gregory Matloff was told that his date was a crazy artist; C Bangs was told that her date was a crazy scientist . . . who was still stuck in a "very bad marriage."

At the cafe, they shared something called a "brownie, all the way," which was a brownie slathered in ice cream, chocolate syrup, and whipped cream. As they took bites out of the brownie, Gregory realized C was more intelligent than their friend had implied, and C noticed the same about Gregory.

Still, the date was awkward and forced and not exactly an instant love connection. Then Matloff, an astrophysicist, began chatting about his work and his theories about the universe. C Bangs asked him, "Have you been to Arecibo?"

The Arecibo Telescope is in Puerto Rico, and it's a key part of the search for extraterrestrial life, or SETI.

Matloff perked up. Now the date was getting interesting. "I've never even been to Puerto Rico," he said, but he knew all about the "Arecibo message," a powerful broadcast sent from the telescope in 1974. The Arecibo message contained a code—expressed in ones and zeroes—that would hopefully be interpreted by aliens, and the missive (when the bits and bites were decoded) included a stick figure of a human and an etching of our solar system.

Both Greg Matloff and C Bangs were fascinated by the idea of communicating with aliens. If aliens live across the galaxy, what kind of letter would we, the people of planet Earth, want to send them?

The question has captivated scientists for decades, and the answer boils down to something surprising: art.

NASA first penned interstellar letters in 1972, and the early version was courtesy of Carl Sagan. Sagan suggested a "message plaque" to accompany the Pioneer space probe, which was the first spacecraft to reach Jupiter. They made the plaque from gold-anodized aluminum, and it depicted a drawing of a nude man and a woman next to the probe itself, for scale. (Sagan's wife at the time, Linda Salzman Sagan, created the artwork.)

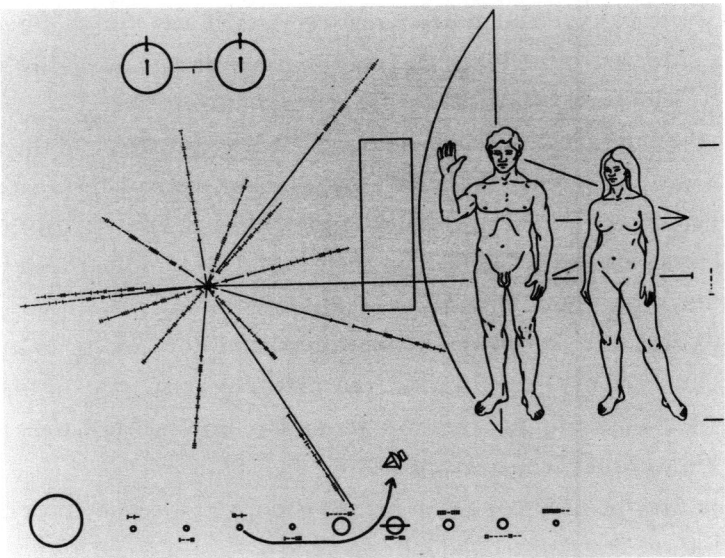

Just to show the aliens that we weren't a bunch of naked rubes, the plaque also contained a drawing of the solar system and a schematic representation of hydrogen, which—since it's the most abundant element in the universe—would hopefully be understood by any extraterrestrials. (Bonus factoid: The male's genitalia are depicted; the female's are left blank, like a Barbie doll. Allegedly, Sagan was worried that NASA would never green-light a vagina.)

Sagan's plaque traveled more than seven billion miles. Impressive, sure, but only a pebble toss in the context of the galaxy. Next came the Voyager 1 and Voyager 2 probes, launched in 1977, each of which carried a "Golden Record" (also courtesy of Sagan) containing sounds and images. The Voyager probes, like the Pioneer, failed to leave the solar system.

How could we go farther? Scientists kept thinking. A brilliant physicist named Robert Forward, who was obsessed with interstellar travel, envisioned a "minimalist probe," or as he called it in a 1985 paper, "an interstellar flyby probe of wire mesh sail with microcircuits at each intersection." The idea was that this itty-bitty probe could travel via beam of light—the particles of light would push its tiny "sails" just as wind propelled a sailboat.

Forward crunched the numbers. He showed that while it would take a conventional spacecraft four thousand years to reach Alpha Centauri, his miniprobe—moving at 10 to 20 percent of the speed of light—could make the trip in just two decades.

What happened next? *Star Trek*. Or at least that was one astrophysicist's theory—a "crazy scientist" who loved chocolate-covered brownies. In the 1990s, "President Clinton hears about *Star Trek*, and he realizes there are two million *Star Trek* fans, and he says, 'How do I get them all to vote Democratic?' And he comes up with a brilliant idea: Let's fund an interstellar propulsion research effort at NASA," says Gregory Matloff, a star protege of Robert Forward (who passed away in 2001) and a current torchbearer for this interstellar journey.

For years, and especially since that brownie he shared with C Bangs, Matloff had been thinking about that journey. In the 1990s, thanks to Clinton's newfound interest in interstellar communication (or at least interstellar politics), Matloff was tasked with figuring out how to send a new "letter" from Earth. So he turned to the most brilliant person he knew, someone who cared about exploring the cosmos just as much as he did: his wife.

Back in 1983, once Matloff left his "very bad marriage," that first date led to a second. Then a third. The crazy artist and crazy scientist were the right kind of crazy. They eventually got married, and they became both life partners and scientific partners. They collaborated on space and interstellar research. C Bangs contributed to Matloff's academic research papers and to most of his thirteen books, which featured titles like *Starflight Handbook*.

In the Clinton era, Matloff helped design plans for a "nanocraft" that could reach Alpha Centauri, building on the work of Robert Forward. The nanocraft would weigh less than a gram. Obviously, it was too small for a person, too small for a puppy, too small for a Carl Sagan–inspired plaque or even a floppy disk. They would need something smaller still.

This is where C Bangs came in. What if the nanocraft could travel with something virtually weightless: holograms? Matloff's team performed test after test and proved that holograms are not impacted by space radiation, making them the perfect medium to travel across the galaxy. "A small hologram can contain nearly infinite amounts of information," says Matloff. Holograms could display art, messages, and data to any aliens across the galaxy.

"I invited a number of artists to submit an image that they would want on a message plaque," says C Bangs, and then she selected some of the images to be sent as a hologram. (C Bangs did more than contribute the art; she later suggested incorporating some of Robert Forward's original ideas into the design, which would help the nanocraft escape Earth's orbit.)

The idea lay dormant for more than a decade. (*Star Trek* nostalgia only took the NASA funding so far.) Then, in 2016, a new initiative brought it roaring back: the Breakthrough Starshot Project cofounded by Stephen Hawking in one of the final acts of his life.

And now, suddenly, they felt a newfound urgency to send this message. In 2016, scientists made the astonishing discovery that Proxima Centauri, the nearest star to the sun, had an Earth-sized planet with a region that maybe—just maybe—could be suitable for life. "That discovery really freaked us out," says Matloff. "It was amazing."

Now the idea of extraterrestrial life didn't seem so theoretical. It felt concrete—even within our grasp—and this made scientists hungry for more information. "Imagine if it's a living planet. You want to take a picture of that," says Matloff. "Imagine if, on the night side of the planet, there are cities. You want to see the lights of those cities."

So now the scope of Breakthrough Starshot has expanded to include two goals: Send messages via hologram to whoever is at the other end of those twenty-five trillion miles, and then (somehow) take photos of this new world and (somehow) beam them back to Earth.

Some of the details are still to be determined, and the theories are still being tested, but Matloff and C Bangs are confident it can work. As a proof of concept, C Bangs's holograms will orbit Earth on a satellite called Alpha Cubesat—the first holograms in outer space. Then, with any luck (and funding), more holograms will be launched via laser beam, hurling toward another corner of the galaxy.

This won't happen overnight, but C Bangs and Matloff are in it for the long game. Their love affair—with each other and with interstellar travel—started more than forty years ago.

They can wait a few more.

THE CLASSIC
LETTERS FROM THE EDGE

Robert Falcon Scott

"For four days we have been unable to leave the tent–the gale howling about us. We are weak, writing is difficult, but for my own sake I do not regret this journey."

NO BOOK OF LETTERS from the edge would be complete without Robert Falcon Scott, the dashing Brit who led a doomed expedition to the South Pole.

Scott's legacy is complicated. It's true that he bungled the expedition at every turn; he succeeded in reaching the coveted Pole, but was beaten to the punch by Roald Amundsen and then perished on the way back, along with two others. But there's more to the story. For all Scott's faults as an expedition leader—and there are many—he was a superb letter writer. As Scott lay hungry and cold and dying, he scribbled page after page of lovely prose that, word by word, crafted his legacy as a tragic hero.

This is arguably the finest example of how letters from the edge are not just a means of correspondence but are, at times, an explorer's way of speaking directly to history. Scott wrote letters to his wife, letters to his commanding officers, letters to friends, letters of condolence, and even a sweeping letter to the public at large.

Scott does a masterful job setting a grim scene but assuring the reader that, despite the hardships, his disposition remains sunny.

This is British stiff-upper-lip at its finest, evident in his letter to J. M. Barrie:

> We are in a desperate state, feet frozen, &c. No fuel and a long way from food, but it would do your heart good to be in our tent, to hear our songs and the cheery conversation as to what we will do when we get to Hut Point.
>
> We are very near the end, but have not and will not lose our good cheer. We have four days of storm in our tent and nowhere's food or fuel. We did intend to finish ourselves when things proved like this, but we have decided to die naturally in the track. As a dying man, my dear friend, be good to my wife and child. Give the boy a chance in life if the State won't do it. He ought to have good stuff in him.

As Scott shivered in the tent, he accepted the grim responsibility of writing condolences letters to the families of his fallen comrades. And they are beautiful.

> My dear Mrs. Bowers, I am afraid this will reach you after one of the heaviest blows of your life. I write when we are very near the end of our journey, and I am finishing it in company with two gallant, noble gentlemen. One of these is your son.
>
> He had come to be one of my closest and soundest friends, and I appreciate his wonderful upright nature, his ability and energy. As the troubles have thickened his dauntless spirit ever shone brighter and he has remained cheerful, hopeful, and indomitable to the end. The ways of Providence are inscrutable, but there must be some reason why such a young, vigorous and promising life is taken. My whole heart goes out in pity for you.

Alas, not every letter was so warm and selfless. He wrote to his superior officers in the military, preemptively exonerating himself and then—brazenly—shifting the fault to his younger companions.

To Vice-Admiral Sir Francis Charles Bridgeman

My dear Sir Francis,

I fear we have slipped up; a close shave; I am writing a few letters which I hope will be delivered some day. I want to . . . tell you how extraordinarily pleasant I found it to serve under you. I want to tell you that I was not too old for this job. It was the younger men that went under first. . . .

After all we are setting a good example to our countrymen, if not by getting into a tight place, by facing it like men when we were there. We could have come through had we neglected the sick. Good-bye.

You'll be hard-pressed to find better examples of understatement. Consider Scott's use of the word "muddle":

My dear Sir Edgar,

I hope this may reach you. I fear we must go and that it leaves the Expedition in a bad muddle. But we have been to the Pole and we shall die like gentlemen. I regret only for the women we leave behind. . . .

If this diary is found it will show how we stuck by dying companions and fought the thing out well to the end. I think this will show that the Spirit of pluck and the power to endure has not passed out of our race.

In one of his final letters, Scott wrote to his wife, Kathleen.

Dearest Darling—we are in a very tight corner and I have doubts of pulling through—In our short lunch hours I take advantage of a very small measure of warmth to write letters preparatory to a possible end—the first is naturally to you. . . .

If anything happens to me I shall like you to know how much

you have meant to me and that pleasant recollections are with me as I depart—I should like you to take what comfort you can from these facts also—I shall not have suffered any pain but leave the world fresh from harness and full of good health and vigour. . . .

Therefore you must not imagine a great tragedy—we are very anxious of course and have been for weeks but on splendid physical condition and our appetites compensate for all discomfort. The cold is biting and sometimes angering but here again the hot food which drives it forth is so wonderfully enjoyable that we would scarcely be without it.

After the reassurances, he gives some parenting advice for their young child.

Make the boy interested in natural history if you can; it is better than games; they encourage it at some schools. I know you will keep him in the open air.

And finally, in something of a rousing summation of how and why the expedition ended in tragedy, Scott wrote a "Message to the Public." It almost reads like a closing argument to a jury.

The causes of the disaster are not due to faulty organisation, but to misfortune in all risks which had to be undertaken.

1. The loss of pony transport in March 1911 obliged me to start later than I had intended, and obliged the limits of stuff transported to be narrowed.

Note: Before the expedition, Scott was counseled many, many times to rely not on ponies, but instead to trust the hardiness of dogs. He ignored this advice until it was too late.

2. The weather throughout the outward journey, and especially the long gale in 83 ° S., stopped us.

Note: Amundsen's team faced the same weather.

> 3. The soft snow in lower reaches of glacier again reduced pace.
>
> We fought these untoward events with a will and conquered, but it cut into our provision reserve.
>
> Every detail of our food supplies, clothing and depôts made on the interior ice-sheet and over that long stretch of 700 miles to the Pole and back, worked out to perfection. The advance party would have returned to the glacier in fine form and with surplus of food, but for the astonishing failure of the man whom we had least expected to fail. Edgar Evans was thought the strongest man of the party. . . . Evans received a concussion of the brain—he died a natural death, but left us a shaken party.

For more than a century, explorers have second-guessed Scott's strategy and tactics. But even the harshest critic must acknowledge that, at the very end, this dying man gives a heroic, stoic message of grit and resolve. As he gasped his last breaths, he jotted down words that would inspire generations:

> For four days we have been unable to leave the tent—the gale howling about us. We are weak, writing is difficult, but for my own sake I do not regret this journey, which has shown that Englishmen can endure hardships, help one another, and meet death with as great a fortitude as ever in the past.

Scott, like almost all explorers, was aware of the risks he assumed. And he was willing to live—and die—with the consequences.

> We took risks, we knew we took them; things have come out against us, and therefore we have no cause for complaint, but bow to the will of Providence, determined still to do our best to the last.

In his very last words, Scott promises that, had he lived, he would have returned home with "a tale to tell of the hardihood, endurance, and courage of my companions which would have stirred the heart of every Englishman."

But he concedes that this is not possible, so gives full-throated expression to why so many write letters from the edge. As Scott wrote in his final hours, "These rough notes and our dead bodies must tell the tale."

THE MARTIAN EXPLORER WHO REFUSED TO QUIT

Tanya Harrison and Oppy

MANY EXPLORERS THINK of themselves as being "born to explore," but for Oppy, that's literally the case. She's a rover that was created to explore Mars.

Her full name is Opportunity, but her family—a large team of NASA scientists—thinks of her as Oppy. Many describe her as "she," so we'll do the same here.

Oppy inherited more than fifty years of Mars ambitions. In 1971, the Soviet Union sent a rover to Mars on a pair of skis, with the idea that it could slither across the red planet. It crashed. Nine days later the Soviet Union sent a second ski-rover. It also crashed.

Decades passed, but the dream survived. In 1997, NASA successfully landed the rover Sojourner. While it covered a hundred meters of exploration before losing communication, this provided just a glimpse.

Enter Oppy.

It took NASA more than a decade to design, build, train, and test Oppy and her identical twin rover, Spirit. Even in those early days, the scientists thought of their work as "parents raising a child." They taught Oppy how to crawl, how to use her arms, how to snap photographs, how to inspect the atmosphere.

When you look at Oppy, it's impossible to miss the human resemblance. Her cameras look like eyes. The long vertical rod supporting the head looks like a neck. (Think: ET.) She has arms that can bend. Her wheels look like little legs. (Granted, there are six little legs, not two; she's not an exact humanoid.) As Tanya Harrison, a NASA sci-

entist who worked on Oppy, said, "We definitely anthropomorphized the heck out of it."

Oppy and Spirit left Earth in 2003. NASA sent two rovers, not one, as redundancy in case of a crash, but both bucked the odds and landed safely. Almost *any* data they could gather would be a massive win. NASA didn't know how long the two rovers could keep roving. So much could go wrong: They could crash into rocks, get stuck in the sand, get buried in a dust storm, lose communication, and on and on. If all went well—a big "if"—the scientists hoped they would each operate for ninety sols, or Martian days.

When Oppy landed, she immediately got to work. Her primary objective was to search for signs of water, which would determine if Mars had conditions that could support life. She functioned as a robotic geologist, zooming across the planet to take photos of rocks and sending data back to NASA.

Of course, "zooming across the planet" is a relative concept. Oppy drew her power from solar panels, and in peak conditions they could only produce nine hundred watt-hours of electricity per day, or about enough juice to run a microwave for an hour. This meant she moved slowly. Her average speed was one centimeter per second, or .02 miles per hour.

Oppy was slow, but she was diligent. Every day she sent NASA her own letters from the edge—constant photos and data logs. And every day she faced obstacles. Early in the mission she slid down a boulder into a crater, almost crashing into a giant rock, but somehow she survived. Her wheels once got stuck in the sand, so that she was literally spinning her wheels—NASA feared that was the end. But she gunned her wheels in reverse, dislodging from the sand trap, and she survived. She endured minus 130 degrees Fahrenheit in the Martian winter, and she survived.

And as the clock was ticking on Oppy's ninety-day journey—only a month remained—she hit pay dirt. Oppy discovered hematite spheres—iron-rich pebbles that are formed in the presence of water. Oppy had done it. She found what is widely viewed as conclusive proof that Mars once contained water.

If the mission had ended there, NASA would have had every reason to pop the champagne and erect a statue of Oppy.

But this was just the beginning.

· · ·

OPPY AND SPIRIT kept roving for ninety days. (The scientists did indeed drink champagne.) Then ninety-one. Then ninety-five. Then one hundred.

In most tales of exploration, surprises from the elements—wind, fire, earthquakes, volcanos—tend to bring chaos or even catastrophe. NASA hadn't planned for one particular element of Mars's atmosphere, but it turned out this surprise element wasn't deadly, wasn't chaotic, and wasn't even a problem. It was wonderful. Even miraculous.

The ninety-day goal for Oppy and Spirit's mission was constrained by how long the solar panels could last. Mars is a planet full of red dust. As Oppy and Spirit trawled through the dirt, the panels would naturally get dusty and would no longer be able to absorb sunlight, causing the power to wane.

Enter the "dust devils"—miniature tornados that occasionally emerge from the Martian dirt, thanks to temperature differences between the ground and the atmosphere. Amazingly, these dust devils swarmed both Spirit and Oppy . . . and blew away the dust. Suddenly, the rovers had a new lease on life.

NASA rejoiced. Now the scientists could give Oppy and Spirit even more objectives. They could go farther, take more photos, gather more data. Oppy and Spirit kept at it for weeks. Months. Years.

In May of 2009, more than *five years* after the mission was supposed to have ended, Spirit got stuck in a patch of soft soil. For months the scientists tried to free Spirit from the trap, but to no avail. Spirit's mission was over. Oppy was on her own.

Day after day, month after month, year after year, Oppy kept delivering the scientific goods. She monitored the planet's atmospheric opacity, helping scientists better understand the Martian climate. She inspected rocks, offering valuable insights into Mars's volcanic history and the impact of meteorites. And she captured stunning 360-degree panoramic photos of the Martian landscape—from eye level, as opposed to a satellite—offering unprecedented views of what it's like to actually be on Mars.

Oppy did more than just respond to commands—she could think and make decisions. That was necessary for NASA. Oppy lived her life (so to speak) operating on Mars sols, as opposed to an Earth day. Each sol is 24 hours, 39 minutes, and 35.244 seconds. At the onset of the mission, every day (on Earth) the scientists had a regular status meeting that operated on sol time. So that might be 8 a.m.

on Monday, then 8:40 a.m. on Tuesday, then midnight a month later.

Communicating with Oppy wasn't simple, and it wasn't real-time. Given the tricky system of orbital satellite windows—pinging a signal from Oppy to a satellite orbiting Mars to a large radio antenna on Earth—NASA could only send and receive messages once per day, or rather, once per sol. Early in the mission, the scientists also sent Oppy a cheerful "wake-up" song to begin each day. And every day, the team at NASA huddled up to determine where Oppy should go and what she should do.

This gave Oppy a say in the matter. Since the communication was not in real time, NASA imbued Oppy with a certain amount of autonomy. She could look at the terrain, analyze it, and then figure out the best way to scoot around rocks or obstacles. If things looked too dangerous, she could stop. When appropriate, she was smart enough to back up, look around, and search for another path forward. (Given that she was created in 2003, she was roughly twenty years ahead of self-driving cars.)

Tanya Harrison loved this about Oppy, and she loved the mission. Her job was to download images from Oppy's camera each day, meaning that she was the very first human to get new glimpses of Mars. She looked at each image from both an engineer's perspective (Is the camera working properly?) and a planetary geologist's perspective (What are we learning?). It was a dream gig.

Harrison was still a college student when Oppy landed on Mars in 2004, and she joined the project in 2016, twelve years after Oppy's mission was supposed to end. By that time, most of Oppy's original crew had moved on to other projects. And by 2016, there were newer, shinier, sleeker rovers on Mars—Curiosity and Perseverance. But Harrison had a soft spot for Oppy. She thought of Oppy as a workhorse that collected data year after year. And she loved that Oppy, now operating years past the original goal, was showing endearing signs of age.

Oppy, in fact, was aging like a human.

Her joints were old and hurting. Her arm couldn't function like it did in her youth, so the scientists kept it permanently extended. One of her wheels stopped working.

Then Oppy's memory began to fade. NASA would give her instructions like "Drive ten meters, then take ten images," and later discover that Oppy drove ten meters but only remembered to take six images.

But even as Oppy's memory faltered, she did her job and kept inching forward and sending us more discoveries. By 2018, more than a thousand scientists, engineers, and technicians had worked on the mission. Most had moved on; some started their careers as junior analysts on Oppy and "graduated" to more cutting-edge projects. There are NASA employees who met and fell in love and got married while working on Oppy. As the cast of characters rotated in and out of this extraordinary mission, there was only one explorer who was there every day and every sol, from the very beginning: Oppy.

When Oppy blasted off from Earth, people still used Blackberries. George W. Bush was the president of the United States. Facebook didn't exist. As the world dramatically changed over the next fifteen years—new tech, new wars, new problems—Oppy never looked back to fuss or complain. She kept roving, kept exploring, kept sending bits and bytes from the edge.

. . .

ON JUNE 1, 2018, Harrison was the first to see Oppy's dispatch: a photo showing dust in the atmosphere. Lots of dust. NASA's weather monitoring satellite confirmed that a dust storm was approaching from the northern polar cap, and it looked to be gaining speed.

This could be trouble, so the scientists huddled up to work on a solution. Their options were limited. "Since the rover moves so slowly, there's not a lot you can do," says Harrison. Oppy couldn't outrun the storm. Oppy couldn't hide from the storm. Oppy could only hope to outlast the storm.

For the next week, Oppy kept sending photos of the gathering dust storm. On June 10, Oppy sent a photo that startled Harrison: a complete dust-out. Normally, Oppy's photos of Mars—even with her faulty memory—were crisp and clear. But this picture looked like snow from a television screen on a channel that doesn't exist. Harrison wondered if something was wrong with the equipment. Was the camera pointed in the wrong direction? Was there a glitch? That wouldn't surprise her, as glitches were more and more common this deep into Oppy's golden years.

Dr. Tanya Harrison ✓ @tanyaofmars · Jun 8, 2018
It's dusty as all heck for Opportunity on #Mars right now. In the span of the last 3 sols, we've lost view of the sun with Pancam. Right is sol 5106, left is 5109 (today).

Harrison began getting frantic messages from her teammates. What was wrong? They knew the dust storm was serious, but Oppy had survived dust storms before. Why was this photo so grainy? When Harrison looked at it again—she stared at it many times—it seemed to her like a shaken-up snow globe.

Oppy then sent a message in bits and bytes that were loosely translated to mean:

My battery is low and it's getting dark.

NASA sent Oppy a message. No reply. They sent another message, and again: no reply. Harrison began to worry, but she still had faith in Oppy's resilience, in her ability to get through this. She always did. The problem with dust, of course, was that it blocked the sun from reaching Oppy's solar panels, which was like depriving humans of water or food. Without sunlight, Oppy would die.

Then again, for fifteen years, the dust on Mars had been remarkably capricious. It came and went. The dust from a storm could vanish as soon as the storm passed.

This storm would eventually pass, but Harrison also knew this storm was a beast. (Prior to working on Oppy, Harrison actually served as a Martian "weatherperson," responsible for monitoring the weather for operational planning.) In all the decades of monitoring Martian weather, NASA had never seen a storm so violent. It felt biblical. The storm would not die down in a matter of hours, days, or even weeks.

Harrison and NASA could only wait.

Every day, Harrison woke up and looked for signs that the storm had passed. Each day she was disappointed. Agonizing weeks passed. Then months.

And then one night, while at home, Harrison received a phone call. It was about Oppy. A friend who worked at NASA's Jet Propulsion Laboratory (JPL) called and told her, as a heads-up, about a certain rumor they had heard at NASA headquarters: They were ready to end the mission.

But Harrison still held out hope. Eventually the storm would clear—it had to—and perhaps Oppy's panels would be restored. Why give up now? Why not give Oppy a fighting chance? Harrison had a platform on social media, so she turned to the public for support and created a new campaign: #SaveOppy.

Practically overnight on Twitter, the hashtags #SaveOppy and #WakeUpOppy showed a swell of support and love from the public. People wrote poems about Oppy. At a gaming conference, hundreds of space enthusiasts shouted in unison, "We love you, Oppy!" One female engineer who worked on the rovers had a personal campaign of #NoRoverNoRazor, vowing not to shave her legs until Oppy revived, tweeting, "I'd really like to shave soon, Oppy. Please phone home soon."

Perhaps in thanks to this outpouring of public support, NASA continued to actively support Oppy. And finally, after the most brutal storm in the recorded history of Mars, the atmosphere at last began to clear. So NASA sent a message to Oppy that essentially said, "Wake up."

And they didn't just send Oppy a command code or a text-based message. For this life-or-death moment in Oppy's journey, the team revived their old tradition of sending Oppy a morning wake-up song. After pinging from antenna to satellite to satellite, the upbeat chords of Wham!'s "Wake Me Up Before You Go-Go" made their way to the slumbering Oppy, 140 million miles from Earth. The music also blasted inside the control room at JPL, where Harrison and the scientists anxiously watched the screens, faces grim, yearning for a response.

Nothing.

But all hope was not lost. After all, in the very beginning, back when Harrison was still a college student, Oppy was miraculously saved by those dust devils, the mini-tornados that gave her a Martian bath, cleaning the panels. Maybe the dust devils could again save the day.

Each year on Mars there's a "dust devil season," which occurs in Martian spring and summer. So NASA waited. The engineers spent Christmas thinking about Oppy. Then New Year's. January passed. In the peak of dust devil season, those mini-tornados that had once rejuvenated Oppy, now in her darkest moment, again paid a visit.

The devils came and went. NASA, nervous but hopeful, again sent her a message. Harrison stared at the screen. "Wake up."

No response from Oppy. It had now been eight months since Oppy had sent that foreboding snow-globe image, and the heads of the mission knew it was most likely the end. Harrison even viewed it as the death knell.

In one last grasp at hope, out of respect, fealty, and even love for Oppy, NASA convened the larger team for a final attempt at a revival. In some ways, this was ceremonial. "We did not think the rover was going to wake up," says Harrison. No one was really needed in the room. The command could be given remotely. That didn't stop many of the scientists and engineers who had worked on Oppy—some of whom had left the project years earlier—from returning for this last goodbye. Some flew across the nation to be there, paying for flights out of their own pockets. Some had spent *decades* with Oppy, including the years spent planning and designing and testing. Perhaps now, in this united show of thanks and community and even family, NASA could revive Oppy. Harrison is a scientist. She's driven by data. But, like all her teammates, she still felt a flicker of hope.

NASA sent the command to Oppy: "Wake up."

Because of the lag in communication, the scientists had to wait twenty-eight agonizing minutes for a response.

No response came.

Harrison sat next to a friend in the control room, and she gripped her friend's hand. They both began crying. NASA planned to try the command two more times before declaring the mission over, declaring Oppy deceased.

The second-to-last attempt: "Wake up."

Harrison and her team again waited twenty-eight minutes.

No response.

In one last attempt, again NASA again tried to reach its most loyal and dogged rover: "Wake up." In those next twenty-eight minutes, it was impossible not to feel the gravity, both scientific and emotional—the significance of all that Oppy had accomplished. Oppy, crawling across the red planet at one centimeter per second, had taught us more about Mars than anyone before. She'd sent scientists a total of 137,444 command files. She'd sent us a staggering 217,000 images, which ranged from close-ups of rocks to sweeping views of craters to an endearing selfie of Oppy herself. She'd even cracked open the possibility that, billions of years ago, Mars contained a living and thriving ecosystem and perhaps an ancient civilization. She opened minds, opened hearts.

Harrison squeezed her friend's hand even harder. She stared at the clock—the twenty-eight minutes were an eternity. The storyteller in her imagined that somehow, *still*, even now, Oppy could pull through.

And then, finally, the twenty-eight minutes ticked by.

No response.

Oppy's mission, after 5,111 sols, was officially over. She'd surpassed her goal by 5,021 sols.

Harrison was crying. So was her friend. Most of the scientists in the room, as Harrison remembers now, were "bawling their eyes out." To mark the moment, the mission director played one final wake-up song for Oppy. He chose Billie Holiday's "I'll Be Seeing You," a song about the end of a relationship, and the nostalgic lyrics flowed through the NASA laboratory.

> I'll be looking at the moon
> But I'll be seeing you

The scientists just stood there, overwhelmed, speechless. Oppy was such a fixture that this moment felt unthinkable. It even felt like a funeral. "It's this mission that nobody thought would be over," says Harrison. "Nobody seemed to know what to do with themselves."

. . .

THE NASA SCIENTISTS eventually realized they needed to do two things. The first was simple: Go to a nearby bar and toast to Oppy.

As for the second, it was easy to guess what Oppy—or at least the spirit of Oppy—would want Harrison, her NASA colleagues, and humanity at large to do. To build on her progress. To keep moving forward, even if only at the speed of .02 miles per hour. To keep exploring.

So that's what NASA is doing. Exploration is not just about one expedition or one person or even one lovable rover. It's a connected story of our quest to better understand the universe. Oppy's baton has been picked up by the newer Mars rovers, who keep sending data back to Earth.

And "returning to Earth" is a key and overlooked part of Oppy's story. The rover's mission was to teach us about Mars, and she succeeded beyond NASA's loftiest hopes—but in some ways, she taught us a lesson about Earth. That's how Harrison sees it. Oppy discovered that Mars had the conditions to support life. Yet, as far as we can tell, there *isn't* life—at least not now.

Why did life flourish on Earth but not on Mars? "If you had all the conditions for life on Mars," wonders Harrison, "but it never happened, why is it that life inhabits every single nook and cranny on this planet?" Harrison searches for life on Mars, but she's awed by life on Earth. "There's life deep within the earth, buried in ice cores and inside of volcanoes. Stuff managed to survive there," she says. "And then you look at Mars. And it's just this barren wasteland."

The insight from Oppy helped Harrison appreciate the miracle of our own planet. "It's not really about Mars," she says. "It's about understanding why the earth is so special."

Oppy, in the end, sent letters from the edge that enriched our understanding of home. This is what explorers do. From Ada Blackjack in the Arctic to Lonnie Schorer in the Soviet Union to Andrés Ruzo and the boiling river to Wallace and Caspari in the dark markets of Hong Kong, explorers go to the edge to discover, learn, share, teach, and inspire.

And in some ways, they will never stop. For the universe, ultimately, has no edge.

ACKNOWLEDGMENTS

SINCE ITS FOUNDING IN 1904, there have been thousands of members of The Explorers Club. Nearly all of them, in one form or another, have sent some type of letter from the edge. So thank you, first and foremost, to all of the explorers who have journeyed to the edge, made a discovery, and then shared their knowledge with the world.

This book is only a tiny slice of that larger story. In the early days of this book's research, The Explorers Club sent a request to all members for letters and tales. Only a small fraction could be included. So thank you to everyone who submitted their letter and did *not* have it appear in this book; your contributions matter, and they quietly informed the book's themes, scope, and direction.

Thank you to every explorer who I interviewed for giving their time, memories, letters, and enthusiasm for this book. That often took courage. In some of the letters, the events described were the most painful and challenging moments of that explorer's life. The edge can be brutal, cruel, deadly. Thank you for returning to this edge to share your story and help others understand.

Specifically, thank you to C Bangs, Juli Berwald, Gino Caspari, Tiffany Duong, Daniel Farber Huang, Peter Flo Grinde-Hollevik, Amanda Fornal, Justin Fornal, Jessica Glass, Jane Hamilton-Merritt, J. R. Harris, Dr. Richard Harris, Robert "Rio" Hahn, Tanya Harrison, Meg Haywood Sullivan, Ben Jordan, Richie Kohler, Evan Kovacs, Heather Kuhlken, George Kourounis, Ulla Lohmann, Meg Lowman, Mike Massimino, Gregory Matloff, Theresa Menders, Peter McMillan, Paul Niel, Martin Nweeia, Donna Oliver, Charlie Pellegrino, Tom Paradise, Robert Peck, Don Pettit, Marcio Pimenta,

Ellen Pikitch, Ed Punchard, Will Roseman, Andrés Ruzo, Lonnie Schorer, Shawn Small, Klaus Thymann, Arnie Weissmann, Jaclyn Whittal, Mariah Wilson, and Trevor Wallace. Oh, and one more: Thank you to Oppy.

As with the first book from The Explorers Club, none of this would be possible without the generous time, patience, and insights from the small-but-mighty team at headquarters. A huge thank you to Executive Director Will Roseman, who once again provided early guidance and inspiration for the book. Thank you to Lacey Flint, the Club's archivist, for both introducing me to Ada Blackjack and for revealing the Research Collections' secrets. Thank you to Director of Media and Programming Kevin Murphy, for the early conversations that helped shape many of the book's themes. And thank you to Gracie Almeida, Heather Bain, Brittany Barbezat, Charlotte Cailliarec, Coleen Castillo, Chris Daniels, Margaret Ferris, Felix Freeland, Cheryl Johnson, Valerie Kilbridge, Tim McGovern, Andrew McInerney, Jenna O'Connor, Austin Raywood, George Shomo, Patryk Trzonkowski, Tomasz Trzonkowski, and Bonnie Wyper for all the support, both direct and indirect.

Thank you to the Club's former president Richard Garriott, for early conversations that helped the book find its way. And a massive thank you to the Club's former and current president, Richard Wiese, for the early vision for this book and for continuing to support and champion it.

And as with the first book, this project quite literally would not be possible without the Club's Director of Grants, Emerald Nash. Thank you for the *years* of weekly meetings, the countless connections, the consistent feedback and direction, and for all of the ideas, inspiration, and insights. I'm in your debt.

I'm also in the debt of Crown and Ten Speed Press, where once again our partnership was crucial to the book's success. Thank you to my longtime brilliant editor, Matt Inman, for believing in the book(s), asking the smartest questions, and providing a compass when we most needed direction. Thank you to Fariza Hawke for all the razor-sharp edits and consistently great feedback. Thank you to Mason Eng, Sohayla Farman, Jessica Heim, Aubrey Khan, Anna Kochman, and Josie McRoberts, as well as Lisa Brousseau, Alissa Fitzgerald, and Mimi Lipson.

Thank you to agent Albert Lee at UTA who was instrumental in bringing the series of Explorers Club books to life, and thank you to my agent (and dear friend) Rob Weisbach for the unfailingly sound wisdom and for always having my back.

And thank you to everyone who has read this book and is now inspired to journey to their own edge—whatever that edge might be. Please don't forget to send a letter.

—JEFF WILSER

CREDITS

PAGE v: courtesy of The Explorers Club

PAGE 22: courtesy of The Explorers Club

PAGE 26: courtesy of Mike Massimino (@ Astro_Mike)

PAGE 30: courtesy of Meg Lowman

PAGE 31: courtesy of Meg Lowman

PAGE 37: courtesy of Donna Oliver

PAGE 37: courtesy of Donna Oliver

PAGE 45: courtesy of Robert Peck

PAGE 53: courtesy of Devlin Gandy

PAGE 88: courtesy of Paul Niel

PAGE 96: courtesy of Ellen Pikitch

PAGE 132: courtesy of Charlie Pellegrino

PAGE 135: courtesy of Tiffany Duong

PAGE 163: courtesy of Tom Paradise

PAGE 238: courtesy of Ulla Lohmann

PAGE 247: courtesy of Lonnie Schorer

PAGE 252: courtesy of CIA Reading Room

PAGE 264: courtesy of NASA

PAGE 275: courtesy of NASA

PAGE 280: courtesy of NASA

ABOUT THE AUTHORS

THE EXPLORERS CLUB is a multidisciplinary professional society dedicated to the advancement of field research, scientific exploration, and resource conservation. Headquartered in New York City with a community of chapters around the world, they have been supporting scientific expeditions of all disciplines and uniting members in the bonds of good fellowship since 1904.

JEFF WILSER is the author of eight books. His work has appeared in outlets such as *The New York Times,* *WIRED, Fast Company,* and *New York* magazine. He hosts the podcast *AI-Curious,* is based in Denver, and has a small puppy named Mojo. Wilser is an explorer at heart.